D1860051

INDIA

IN THE
FIFTEENTH CENTURY

INDIA

IN THE

FIFTEENTH CENTURY

BEING A COLLECTION OF

NARRATIVES OF VOYAGES
TO INDIA,
IN

THE CENTURY PRECEDING THE PORTUGUESE DISCOVERY
OF THE CAPE OF GOOD HOPE;
FROM

Latin, Persian, Russian, and Italian Sources,
Now First Translated Into English,

Edited, with an Inroduction
By

R. H. MAJOR, ESQ., F.S.A.

GYAN

Published by

GYAN

Gyan Publishing House
5, Ansari Road
Daryaganj, New Delhi-110002
Phone: 011-47034999, 9811692060
E-mail: books@gyanbooks.com

Distribution Network
gyanbooks.com
India, USA, Canada, UK, Australia, France

© Publisher

All rights reserved. No part of this work may be reproduced, stored, adapted, or transmitted in any form or by any means, electronic, mechanical, photocopying, micro-filming, recording or otherwise, or translated in any language, without the prior written permission of the copyright owner and the publisher.

ISBN : 978-81-212-3591-4 (PB)
First Published, 1857

2nd Impression 2020

Printed at: Gyan Press, Delhi.

The book is sold subject to the condition that it shall not, by way of trade or otherwise, be lent, resold, hired out, or otherwise circulated without the prior publisher's written consent.

India in the Fifteenth Century
Author: R. H. Major

THE HAKLUYT SOCIETY.

SIR RODERICK IMPEY MURCHISON, G.C.St.S., F.R.S., D.C.L., Corr. Mem. Inst. Fr.
Hon. Mem. Imp. Acad. Sc. St. Petersburg, &c., &c., President.

The Marquis of LANSDOWNE.
Rear-Admiral C. R. DRINKWATER BETHUNE, C.B. } Vice-Presidents.

Rear-Admiral Sir FRANCIS BEAUFORT, K.C.B., F.R.S.
Rt. Hon. LORD BROUGHTON.
JOHN BRUCE, Esq., F.S.A.
The LORD ALFRED CHURCHILL.
The Right Rev. the LORD BISHOP OF ST. DAVID'S.
CHARLES WENTWORTH DILKE, Esq., F.S.A.
Rt. Hon. Sir DAVID DUNDAS.
Sir HENRY ELLIS, K.H., F.R.S.
Lieut-Gen. CHARLES RICHARD FOX.
R. W. GREY, Esq., M.P.
JOHN WINTER JONES, Esq., F.S.A.
His Excellency the COUNT DE LAVRADIO.
P. LEVESQUE, Esq., F.S.A.
Rt. Hon. ROBERT LOWE, M.P.
Sir ERSKINE PERRY, M.P.
Sir HENRY RAWLINSON, K.C.B.
The Rev. W. WHEWELL, D.D.

R. H. MAJOR, Esq., F.S.A., Honorary Secretary.

CONTENTS.

NARRATIVE OF THE VOYAGE OF ABD-ER-RAZZAK, Ambassador from Shah Rukh, A.H. 845, A.D. 1442. Translated from the Persian into French by M. QUATREMÈRE. Rendered into English, with Notes, by R. H. MAJOR, ESQ., F.S.A.

THE TRAVELS OF NICOLÒ CONTI IN THE EAST IN THE EARLY PART OF THE FIFTEENTH CENTURY. Translated from the original of POGGIO BRACCIOLINI, with Notes, by J. WINTER JONES, ESQ., F.S.A., Keeper of the Printed Books, British Museum.

THE TRAVELS OF ATHANASIUS NIKITIN, a native of Twer. Translated from the Russian, with Notes, by COUNT WIELHORSKY, late Secretary of the Russian Legation at the Court of St. James's.

THE JOURNEY OF HIERONIMO DI SANTO STEFANO, a Genoese. Translated by R. H. MAJOR, ESQ., F.S.A.

present Keeper of the Printed Books in the British Museum, was requested to edit such a volume, which he obligingly undertook to do, though with much hesitation, in consequence of the increasing pressure of his important duties in the Museum. After translating and annotating the voyage of Nicolò de' Conti and seeing it through the press, he felt compelled by the claims of his present responsible position to give up a task which he would otherwise gladly have completed, but which he could not continue with justice to the members of the Society or to himself. In the spring of the present year, the Honorary Secretary of the Society volunteered to complete what Mr. Jones had left undone, a task which, although laborious, has been performed under the advantage of not having in any way to interfere with the labours of his predecessor.

While thus called upon to refer to the contributors to this volume, the editor cannot deny himself the satisfaction of recording in this place the following exalted testimony to the generous conduct of his lamented friend, Count Wielhorsky, after his return to Russia. The following autograph letter from the present Empress of Russia to the Count's father, the Count Michel Wielhorsky, was published in the *Journal de St. Petersbourg* of the 3rd January, 1856, and its translation into English appeared in *The Times* of the 12th of the same month.

"Count Michel Yourievitch,—Appreciating the generous sentiment which led your son to express the desire to go to the aid of the suffering among our brave soldiers wounded in the army of the Crimea, I intrusted to him, in this sacred work, the accomplishment of my views and intentions.

"Count Wielhorski Matuschkine completely justified my choice and my confidence, by wise measures and indefatigable activity, which were joined, in the midst of incessant labours, to his feelings of humanity and ardent zeal. Thousands of wounded men, thousands of mourning families have blessed, and still bless, the attentions, so full of humanity and Christian sentiment, which your son lavished upon them. It gave me pleasure to think that, on his return to St. Petersburg, I should have the heartfelt joy of expressing to him my sincere gratitude for his arduous labours, and for having so well divined my wishes and carried them out with so much success. He had already worthily received a testimony of the high satisfaction of His Majesty the Emperor, at the period of his visit to the Crimea.

"The Most High has otherwise ordained. It is with keen sorrow that I have learned the premature and unexpected death of your son. I appreciate the extent of your grief, and I am unable to express the interest and sympathy with which it inspires me. One consolation remains to your sorrow—it is the secret thought that your son, in his short career, has known how to distinguish himself by a useful activity in the performance of his professional duties, and that Divine Grace has granted him an end that every Christian may envy.

"Deprived of the satisfaction of expressing my thankfulness to your son himself, it is in his name and in remembrance of him that I address myself to you. It was in the paternal house and in the example of the family that he imbibed the principles which formed the rule of his life, and which, after his death, will assure to his memory an imperishable fame.

"I remain, ever yours, very affectionately,

"MARIE."

"St. Petersburg, Dec. 26, 1855."

To those who knew Count Wielhorsky in England the noble conduct thus feelingly appreciated by the Empress will occasion no surprise; while, by those who did not, it is hoped that this testimony to the worth of one, now gone, who obligingly rendered his best services to our Society, will not be deemed superfluous.

R. H. M.

INTRODUCTION.

BEFORE the days when Alexander of Macedon sought to add to his triumphs the conquest of the Eastern world, India had been pronounced by Herodotus to be the wealthiest and most populous country on the face of the earth. The subsequent history of commerce has proved the correctness of his assertion. Yet, though endowed with a soil and climate on which nature has poured forth her choicest gifts with the most partial profusion, and at the same time boasting a civilisation even far beyond the limits of authentic history, it is remarkable that India has never been thoroughly explored till within the last century. No era in the history of the exploration of such a country can be without its interest, but the period treated of in the collection of documents which are here for the first time laid before the English reader, claims a peculiarly honourable place in the chain of our information respecting it. It is true that it was no longer possible at that period to speak, as Horace poetically did of old, of the "intacti thesauri divitis Indiæ", yet the time had not yet come when Vasco de Gama, by rounding the

Cape of Good Hope, had opened up a readier track to that more active commerce, by which these riches should become the property of the whole western world. The interest which attaches to these documents, however, will be best appreciated by our taking a brief retrospect of the intercourse of the West with India, and bringing under review the earlier voyages made to that country; it being premised that the word India is here used in its most extended sense, comprising India within and beyond the Ganges, with the East Indian Islands.

Although it is now well ascertained that India was the country from which the Phœnician pilots of King Solomon's fleets "brought gold and silver, ivory, apes and peacocks", inasmuch as the original designations of these various importations are not Hebrew but Sanscrit, yet even so late as the days of Herodotus the knowledge of that country was extremely limited. The earliest fact which he has recorded respecting the intercourse of Indians with other nations, is the conquest of the western part of Hindostan by Darius I. He also states that Indians served in the Persian armies. The sway of the Persians over that country was, however, but of brief duration. With the conquest of Darius III by Alexander, and the death of that prince in the year 330, A. C., the Persian empire ceased.

Alexander, in his famous expedition, when he had reached the Hyphasis, or Gharra, one of the five great affluents of the Indus constituting the Punjab, was compelled, by the discontent of his troops, to relinquish the design of advancing any further. To this expedition, nevertheless, apparently so unsuccessful, was due the commencement of that Indian trade, which has subsequently proved of such vast importance to Europe. The Macedonian conqueror, by founding several cities on the branches of the Indus, and by commissioning Nearchus to survey the coasts from the mouth of the Indus to that of the Tigris, laid open the means of a communication with India both by land and by sea. It was evidently his plan that the treasures of that country might thus be carried through the Persian Gulf into the interior of his Asiatic dominions, while by the Red Sea they might be conveyed to Alexandria. The untimely death of this great monarch, however, suddenly arrested the prosecution of these grand conceptions.

The narratives which we have had handed down to us respecting India, through a long series of ages, have been mixed up largely with the fabulous. The earliest dealer in these fictions was Megasthenes, who was sent by Seleucus, one of the immediate successors of Alexander, to negociate a peace with Sandracottus [Chandra-gupta], an Indian prince; Seleucus himself being compelled to withdraw from India to encounter Antigonus, his rival for the throne. Megasthenes was, perhaps, the first European who had ever beheld the Ganges. He dwelt for several years in Palibothra, on the banks of that river,—a city supposed to have occupied the site of the modern Patna,—and afterwards wrote an account of the country, which, though now lost, has probably been transmitted to us pretty closely in the narratives of Diodorus Siculus, Strabo, and Arrian. Yet though his minuter details seem—nay, in many respects, are—totally undeserving of credit, his geographical description of India may, curiously enough, be commended for its accuracy. Moreover, it is to Onesicritus, one of the companions of Megasthenes, that we are indebted for the earliest account of Ceylon or Taprobane. From him we first hear of its trained elephants, its pearls, and its gold.

The development of the plans of Alexander was not lost sight of under the enlightened government of the Ptolemies. By the establishment of the port of Berenice, on the Red Sea, goods brought from the East were conveyed by caravans to Coptus on the Nile, and hence to Alexandria. Thus Egypt became the principal point of communication between India and Europe.

Meanwhile the Persians, notoriously addicted to refined and effeminate luxuries, could by no means dispense with the costly productions and elegant manufactures of India. These people, however, seem to have had an unconquerable aversion to the sea,—a ludicrous example of which we have in the singular instance of the voyage, now first rendered into English in the following pages, of Abderrazzak, the ambassador of Shah Rokh to the Court of Bijnagar. The droll pathos with which he bemoans his sad lot in having to undergo so many hardships, loses nothing from the florid exaggeration of oriental hyperbole. But of this hereafter. The supply of Indian commodities to the various provinces of Persia was effected by camels, from the banks of the Indus to those of the Oxus, down which river they were conveyed to the Caspian, and thence circulated either by land-carriage, or by the navigable rivers, through the various parts of the country.

It was the opinion of Major Rennell, an authority always deserving to be listened to with deference, that "under the Ptolemies the Egyptians extended their navigations to the extreme points of the Indian continent, and even sailed up the Ganges to Palibothra"; and it is certain that Strabo, who wrote a little before the commencement of the Christian æra, states that some, though few, of the traders from the Red Sea had reached the Ganges.

By this time, however, Rome had become the mistress of Egypt,—the great highway of Indian maritime commerce to the west,—and the luxurious and costly articles which that distant country alone could furnish, became necessary to feed the pleasures and maintain the grandeur of an empire glutted to satiety with the successes of conquest. It was about eighty years after Egypt had been annexed to the Roman empire,—that is, about the year A.D. 50,—that a discovery was made of the greatest importance both to geography and commerce. During the many voyages made by the navigators of Egypt and Syria, it was scarcely possible that the regular shiftings of the periodical winds, or monsoons, blowing during one part of the year from the east, and during the other from the west, could have failed to be observed. It is by the author of the *Periplus of the Erythrean Sea* (supposed to be Arrian, to whom we are indebted for the earliest mention of the peninsula of the Deccan, and whose details are remarkable for their correctness), that we are informed that Hippalus, the commander of a vessel in the Indian trade, had the hardihood to stretch out to sea from the mouth of the Arabian Gulf, and practically tested the more theoretical observations of his predecessors. His experiment was successful, and he found himself carried by the south-western monsoon to Musiris, a port on the coast of Malabar, in all probability Mangalore. This bold adventure gained for him the honour of having his name attached to the wind by which he was enabled to perform this novel voyage.

Pliny has very fully described to us the shortened route thus gained. He says: "The subject is well worthy of our notice, inasmuch as in no year does India drain our empire of less than five hundred and fifty millions of sesterces, giving back her own wares in exchange, which are sold at fully one hundred times their prime cost." The sum here mentioned may be computed at about £1,400,000 of our money. The first point he mentions, from Alexandria, is Juliopolis, which Mannert considers to be that suburb of Alexandria called by Strabo Eleusis. From Juliopolis to Coptos, on the Nile, is three hundred miles. From Coptos to Berenice are noted various *ὑδρευματα*, or watering places, at which the travellers rested during the day time, the greater part of the distance being travelled by night, on account of the extreme heat. The entire distance from Coptos to Berenice occupied twelve days. The traces of several of these *ὑδρευματα* were found by Belzoni, and the site of Berenice, whose ruins still exist, was ascertained by Moresby and Carless, at the bottom of the inlet known as the Sinus Immundus, or Foul Bay. The distance from Coptos was two hundred and fifty-seven miles. The voyage from Berenice was generally commenced before or immediately after the rising of the Dog-Star, and thirty days brought them to Ocelis, now called Gehla, a harbour at the south-western point of Arabia Felix, or else to Cave, which D'Anville identifies with Cava Canim Bay, near Mount Hissan Ghorib, at the foot of which ruins are still to be seen. Pliny states that Ocelis was the best place for embarkation, and if *Hippalus*, or the west wind, were blowing, it was possible to reach Musiris, to which we have already referred, in forty days. He describes this place, however, as dangerous for disembarcation, on account of the pirates which frequent the neighbourhood, and as the roadstead was at a considerable distance from the shore, cargoes had to be conveyed thither in boats. A much more convenient port was Barace, to which pepper was conveyed, in boats hollowed out of a single tree, from Cottonara, the Cottiara of Ptolemy, supposed to be either Calicut or Cochin.

In the present advanced stage of our acquaintance with India, we are accustomed to receive from that country, in large supply, a vast variety of important articles, such as cotton, silk, wool, gums, spices, indigo, and coffee. In the days of which we write, commerce was confined to commodities more immediately meeting the requirements of the most luxurious subjects of a very luxurious kingdom. The importations at that time consisted mainly of precious stones and pearls, spices and silk. Diamonds and pearls, which history tells us were so much in demand amongst the Romans, were principally supplied from India. Spices, such as frankincense, cassia, and cinnamon, were largely used, not only in their religious worship, but in burning the bodies of the dead; and silk, at that time derived alone from India, was sought for eagerly by the wealthiest Roman ladies, and so late as the time of Aurelian, in the later half of the third century of our era, was valued at its weight in gold.

The great geographer Ptolemy, who wrote at the commencement of the second century, describes the peninsula of India with far less accuracy than Arrian, who wrote but shortly after him and in the same century, and who correctly represented it as extending from north to south, while Ptolemy commits the egregious error of making the coast line run nearly west and east, the mouths of the Ganges being removed sufficiently eastward to allow room for the insertion of the numerous names of places of which he had gained information. The abundance of topographical information, for which his writings are remarkable, was due to the great extension which commercial intercourse had received in the century immediately preceding, and to the facility which his residence in Alexandria, the centre of a large proportion of the commerce of the day, afforded him of consulting the itineraries of various merchants. He was, in short, the Hakluyt of that day. He first acquaints us with the names of six different mouths of the Ganges, and describes their positions. He delineates, with great inaccuracy as to its general form, but with wonderful copiousness of detail as to the names of towns, rivers, and headlands, that part of India which lies beyond the Ganges. His Aurea Chersonesus has been shown by D'Anville to be the Malay Peninsula, and his Sin-hoa, the western part of the kingdom of Cochin China.

We have already spoken of the trade which had long before been opened into the interior of Persia, and to the countries bordering on the Caspian and Black Sea by land carriage through the provinces that stretch along the northern frontier of India. Of the distant inland regions thus traversed Ptolemy was enabled to gain some general information, though the inaccuracy of his geographical delineations throws great obscurity over the identification of most of the points he lays down.

From the age of Ptolemy until the reign of the Emperor Justinian but small addition was made to geographical knowledge concerning India. That the communication between the east and west in the fourth century was tolerably frequent and regular, may be gathered from the language of Ammianus Marcellinus, who, wishing to pay homage to the memory of the Emperor Julian, says that on the first rumour of his accession to the throne, deputations came from the farthest east to congratulate him. His words are:

"Inde nationibus Indicis certatim cum donis optimates mittentibus ante tempus abusque Divis et Serendivis. (Lib. 22, cap. vii.)

After the partition of the Roman empire, the intercourse between Rome and India by way of the Red Sea began to decline; but while the Greek empire flourished, Constantinople was the centre of commerce between Asia and Europe. The caravans came by Candahar into Persia, but through Egypt especially the Greeks received an enormous quantity of the costly products of the East. This latter channel of commerce, however, was doomed to receive an almost fatal blow under the following circumstances. The Persians, who, as we have already said, had in earlier times manifested an extreme dislike to maritime commerce, began, after the subversion of the Parthian empire, to entertain a more reasonable notion of its importance and value. Having learned from the small Indian traders who frequented the various ports in the Persian Gulf, with what safety and rapidity the voyage from thence to Malabar and Ceylon might be performed, they fitted out vessels which made this voyage annually, and thus, in exchange for specie and some of the commodities of their own country, they brought home not only the costly products of India, but also those of China, which they were enabled to procure at Ceylon. By this channel the luxurious inhabitants of Constantinople were furnished in large abundance with the manufactures of Hindustán; and by this means, in conjunction with other causes, the Egyptian trade was subjected to a depression almost amounting to annihilation.

The success of the Persians in their commerce with India, which was mainly due to the advantages of their physical situation, increased to such an extent, that at length the whole of the silk trade, which from time immemorial had been imported into Ceylon from China, fell into their hands. As at the same time the frequent wars between the Persians and the Imperial government of Constantinople afforded the former a pretext for seizing the caravans by which the manufactures of China were conveyed through Tartary into Greece, it followed that the Greeks were obliged to purchase from their enemies at an exorbitant rate all those valuable commodities of the East, which had now become to them almost a necessity. The Emperor Justinian, after making some fruitless efforts to rescue the commerce of his subjects from the exactions of the Persians, had the satisfaction of seeing his wish partially gratified by the occurrence of a curious and unexpected circumstance. Two monks of the Nestorian persuasion, who had been sent as missionaries to India and China, and had during their residence in the latter country acquired a knowledge of the methods not only of training the silkworm, but of manufacturing silk into those beautiful fabrics that were so much admired in Europe, returned to Constantinople and imparted to Justinian the important discovery which they had made. The emperor encouraged them to go out again to China, and in the course of a few years the monks returned from their mission, bringing with them the eggs of the silkworm concealed in a hollow cane. They were hatched by the heat of a dunghill, and fed with the leaves of the mulberry. They multiplied rapidly, and extensive silk manufactures were soon established in the Peloponnesus and in some of the Greek Islands. The subjects of the Greek emperors were no longer indebted to the Persians for their silks: even Chinese silks underwent a temporary depreciation in the European markets, and thus an important change was effected in the commercial intercourse between Europe and India. In spite, however, of the advantage thus suddenly obtained by the Greeks, the merchants of Constantinople, narrowed in their fortunes by the repeated exactions of Justinian, were but little able to contend with their wealthy rivals in commercial pursuits, and even the wealth and mercantile influence of the latter had not yet so entirely destroyed the Egyptian trade but that some of the commodities of Hindustán were still imported into Egypt, and thence found their way into Italy and the Grecian States.

It was in the reign of Justinian that Cosmas, an Egyptian merchant, made some voyages to India, on account of which he received the surname of Indicopleustes. Retiring in the later years of his life into a monastic cell, he composed various works, of which one, entitled *Topographia Christiana*, has been preserved to our own times. This work contains a particular description of India. It is from his account, together with that of the cotemporary Greek historian,

Procopius, that the above events connected with Indian commerce in the reign of Justinian have been derived.

In the course of the succeeding century other events occurred, by which the nations of Europe became almost entirely excluded from any share in the old modes of intercourse with the East. The disciples of Mahomet, stimulated alike by the love of gain and the desire of propagating their new religion, laid aside the pristine peaceful habits of their race, and betook themselves with enthusiastic ardour to the task of promulgating the doctrines of their prophet and extending the dominion of his successors. This new and vehement spirit with which the Arabs had become imbued, was, after the death of Mahomet, fostered and brought into action by his successor, the intrepid Omar, who, at the head of a numerous army of the faithful, marched into Persia, and in the course of a few years subdued the whole of that ancient empire, and established the dominion of the Khalífs and the faith of his great predecessor on the ruins of the dynasty of the Sassanides and the religion of Zoroaster. The rapidity of the successes of the Muhammedans stands unrivalled in the history of mankind. Egypt soon fell beneath their sway, and as they not only subdued but took possession of that country, the Greeks were excluded from all intercourse with Alexandria, which had for a long time been their principal resort for Indian goods. The Arabs thus becoming sensible of the enormous advantages derivable from Eastern commerce, soon entered upon the pursuit of mercantile enterprize with the same ardour which had characterized their efforts as warriors. They speedily outstepped the limits of previous nautical investigation, and imported many of the most costly commodities of the East immediately from the countries which produced them. In order to give every possible encouragement to commerce, the Khalíf Omar founded the city of Busrah on the west bank of the Shat el Arab, between the junction of the Tigris and Euphrates and the Persian Gulf, a station scarcely inferior to Alexandria for the shipping engaged in the Indian trade.

We find from the narratives of the celebrated Arabian traveller and historian Masúdi, who wrote at the beginning of the tenth century, and of Ibn Haukal, also an Arabian traveller, who visited India a short time after Masúdi, that although the Arabs, who in the course of the seventh and eighth centuries made several descents upon the coasts of Guzerat, the Gulf of Cambay, and Malabar, made no fixed stay on these coasts, nevertheless a considerable number of individual merchants established themselves there, and the Arab name was held in high respect in the country. They both agree that Muhammedanism had begun to develope itself. The Mussulmans had erected mosques, and were in the habit of publicly celebrating their five prayers in the day. The part of India with which the Arabs had the least intercourse was Hindustán properly so called, namely, the country watered by the Jumna and the Ganges, from the Panjab to the Sunderbunds. Ibn

Haukal, after making mention of some cities in the Gulf of Cambay and on the neighbouring coasts, says: "These are the towns with which I am acquainted. There are other cities, such as Canooj, which lie in deserts at great distances. These are desolate countries, which the native merchants alone can penetrate, so wide apart are they and so encompassed with dangers."

But whatever limit may be assigned to the advance of the Muhammedans into the interior of the country, it is certain that they obtained a monopoly of the Indian commerce, and a consequent enormous increase in wealth and prosperity. Nor were their successes confined to the East. The whole of the north coast of Africa, from the Delta of the Nile to the Straits of Gibraltar, together with a great part of Spain, had submitted to their sway. Meanwhile, during this same period, the continued hostilities in which they were engaged with the Christians precluded the latter from deriving any of the benefits which had previously been open to them through the medium of commerce. It was by the inland intercourse through Tátary alone that they received the productions of the East, and then only enough to stimulate their desire to obtain more. About the commencement of the tenth century, however, a remarkable spirit of industry, particularly in the cultivation of the mechanical arts and in the pursuit of domestic traffic, began to manifest itself in the free cities of Amalfi and Venice, and this with an earnestness of purpose which the wealth they thereby acquired only served to augment. The new desires and increasing ardour for commercial enterprize thus engendered, tended gradually to soften the feelings of alienation which had grown up between the Christians and Muhammedans; the ancient channel of intercourse with India by Egypt was again laid open, and under the auspices of these Italian merchants the Eastern trade diffused its beneficial influence over all the west of Europe.

About the middle of the eleventh century the empire of the Khalífs began to decline, and its decline paved the way for the irruptions of the Turks, whose invasion of Syria and Palestine was one of the proximate causes of the crusades. These expeditions, the religious object of which it is not our purpose now to dwell upon, while they naturally revived the old hostility between the Christians and Muhammedans, and thus caused a suspension of their growing intercourse, yet by more fully opening the eyes of the sovereigns of the West to the wealth which was to be gained by the lucrative commerce of the East, laid the basis of that mercantile prosperity which Western Europe has never since lost sight of.

The illustrious warriors of the West who led their armies into Palestine, themselves became the sovereigns of the very states and cities into which the costly products of India were so largely imported; and though the commercial intercourse with the East was doubtless not the primary object with the distinguished commanders of the Crusades, it became a matter of paramount importance to the merchants who were associated in the enterprize. They gained permission to settle at Acre, Aleppo, and other trading towns on the coast of Syria, together with a variety of privileges which greatly enhanced the advantage of their position. By this means the cities of Venice, Genoa, Amalfi, Pisa, and Florence entirely engrossed the Indian trade, and every important port in Europe was at that time visited by their mariners.

On the partition of the Grecian States in 1104 by the leaders of the fourth Crusade, the Venetians obtained possession of part of the Morea, and of some of the most important islands of the Archipelago, and were thus enabled to secure essential advantages in the Indian trade over the rival states of Italy. The Genoese, jealous of this superiority, conspired with the disaffected Greeks under the command of Michael Palæologus, and drove the Venetian merchants from Constantinople; and thus the entire commerce by the Black Sea, and consequently the inland trade with India, fell into their hands. The Venetians in retaliation procured a Bull of dispensation from the Pope, by which they were permitted to open a free trade with the infidels; and accordingly, by the settlement of their merchants at the different trading cities of Egypt and Syria, established their intercourse with India upon a more solid basis than that which they had heretofore possessed.

While these rivalries were pending between the Venetians and the Genoese, we find the republic of Florence bestirring itself so actively in the pursuit of commercial influence, that by their success both in manufactures and in banking transactions, they were enabled, under the administration of Cosmo de Medicis, to procure, through ambassadors sent to Alexandria, a participation in the commercial privileges which were enjoyed by the Venetians. The Genoese, however, still carried on the northern trade between India and Constantinople, until, by the conquest of the Greek empire by Mahmúd II in 1453, they were finally expelled from that city. At this time the Turkish government became permanently established in Europe, Constantinople was no longer a mart open to the nations of the West for Indian commodities, and no supply of them could now be obtained but in Egypt and the ports of Syria, subject to the Sultáns of the Mamlúks, and as the Venetians by their commercial treaty with those powerful princes commanded these channels of intercourse, they were enabled to monopolize the supply of the products of the East to the countries of the West, until the close of the fifteenth century. At this period, the grand turning point of geographical discovery, two of the most memorable events in the annals of the world, viz., the discovery of America and the rounding of the Cape of Good Hope, produced an effect which proved fatal to the commerce of the Venetian Republic and opened the commerce of India to the Portuguese, whose perseverance, enterprize, and nautical skill so eminently qualified them to follow up the advantage with success.

Having endeavoured thus briefly to trace the political changes which affected the intercourse of India with the western world during several centuries, it is now time that we should refer to those voyages which were made within that period, and the accounts of which have been handed down to our times.

The earliest of these is one of most striking interest, for which we are indebted to the labours of the learned Chinese scholar, M. Stanislas Julien. In the first volume of a work entitled *Les Pelerins Bouddhistes*, published in 1853, he gives the biography of Hiouen-thsang, who passed seventeen years (from 629 to 645) in the countries lying to the west of China, and especially in India. The second volume, published in the beginning of this year, contains the first portion of Hiouen-thsang's own diary. This traveller passed through countries which few had visited before him, and he describes some parts of the world which no one has explored since. His observations, geographical, statistical, and historical, are characterized by great minuteness and precision. Though some Chinese pilgrims had visited India before, and several after his time, yet Hiouen-thsang is regarded by the Chinese themselves as the most distinguished of these pilgrims. As the chief purpose of his journey, however, was not so much to advance geographical science as it was to study the religion of Buddha, we propose merely to present the reader with an abridgment of the summary made by M. Stanislas Julien of the route which he followed from China into India.

Starting from Liang-tcheou, at the north-west extremity of China, a city which was then the general rendezvous of the people dwelling west of the Hoangho, he arrived shortly after at Kona-tcheou, a city still bearing the same name, south of the river named by Klaproth, from the Chinese maps, Sou-lai-ho. For several days our traveller journeyed painfully across the sandy desert, which stretches north and north-west of this river, and at length reached the city of Igou, the capital of the kingdom of the same name (Oigour). This city seems to correspond with that now known as Kamil, the capital of one of the districts of Eastern Turkistán. Six or seven days journey westward from Igou brought him to the capital of the kingdom of Kao-tchang. After leaving this capital, the itinerary continues to lead us westward through cities and kingdoms, the identification of which would carry us beyond the limits of this analysis; suffice it that it at length brought him to the mountain Ling-chan, at the northern extremity of the Tsong-ling mountains. Of this mountain and its formidable glaciers he gives a fine description. M. Julien here remarks upon the exact agreement of his geographical details, given in this part of the itinerary, with the notions which the recent labours of the illustrious Humboldt have given us in reference to central Asia. It had been till recently believed, that from the plateau of Pamir, where the Oxus takes its rise, to the Altai mountains, which edge the southern coasts of Lake Baikal, there existed an uninterrupted chain of almost impassable mountains. The Baron von Humboldt was the first to show, from documents hitherto unknown or misemployed, that an immense depression separates the group of Pamir from that of the Altai. It was by this natural pass, that from the most ancient times the numberless migrations have been made in the direction of the Caspian Sea. It is the only route which the caravans could have followed, and it was by this route that our traveller took his course. We will not weary the reader by following him through a course of unrecognizable names of places. Hiouen-thsang passed by Samarcand, and at length reached Pesháwur, a name rendered familiar to every Englishman by recent occurrences. He penetrated the mountainous districts which lie to the north of Cashmír, and reached that part of the valley of the Indus near the modern Iskardo. He appears then to have redescended the valley of the Indus on its western bank (which no European has hitherto explored at this part of its course), and then to have crossed the river a second time near Attok. Our traveller made a prolonged stay in the northern parts of the Panjáb, but the difficulty of tracing the various points of which he treats in this part of his journey arises not only from the fact that his journal was made up for an object quite distinct from that of geographical research, but from the imperfection of modern maps, by which the places which he mentions might be identified. Before descending to the lower countries watered by the Ganges, Hiouen-thsang visited in detail those which lie along the upper part of the river. The route of the traveller through the region comprised between the Ganges, the Gandakí, and the mountains of Nípál, becomes more circumstantially traced. That part of the plain of the Ganges, which now forms the province of Oude, and the north of Allahabad, was at that time divided into twelve little kingdoms. The most celebrated of these kingdoms were those of Ayodhya, whose renown is carried back to the remotest times of the heroic period of India: Prayága, with its capital seated on the confluence of the Ganges and the Yamuna, and which owes to this position the profound religious veneration which has always been entertained for it: Kapilavastu, where the Buddha Sakyamúni was born: Kasínagar, where he died, and lastly Váranásí, the modern Benares, the only place which through the range of time has preserved his renown from the days of old.

From Benares, our traveller has but to cross the Ganges to enter the territory of Magadha, which corresponds with that part of the present Bahár extending along the south of the river. It is here, in especial, that his narrative is enriched with local topographical details, as well as with an account of historical traditions and religious legends. Here we find new and curious information respecting the Palibothra of the Greek and Latin authors; and from his account there is abundant room for the ancient map of India to be remodelled. After Magadha the narrative become more hasty. Hiouen-thsang pursues his route eastwards. He passes through the north-east part of Bengal, and then downwards to the south-west point of the delta of the Ganges.

Not content with having studied for many years those parts of Northern India in which Buddhism had its birth, he traversed a great part of the peninsula of Hindustán. He coasted down to the Godávarí, and then turned inland towards Kantchi, the capital of the kingdom of Drávida, on the Lower Palaru, between Pondicherry and Madras. This was the southernmost point which he reached. Turning back again north-west, he visited Concan, on the opposite coast of the peninsula, and arrives at length at the kingdom of Malwa, the name of which is well known at the present day. He then resumes his journey westward towards Sindh, again enters Multán, and thence a second time visits Magadha. Finally, after this long course of journeyings throughout India, he made his return homeward to China.

The second voyage of which we have to speak is that by the Muhammedan merchant, Soliman, made in the beginning of the ninth century, who most probably had his principal establishment in Busrah. The narrative of this voyage was first translated from the Arabic into French by the learned M. Eusèbe Renaudot, from the manuscript in the library of the Comte de Seignelay, and published at Paris in 1718. A translation appeared in English in 1733. It has more recently passed under the able revision of M. Reinaud, who in 1845 gave a new translation of these voyages, with corrections and additional illustrations; and still more lately it has received some most valuable corrections at the hands of M. Alfred Maury, in a memoir published in the fifth volume of the *Bulletin de la Société de Géographie*, p. 203. The work thus published by M. Renaudot consists of two parts; the first containing the narrative of the above-named traveller, Soliman, and the second a commentary on Soliman's voyage, written some twenty-seven years after by Abú Said Hassan, an amateur in geographical science, who belonged to the town of Siraf in Farsistan.

The period of Soliman's voyage was one in which the commercial relations of the empire of the Khalifs with the East were at the highest point of their activity. Several leaves of the earliest part of the original manuscript are wanting. It commences by indicating seven seas which have to be crossed in passing from the mouths of the Tigris and Euphrates to China. The two first which are missing in the manuscript, are shown by M. Reinaud to be the Persian Gulf and the Sea which stretches from the mouths of the Indus to Goa. The third the manuscript describes as the Sea of Herkend, bounded on the north by the Sea of the country of Lar, the Larice of the ancients, on the west by the Laccadives and Maldives, and on the east and southeast by the peninsula of Hindustán and the island of Ceylon. He makes the number of islands of which the Maldives and Laccadives consist to amount to one thousand nine hundred. Ptolemy reckoned them at thirteen hundred and seventy-eight. The name which he gives them of Dybadjits, seems to respond to that of Divi, used by Ammianus Marcellinus in the passage we have already quoted.

Cosmas had already spoken of these islands in terms similar to those used by Soliman. The sea of Herkend extended as far as the chain of rocks which stretches from the Indian continent to the island of Ceylon, known as Adam's Bridge. Beyond this began the fourth sea, called Schelaheth, answering, as M. Maury shows, to the Straits of Malacca. Soliman also speaks of three other seas to be crossed on the voyage to China, but here there is a defect in the manuscript of one or more leaves.

By Soliman's account one month's sail from Muscát brought the ships to Koulam (Quilon), a little to the north of Cape Comorin, and at that time the most considerable port of southern India. From Koulam they sailed to the islands Lendjebalous in the Sea of Schelaheth, supposed by M. Maury to be the Nicobar Islands; and thence, after ten days sail, they reached Betoumah, which Renaudot understands to mean Beit-Touma, the house or church of Saint Thomas, otherwise Maliapúr, where Saint Thomas was believed to have been buried. Ten days from Betoumah brought the ships to a place called Kedrendj, and other ten days to the Islands of Sumatra and Java. In pursuing the route of Soliman M. Reinaud remarks: "It will be remembered that he started for India from the Persian Gulf, sailing with the monsoon. The first country which attracts his attention is naturally that near the Gulf of Cambay, before which those Arab ships were accustomed to pass which made for the coast of Malabar and in the direction of the Island of Ceylon. This region, which stretched far inland towards the north-east, comprehended Guzerat, the Gulf of Cambay, and Malabar. On the south it terminated at the province of Concan, which is called by Edrisi the country of Sadj or of the Teak, from the forests of that valuable wood which crown the western slope of the chain of the Ghâts. This tree at that time furnished the inhabitants of Siraf in Farsistan with the wood of which they built their houses, and of it the English government at this day build their vessels of war at Bombay.

The provinces which encircle the Gulf of Cambay formed the empire which, shortly before the Christian era, under the reign of the great Vikramaditya, absorbed all the other empires of India, and had for its capital Ujain, or as the Indians pronounce it, Ujjayini. Masúdi, in his *Moroudj-al-dzeheb*, relates that the principal centre of Indian civilization was at Canooj, to which he gives the epithet of Hauzé, signifying "centre". The affairs of the government having fallen into disorder, at a period apparently corresponding to the year 607 of our era, the empire was divided, and from its ruins several kingdoms were formed, namely, Canooj, Sindh, Cashmír, and the empire of which we are now speaking, and which, according to Masúdi, received on account of its preeminence the title of "the grand centre". Its prince was known by the title of Balhara, which M. Reinaud presumes to be "derived from Malvaradja, or Rajah of Malwa". Masúdi adds that in his time this empire still existed. According to

Soliman the Balhara was the chief of the princes of India, and all the Indians acknowledged his preeminence. The Arabs enjoyed great favour in his dominions.

Respecting this name of Maha-raja, which we find mentioned not only by the Muhammedan writers but also by the authors whose narratives are printed in this volume, the learned Baron Walckenaer writes as follows. "The paranas and Hindú books show that the title of Maha-raja or great king was originally applied to the sovereign of a vast monarchy, which, in the second century, comprised a great part of India, the Malay peninsúla, Sumatra, and the neighbouring islands. This dynasty continued until the year 628; but after the subdivision of the empire into several sovereignties, the custom continued of giving the name of Mehradje or Maha-raja to one of the sovereigns of the dismembered empire, who reigned over the largest and richest portion of it, and also of designating India itself by the name of the country of the Maha-raja."

Next to the Balhara, Soliman places the king of the Djorz, which, according to Abú Said, seems to be the king of Canooj. Next to Djorz, he places the kingdom of Thafec, which he says was not large, but the women in it were white and more beautiful than those of the rest of India. Contiguous to these kingdoms he places the empire of Rohmy, whose sovereign possessed a vast number of troops, and, when he went to battle, was accompanied by fifty thousand elephants. In this country cotton stuffs were manufactured of such exquisite delicacy, that a robe made of it would pass through a signet ring. This M. Reinaud conceives to be the ancient kingdom of Vijyapur, or Vijinagar. Soliman then speaks of an inland kingdom named Kascheb or Kaschibyn, which probably answers to Mysore. It is remarkable that he makes no allusion here to Cape Comorin or the neighbouring territory; but Abú Said supplies the omission and with great correctness. From the kingdom of Kascheb Soliman passes to that whose king is named Kyrendj, and which is situated on the sea coast, which M. Reinaud places in the environs of Madras and Masulipatam; an inference which he holds to be confirmed by the expression of Soliman immediately afterwards: "After this we come upon several kingdoms, the number of which God only knows." These words, says M. Reinaud, seem to show an interruption in the enumeration of the principalities of India, which could scarcely occur except in reference to the coasts of Orissa, Bengal, and Aracan. A passage from Edrisi seems to lead to the same conclusion. He says: "The greatest king in India is the Balhara, a title equivalent to *king of kings.* Then comes Komkam (or Concan). After that the king of Thafec; then the king of Djaba (Java); then the king of Djorz; and lastly, the king of Camroun (Kamboja), whose dominions border on China. Such," continues M. Reinaud, "appear to have been the divisions of India in the ninth century. It is to be regretted that the names of places had not been more distinctly fixed. Some of these names seem to have been those attached to certain dynasties, and not the proper names of the countries. Indeed, they would all seem to be in this predicament if we go by the evidence of Ibn Khordadbeh, an Arabian writer of the last half of the ninth century."

After crossing the Gulf of Bengal, Soliman landed in the country of Moudjah, where the influence of China was found to have obtained a footing, and which was probably near Cape Martaban. His narrative suggests the idea that the country of Moudjah was near the seaport called Senef, which gave its name to the surrounding region. He thus expresses himself. "From Kendrendj the ships sail for Senef, a sail of two days." Some authors have connected the name of Senef with that of Tsiampa, a name then and to this day borne by the southern part of Cochin China. But Soliman and Masúdi seem to agree in representing the Sea of Senef as west of the Straits of Malacca and the Islands of Sumatra and Java, which makes it not unlikely to mean the sea of Naafi, on the coast of Aracan. But according to Masúdi the passage through the Straits of Malacca and those of Sunda, led into the sea called Sandji, a name which M. Reinaud conjectures to be an alteration of the word Manji, which was the name in the middle ages known to apply to the south of China, in which case another origin must be attributed to the name of Senef. Beyond this Soliman describes the states of Mabed, in which are a great number of towns, and whose inhabitants more and more resemble the Chinese. The kingdom of Mabed was separated from China by mountains, which gives M. Reinaud the belief that it corresponds with the kingdom of Siam. From this point the Arabian ships took their course towards China.

We have thus closely followed the course of this voyage with the comments made thereupon not only by the cotemporaneous writer Abú Said, but its more recent commentators, because unquestionably it is the most important, when its details and its early period are considered, that we possess before the grand epoch of the discoveries of Marco Polo, of whose account we shall hereafter have to speak.

The Baron Walckenaer, in a paper read before the Academie des Belles Lettres, on 22nd July, 1831, and published in the *Nouvelles Annales des Voyages*, tom. liii, p. 6, calls attention to another document preserved to us in Arabic, whose importance in a geographical point of view had been previously ignored. He claims for it a value equal to the narratives of Solimán and Abú Said. The voyages of *Sindbad the Sailor* have by most of us been regarded as nothing better than one of the responses of the fair princess Sheherazade to the never ending request of her sister, Dinarzade. "Sister, if you are not sleepy, tell us one of those beautiful stories of yours." The learned Baron Walckenaer was by no means of the same opinion. Although the voyages of *Sindbad the Sailor* have been inserted into the *Thousand and One Nights*, they form in Arabic a distinct and separate work, a translation of which into French was made by M. Langlès, and published in Paris in 1814.

The Baron Walckenaer ascribes to the voyages of Sindbad a date about coincident with that of Solimán. Although, doubtless, these voyages may be imaginary when regarded as the explorations of one individual, they are not the less certainly based upon real facts within the knowledge of the Arabs of the time.

The first country which Sindbad reaches is that of the Maha-raja or great king. The story which Sindbad tells of the mare of the king of Mahradje, which goes to the shore to meet a stallion which emerges from the sea, and also of an island named Kacel, where the beating of a drum was heard, occurs also in the *Malay Annals*, translated from the Malay by Mr. Leyden. The author of these annals connects this tradition with the foundation of the city of Vijnagar, nearly in the centre of the Dekhan. Hence it may be inferred that Sindbad's Maha-raja was the sovereign of the Dekhan, and that the city of Mahradje of which he speaks is the city of Vijnagar, the ruins of which are still seen near the banks of the Tungabudra, opposite Anagundi, which is supposed to have formed a portion of the ancient city itself. Katib-tchelebi, or "the Turkish geographer," describes this city as the most magnificent and the wealthiest in its commerce of the two capitals of Narsinga. (See *Ghihan-Numa, geographia orientalis ex Turcico in Latinum versa Matth. Norberg, Londini Gothorum*, 1818, t. i, p. 126.) The magnificence of this city is also fully spoken of by Nicolò de Conti and by Abd-er-razzak in the text of the present volume.

In his second voyage Sindbad mentions but one country, namely, the peninsula of Riha, in which were high mountains, and which produced camphor. He describes with great correctness the mode of extracting the camphor by making incisions in the tree which produces it. He also describes minutely the rhinoceros and the elephant. The Arabs were the first to mention camphor, which was unknown to the Greeks and Romans. The best is procured from Sumatra, Borneo, and the Malay peninsula. It may therefore be inferred that the latter, which is the nearest of these countries to Persia, where camphor is gathered and where the elephant and rhinoceros are found, was the country visited by Sindbad in his second voyage.

In his third voyage Sindbad lands on an island of tatooed and ferocious savages, which would seem exactly to correspond with the character which orientalists and European navigators have always ascribed to the Andamán Islands. It has been already stated that Selaheth, or the island of the strait mentioned by Soliman, was supposed by M. Maury to mean the Straits of Malacca. This opinion had been already propounded by the Baron Walckenaer. Sindbad speaks of a fish in the Island of Selaheth, partaking of the nature of the ox, and breeding and milking its young in like manner. It has been stated by Marsden that the hippopotamus exists in Sumatra, but this is now known, from the researches of modern naturalists, to be the Malacca tapir, and it may be accepted almost with certainty that Sindbad's description applies to the dugong, a sort of sea-calf, which is known on those coasts.

In his fourth voyage Sindbad is again carried to an island (for all countries were regarded as islands by navigators who were unable to complete their explorations). He gives no name to this island, but relates that he found there men gathering pepper. This would seem to be the coast of Malabar. In the district of Cottonara, on this coast, the best pepper is gathered and in the largest quantity to the present day. On this coast Ptolemy places the island of pepper. On this coast Cosmas, in the middle ages, mentions five ports whence pepper was exported; and it is here that Ibn Batuta, an Arab, whose travels in the fourteenth century we have yet to mention, saw and well described the plant, and says that it was the principal source of wealth of the country.

Hence Sindbad went to the Island of Nacous, apparently the Island of Nicobar. "Thence," says he, "we came in six days to the Island of Kêlâ. We travelled into the interior of the kingdom of Kêlâ. It is a large empire bordering on India, in which are mines of tin, plantations of sugar cane, and excellent camphor." The Baron Walckenaer recognizes Sindbad's kingdom of Kêlâ in the province of Keydah, in the Malay peninsula, watered by the river Calung. In this province, which is opposite to Sumatra, the trade in Malacca tin and camphor was principally carried on.

In his fifth voyage, Sindbad, after suffering shipwreck, is cast upon an island, where he becomes the victim of the Old Man of the Sea, whom he is obliged to carry on his back. The Baron Walckenaer believes that the country of the Old Man of the Sea is again a portion of the coast of Malabar. Ibn Batuta, who in the early part of the fourteenth century visited this coast, tells us that in his time there were no horses or beasts of burthen, and that everything had to be carried on men's backs, who hired themselves for this purpose. A proof of the correctness of his inference is drawn by the Baron from the fact that after escaping from the Old Man of the Sea, and setting sail again, he arrives almost immediately at a place where they gathered cocoa nuts, that is, in the Maldives, which lie opposite to the coast of Malabar. "Doubtless," he says, "the cocoa grows in all the islands of the Asiatic Archipelago, but by all oriental geographers the cocoa nut islands are understood to be the Maldives." "Thence," says Sindbad, we sailed to the island of pepper and to the peninsular of Comorin, in which is found the aloes wood, called *santy*. Thence we went to the pearl fisheries. I made a bargain with the divers, who brought me up a considerable number of beautiful pearls, and God heaped me with blessings; after which I travelled without interruption from country to country until I arrived at Bagdad." The Baron Walckenaer well expresses surprise at any mistake having been made respecting a track bearing such clear indications as this. From the Maldives Sindbad sailed to the island of pepper on the coast of Malabar. Thence he goes to the coast of Comorin, in the region of Komar, where he finds the aloes wood, called, as Ibn Batuta informs us, Houd al Komar, or wood of Komar. Thence he proceeded to the Gulf of Manaar, where the pearl fishery is carried on, and which is a sort of dependency of Ceylon, and after making great profit by his rich cargo he returns to his own country.

There is no difficulty in determining the places visited by Sindbad in his sixth voyage. He is thrown by a tempest upon an island, which is placed as in a gulf in the midst of the sea. The trees are all superb aloes, of the species named *santy* (Hindi or Sindí ?) and *comary* (Kumárí ?), names taken from the countries; and thence he passed by a subterraneous passage or cavern into the island or kingdom of Serendib or Ceylon. This passage was doubtless the succession of small islets or bank of sand known by the name of Adam's Bridge. Sindbad speaks with tolerable correctness of the dimensions of Serendib, which he describes as eighty leagues long and thirty leagues in its average breadth.

The seventh and last voyage of Sindbad is again to Serendib or Ceylon, whither he was sent as ambassador by the Khalíf Harún-al-Rashíd. It is worthy of notice, that in each of Sindbad's voyages two or three names only are mentioned, and very frequently only one, namely, that of his principal destination, and his details on the products and natural history of these places are exact; while he never names the countries which he makes the scenes of his extravagant fictions, and says nothing of their productions, showing thereby that the fictitious is only laid like a coat of varnish over the real.

With respect, however, to some of the marvellous stories related by Sindbad, it is to be observed, that as they are repeated by other travellers of veracity, and as all that is marvellous is not necessarily untrue, a little consideration is due to such stories before they are discarded as entirely fictitious. Some excellent observations on this subject were published by R. Hole, in a work entitled *Remarks on the Arabian Nights' Entertainments*, London, 1797, 8vo., from which, having verified the references, we give some quotations. The first of these stories is that of the gigantic bird called the *rukh*.

"Sindbad climbs a mountain, and beholds on one side nothing but skies and seas. On the other something white attracts his notice, and, on approaching to examine it, he perceives it to be a huge round bowl, about fifty paces in circumference, with a smooth polished surface.

"The sun was now ready to set, and the sky suddenly grew dark, as if covered with a thick cloud. His surprise and terror are not diminished on perceiving that it was caused by the shadow of a stupendous bird directing her flight towards him. He apprehends, and justly, that this was the winged monster, of which he had heard sailors talk, called the roc, and that the 'huge white bowl' was its egg. The bird descends, and sits on it in the act of incubation; Sindbad, who had crept close to the egg, being blessed with an admirable presence of mind, fastens himself to one of the bird's legs with the linen cloth which was wrapped round his turban. In the morning, agreeably to his hopes, the roc takes her flight; and soaring above the clouds, urges her course with such rapidity, as almost to deprive him of his senses. She, at length, descends to the earth: he unties the knots with which he had fastened himself to her leg; and the bird, soon afterwards, picks up a monstrous serpent and flies away with it.

"If any one chooses to look into Bochart's *Hierozoicon*, vol. ii, p. 84, he may find a more extravagant account of this bird, extracted from Arabian authors, than what is here given by Sindbad."

In Wilford's paper on Egypt and other countries, *Asiatic Researches*, vol. viii, p. 343, we read:—

"In the language of mythology, the *nagas* or *uragas* are large serpents, and the *garudas* or *supernas*, immense birds, which are either the condors of M. Buffon and vulture griffons of Linnæus, called rokhs by the Arabian fabulists and by Marco Polo, or mere creatures of imagination, like the *Simorg* of the Persians, whom Sadi describes as receiving his daily allowance on the mountain of Káf: whatever be the truth, the legend of Sanc'ha-naga and Garudá is thus told in the ancient books of the Hindús.

"'The King of Serpents formerly reigned in Chacragiri, a mountain very far to the eastward, but his subjects were obliged by the power of Garudá to supply that enormous bird with a snake each day.'

"Thus much for the mythological part of the story. From Marco Polo we get the following account of the rukh, which enables us to speak with greater approximation to certainty of the locality from which it came. He says: 'The people of the Island Magaster, now called San Lorenzo (Madagascar), report that at a certain season of the year, an extraordinary kind of bird, which they call a *rukh*, makes its appearance from the southern region. In form it is said to resemble the eagle, but it is incomparably greater in size; being so large and strong as to seize an elephant with its talons, and to lift it into the air; from whence it lets it fall to the ground, in order that when dead it may prey upon the carcase. Persons who have seen this bird assert, that when the wings are spread they measure sixteen paces in extent from point to point; and that the feathers are eight paces in length, and thick in proportion. Messer Marco Polo conceiving that these creatures might be griffins, such as are represented in paintings, half birds and half lions, particularly questioned those who reported their having seen them, as to this point; but they maintained that their shape was altogether that of birds, or, as it might be said, of the eagle."

"'The Grand *Khan* having heard this extraordinary relation, sent messengers to the island, on the pretext of demanding the release of one of his servants who had been detained there, but in reality to examine into the circumstances of the country and the truth of the wonderful things told of it. When they returned to the presence of his majesty, they brought with them (as I have heard) a feather of the *rukh*, positively affirmed to have measured ninety spans, and the quill part to have been two palms in circumference. This surprising exhibition afforded his majesty extreme pleasure, and upon those by whom it was presented he bestowed valuable gifts.'"

In a note to M. I. Geoffroy Saint-Hilaire's Notice of bones and eggs found in Madagascar, printed in the *Annales des Sciences Naturelles*, 3ème Serie, tom. xiv, p. 213, where he is speaking of the Epyornis, one of the giant birds of that island, that naturalist says:—"The stories about the roc may easily have had some connection with the discoveries of gigantic eggs, doubtless made from time to time in the island of Madagascar, and with the opinions to which they gave rise among the natives." M. Geoffroy St. Hilaire, however, objects to Mr. Strickland having fixed the identity of the roc as a Madagascar bird, because Marco Polo, to whose account Mr. Strickland refers, describes the bird as coming to Madagascar from the southern region.

In confirmation of this correction, the editor would call attention to a fact which, as far as he is aware, has not been previously noticed. On maps of the close of the sixteenth century, where the great Terra Australis Incognita, or Magellanica, is laid down, there will be found immediately south of the Cape of Good Hope, and therefore tallying with Marco Polo's account, this legend: "Psittacorum regio, sic a Lusitanis appellata ob incredibilem earum avium ibidem magnitudinem." The editor has been unable to discover the voyage in which these birds were observed, but it is alike certain that many early voyages of the Portuguese have been lost to us, and that portions of the great southern continent have been from time to time more recently discovered. Whatever doubt may exist as to the probability of large birds, like parrots, being found in a country as yet undiscovered south of Africa, it is at least remarkable that Portuguese navigators should have indicated the existence of birds of incredible size in the same regions as those from which Marco Polo makes the rukh to have come.

In any case, it is satisfactory to know that modern investigation has proved the existence of birds in former times, whose size would alike show that the ancient fable was based upon truth, and would present no small temptation to the exaggerative tendencies of orientalists.

But to return to Sindbad: "On looking around him, he perceives his present to be no less deplorable than his former situation. He finds himself in a deep valley, surrounded by inaccessible precipices, strewed with diamonds of an immense size and exquisite beauty; the contemplation of which would have afforded pleasure, had not other objects inspired sensations of a very different nature. This valley, it is said, abounded with serpents of such a prodigious magnitude, that 'the least of them was capable of swallowing an elephant.' A cave, whose entrance was 'low and strait,' and which Sindbad barricadoed with a large stone, protects him from their fury during the night; at the appearance of morn they retire to their hiding places. He supports himself for some time on a scanty stock of provisions, which he had prudently taken with him, inclosed in a leathern pouch. One day, after having eaten a sparing meal in the valley, he falls asleep; but his rest is interrupted by a large piece of fresh meat which fell near the place where he lay, and he soon after beholds other pieces tumbling down the surrounding precipices.

" He now recollects having heard (but he 'always considered it as a fable') of a valley of diamonds, and of the stratagems adopted by merchants to procure them: of its being the custom, at the season when eagles bred in the surrounding mountains, to throw vast joints of meat into the valley, and the diamonds, on whose points the meat fell, would adhere to it. On the sight of such unusual dainties, these eagles ('much stronger in this country than anywhere else') would descend from their lofty station, in hopes of conveying the prey to their nests on the rocky summits. Whilst they were thus employed, it was the merchant's occupation to watch their proceedings, to appear at the proper time, and, by extreme vociferation, compel them through fear to drop their precious morsels; which commonly afforded these adventurers an ample compensation for their labour.

" Sindbad now begins to entertain some hopes of escaping: he fills his pouch with the most valuable diamonds; ties himself with the cloth of his turban to the largest piece of meat he could find; and, placing himself beneath it, awaits, we may suppose with no very perfect composure, the event.

"A huge eagle descends, and having seized on the meat and its appendage, she deposits them near her nest; the merchants advance with loud shouts, which cause her to fly away, and Sindbad, to their no small surprise, makes his appearance. This story need not be pursued any farther. It is sufficient to add, that the fortunate aeronaut enriched both himself and the other merchants."

However wild this narrative may seem, it is countenanced by writers of a different cast from our author.

Epiphanius, archbishop of Salamis in Cyprus, who died in the year 403, in a little treatise, *De duodecim gemmis rationalis summi sacerdotis Hebræorum Liber*, *operâ Fogginii*, Romæ, 1743, p. 30, gives a precisely similar description of the mode of finding jacinths in Scythia. "In a wilderness in the interior of great Scythia," he says, "there is a valley begirt with stony mountains as with walls. It is inaccessible by man, and so excessively deep that the bottom of the valley is invisible from the top of the surrounding mountains. So great is the darkness, that it has the effect of a kind of chaos. To this place certain criminals are condemned, whose task it is to throw down into the valley slaughtered lambs, from which the skin has been first taken off. The little stones adhere to these pieces of flesh. Then the eagles, which live on the summits of the mountains, following the scent of the flesh, fly down and carry away the lambs with the stones adhering to them. They then who are condemned to this place, watch until the eagles have finished their meal, and run and take away the stones." Epiphanius, who wrote this, is spoken of in terms of great respect by many ecclesiastical writers, and St. Jerome styles the treatise here quoted "Egregium volumen, quod si legere volueris, plenissimam scientiam consequeris;" and, indeed, it is by no means improbable that it was from the account of Epiphanius that this story was first translated into Arabic. A similar account is given by Marco Polo and by Nicolò de Conti, as of a usage which they had heard was practised in India, and the position ascribed to the mountain by Conti, namely, fifteen days journey north of Vijanagar, renders it highly probable that Golconda was alluded to. He calls the mountain Albenigaras, and says that it was infested with serpents. Marco Polo also speaks of these serpents, and while his account agrees with that of Sindbad, inasmuch as the serpents, which are the prey of Sindbad's rukh, are devoured by the Venetian's eagles, that of Conti makes the vultures and eagles fly away with the meat to places where they may be safe from the serpents.

Another wonder deserving notice occurs in this voyage as having attracted Sindbad's observation: namely, an enormous tortoise, twenty cubits in length and breadth.

The account of these animals is not to be attributed to a licentious exuberance of fancy in the Arabian author. He might have seen in Ælian that the tortoises (*De Naturâ Anim.*, l. xvi, c. xvii), whose shells were fifteen cubits in length, and sufficiently large to cover a house, were to be found near the island of Taprobana. Pliny and Strabo mention the same circumstance (*Nat. Hist.*, l. ix, c. 10): they likewise turn them upside down, and say, that men used to row in them as in a boat (*Geog.* ,l. xvi, 16). Diodorus Siculus adds to their testimony, and assures us, on the faith of an historian, that the *chelonophagi* (shell fish eaters, L. iiii, c. 1), derived a threefold advantage from the tortoise, which occasionally supplied them with a roof to their houses, a boat, and a dinner.

In this colossal tortoise we recognize the *Colossochelys Atlas*, the first fossil remains of which were discovered by Dr. Falconer and Major Cautley in 1835, in the tertiary strata of the Sewalik Hills or Sub-Himalayahs, skirting the southern foot of the great Himalayah chain. They were found associated with the remains of four extinct species of mastodon and elephant, species of rhinoceros, hippopotamus, horse, and a vast number of other mammalia.

The remains of the Colossochelys were collected during a period of eight or nine years, along a range of eighty miles of hilly country ; they belong, in consequence, to a great number of different animals, varying in size and age. From the circumstances under which they are met with, in crushed fragments contained in elevated strata, which have undergone great disturbance, there is little room for hope that a perfect shell, or anything approaching a complete skeleton, will ever be found in the Sewalik Hills. It is to be mentioned, however, that remains of many of the animals associated with the

Colossochelys in the Sewalik Hills have been discovered along the banks of the Irrawaddi in Ava, and in Perim Island in the Gulf of Cambay, showing that the same extinct fauna was formerly spread over the whole continent of India. (See a paper by Dr. Falconer and Captain Cautley, read May 14th, 1845, at the Zoological Society, and printed in the *Annals and Magazine of Natural History*, vol. xv, p. 55.)

An idea of the vast size of this tortoise is afforded by the cast in the upper galleries in the British Museum.

We have, however, already dwelt at too much length on these interesting details, and must now lead the reader on to the account of the next voyage in chronological sequence bearing upon India. It is one which is eccentric alike as regards the nation and the object of him who performed it. We allude to that of the Spanish Jew, Benjamin of Tudela, who, in the year 1159 or 1160, started from Tudela on a journey of some thirteen or fourteen years, during which he traversed the greater part of the then known world. Nothing certain is known, either as to his profession or whether his object was the acquirement of riches or of scientific information. The only conclusion suggested by his narrative is, that he was anxious to ascertain the number of the Jews who were dispersed throughout the different countries of the world, and to make himself acquainted with their moral and religious condition. As that portion of his wanderings which relates to India is comparatively short, we extract it entire from the best translation which has been made of his narrative, namely, that by the late learned and respected Mr. Asher, of Berlin. The extract is taken from pages 136 to 143 of his valuable work.

"This river (the Tigris) runs downward and falls into the Indian Sea (Persian Gulf), in the vicinity of an island called Kish. The extent of this island is six miles, and the inhabitants do not carry on any agriculture, principally because they have no rivers nor more than one spring in the whole island, and are consequently obliged to drink rain water.

"It is, however, a considerable market, being the point to which Indian merchants and those of the islands bring their commodities; while the traders of Mesopotamia, Yemen, and Persia import all sorts of silk and purple cloths, flax, cotton, hemp, mash (a kind of pea), wheat, barley, millet, rye, and all sorts of comestibles and pulse, which articles form objects of exchange; those from India import great quantities of spices, and the inhabitants of the island live by what they gain in their capacity of brokers to both parties. The island contains about five hundred Jews.

"Ten days passage by sea lies El-Cathif, a city with about five thousand Israelites. In this vicinity the pearls are found: about the twenty-fourth of the month of Nisan (April) large drops of rain are observed upon the surface of the water, which are swallowed by the reptiles, after this they close their shells and fall upon the bottom of the sea; about the middle of the month of Thishri (October), some people dive with the assistance of ropes, collect these reptiles from the bottom and bring them up with them, after which they are opened and the pearls taken out.

"Seven days from thence is Chulam, on the confines of the country of the Sun-worshippers. They are descendents of Khush, are addicted to astrology, and are all black.

"This nation is very trustworthy in matters of trade, and whenever foreign merchants enter their port, three secretaries of the king immediately repair on board their vessels, write down their names and report them to him. The king thereupon grants them security for their property, which they may even leave in the open fields without any guard.

"One of the king's officers sits in the market, and receives goods that may have been found anywhere, and which he returns to those applicants who can minutely describe them. This custom is observed in the whole empire of the king.

"From Easter to new year (from April to October) during the whole of the summer the heat is extreme. From the third hour of the day (nine o'clock in the morning) people shut themselves up in their houses until the evening, at which time every body goes out. The streets and markets are lighted up and the inhabitants employ all the night upon their business, which they are prevented from doing in the day time, in consequence of the excessive heat.

"The pepper grows in this country; the trees which bear this fruit are planted in the fields, which surround the towns, and every one knows his plantation. The trees are small and the pepper is originally white, but when they collect it, they put it into basins and pour hot water upon it; it is then exposed to the heat of the sun and dried in order to make it hard and more substantial, in the course of which process it becomes of a black colour.

"Cinnamon, ginger, and many other kinds of spices also grow in this country.

"The inhabitants do not bury their dead, but embalm them with certain spices, put them upon stools and cover them with cloths, every family keeping apart. The flesh dries upon the bones, and as these corpses resemble living beings, every one of them recognises his parents and all the members of his family for many years to come.

"These people worship the sun; about half a mile from every town they have large places of worship, and every morning they run towards the rising sun; every place of worship contains a representation of that luminary, so constructed by machinery (our author calls it witchcraft) that upon the rising of the sun it turns round with a great noise, at which moment both men and women take up their censers, and burn incense in honour of this their deity. 'This their way is their folly.' (Psalm xlix, 13.) All the cities and countries inhabited by these people contain only about one hundred Jews, who are of black colour as well as the other inhabitants. The Jews are good men, observers of the law, and possess the Pentateuch, the Prophets, and some little knowledge of the Thalmud and its decisions.

"The island of Khandy is distant twenty-two days

journey. The inhabitants are fire worshipers, called Druzes, and twenty-three thousand Jews live among them. These Druzes have priests everywhere in the houses consecrated to their idols, and those priests are expert necromancers, the like of whom are to be met with nowhere. In front of the altar of their house of prayer you see a deep ditch, in which a large fire is continually kept burning; this they call Elahuta, Deity. They pass their children through it, and into this ditch they also throw their dead.

"Some of the great of this country take a vow to burn themselves alive; and if any such devotee declares to his children and kindred his intention to do so, they all applaud him and say: 'Happy shalt thou be, and it shall be well with thee.' (Psalm cxxviii, 2.) Whenever the appointed day arrives, they prepare a sumptuous feast, mount the devotee upon his horse if he be rich, or lead him afoot if he be poor, to the brink of the ditch. He throws himself into the fire, and all his kindred manifest their joy by the playing of instruments until he is entirely consumed. Within three days of this ceremony two of their principal priests repair to his house and thus address his children: 'Prepare the house, for to-day you will be visited by your father, who will manifest his wishes unto you.' Witnesses are selected among the inhabitants of the town, and lo! the devil appears in the image of the dead. The wife and children inquire after his state in the other world, and he answers: 'I have met my companions, but they have not admitted me into their company, before I have discharged my debts to my friends and neighbours.' He then makes a will, divides his goods among his children, and commands them to discharge all debts he owes and to receive what people owe him ; this will is written down by the witnesses......[1] to go his way, and he is not seen any more. In consequence of these lies and deceit, which the priests pass off as magic, they retain a strong hold upon the people, and make them believe that their equal is not to be met with upon earth."

We now come to the account of a voyage which, before all others, claims attention as regards the detailed observation by which it is characterized, namely, that of the great father of modern geography, Marco Polo. "This account," as Sprengel observes, "was long the general manual of Asiatic geography throughout entire Europe, especially after the voyages of the Portuguese had confirmed many of his supposed rhodomontades." In company with his father and his uncle, natives of Venice, who had many years before made a trading journey to Tártary, Marco Polo started in 1271, and after travelling for three years and a half across Asia and encountering a variety of dangers and disasters, at length reached the court of Kublai, Grand Khán of that country. Marco became a great favourite with the Khán, and was employed by him in several important missions to distant provinces. After a residence of seventeen years at the court of Kublai, the three Venetians became extremely anxious to return to their native

[1] A blank occurs here in both the first editions.

country, and at length obtained permission to accompany the ambassadors of a king of Khorassan, who had come to demand a princess of the Khán's family in marriage for their sovereign. The voyage occupied a year and a half, through the Indian seas, before they reached the court of this king, named Arghún. Thence they travelled to Constantinople, and finally reached Venice in 1295. It is with this return voyage that we now have to do.

He touched at the kingdom of Ziamba (Tsiampa), where he learned much of Great Java or Java, though he did not himself visit either that island or Borneo. He then sailed southward, and passing the small island of Pentan (Bintang) came to Java Minor, under which name he designates Sumatra. He appears then to have sailed along its coast through the Straits of Malacca to Seilan [Ceylon], noticing on his way the island Angaman (Andaman Islands). After some stay at Ceylon he sailed to Maabar, which, however, must not be confounded with Malabar, but is the coast of Coromandel. He notices its fine cottons; also its various superstitions, as the worship of the cow, the abstinence from animal food, the courtezans dedicated to the service of the temple, and the acts of voluntary self-sacrifice to their gods, as well as the custom of females burning themselves after the death of their husbands. Then passing Cape Comorin he sailed along the coasts of Malabar, where he notices the abundance of pepper and ginger; then along those of Guzerat and Cambaia, and so, across the Indian Ocean, home.

In the course of his inquiries and explorations, Marco Polo took pains to make himself acquainted with the natural history of each country, and especially with such products as by their costliness or usefulness might become valuable as articles of commerce. By his observations on the manufactures and navigation of different countries, he constantly shows his sense of what would be chiefly interesting to a maritime and commercial people like the Venetians, to whose nation he belonged; and a rich field for such observation lay before him. The commerce of India he found stretching, like an immense chain, from the territories of Kublai Khán to the shores of the Persian Gulf and of the Red Sea. He found the shores and the islands of the Indian Sea luxuriantly covered with nature's choicest productions. In lieu of wine, the palm tree gave its milk, and the bread fruit tree afforded its wholesome food. The betel nut, and spices, and everything which might flatter the palate of man, he found in rich abundance in these climates, and if he does not minutely describe them, he at least names the different plants from which these luxuries were procured. Nor is he silent upon those less useful but not less highly prized productions of India which are derived from beneath the surface of the earth. He tells us of the topaz, the amethyst, and the emerald, of the sapphires of Ceylon, and the diamonds of Golconda, and the rubies from the mountains of Thibet.

He furthermore traces down as far south as the island of Madagascar the nautical explorations of the

Asiatics of the middle ages, and suggests to us an explanation of the reasons why those early navigators failed in discovering the southernmost point of Africa. "They cannot go," he says, "further south than this island and that of Zanguebar, because the current draws them so strongly towards the south that they cannot turn back again. The vessels from Maabar (Coromandel) take twenty days in reaching this island and three months in returning, so strong does the current lie towards the south and never has any other direction." Some attempts had doubtless shown that vessels driven southward of Madagascar had met with no land in that direction, and that an immense tract of ocean lay beyond. Those who escaped the dangers of this navigation, and were brought back to India by the spring (?) monsoon, would warn other explorers from venturing upon similar risks. The age of great maritime discovery had not yet arrived, and if the monsoons presented opportunities of boldly sailing out of sight of land, they at the same time exposed adventurous navigators to a new kind of danger, by carrying them far away to the south across an ocean to which they found no limit.

In the long interval between the travels of Marco Polo (1271-94) and the awakening of the spirit of discovery in Portugal in the fifteenth century, nearly all our knowledge on the state of manners and civilization among the population of Further Asia is derived from the accounts of Muhammedan geographers and travellers; and at the head of the latter class, if preeminence be regulated by the extent of ground passed over, we may safely place Ibn Batuta. This indefatigable explorer started in the year of the Hegira 725, A.D. 1324, from his native city, Tangier, at the age of twenty-two or twenty-three, and continued for thirty years with unwearied diligence travelling about in different countries.

A valuable translation of these important travels, from the abridged Arabic manuscript copies in the Public Library of Cambridge, with notes on the history, geography, botany, antiquities, etc., of the countries visited, was made by Professor Lee, and printed for the Oriental Translation Committee, London, 1829, 4to.

The name, style, and titles of Ibn Batuta, as stated at length, were "the Sheikh Abu-Abdallah Mohammed Ibn Abdallah Al-Lawati Al-Tandij, surnamed Ibn Batuta." He was a Moor by birth, and a doctor of the Muhammedan law and traditions by profession. He set out with the purpose of accomplishing the pilgrimage to Mekka, and proceeded by land towards Egypt.

The adventures which befell him during his long sojourn in India, form one of the most curious and eventful chapters of his peregrinations; and this part of his narrative derives additional interest from the details which he introduces, not only of the natural productions and agriculture of the country, but of the manners, institutions, and history of Hindustán, under the Affghan dynasties, which preceded for nearly three hundred years the establishment of the

Mogul power. He gives an historical retrospect, extending from the first conquest of Dehli by the Muhammedans under Kotbed-dín Ai-bek, in 1188, to the accession of the reigning sovereign, Sultan Muhammed, the son of Tughlak, in 1325; which is especially valuable from the additional facts which it supplies, and the light thrown on many of the transactions recorded by Ferishta. This preliminary sketch is continued by the personal narrative of Ibn Batuta himself, whose fortune led him to India at the crisis when the unity of the Patan power (at all times rather an aristocracy of military leaders, than a consolidated monarchy) was on the point of dissolution, from the mad tyranny of Sultan Muhammed, which drove all the governors of provinces into open revolt, and led to the erection of independent kingdoms in Bengal, the Dekhan, etc. On the arrival of an embassy from the emperor of China, he gladly accepted an appointment as one of the envoys destined to convey the gifts sent in return by Sultan Muhammed; and receiving his outfit and credentials, quitted without delay the dangerous walls of Dehli early in the year of the Hejira 743 (A.D. 1342).

He had not advanced many days journey towards the coast, when his escort was overpowered in a conflict with the Hindús, his colleague in the embassy killed, and he himself, escaping with difficulty from his captors, made his way back, alone and on foot, to the presence of the emperor. After renewing his equipments, he again set forward, and this time reached without molestation the distant port of Calicut, where the Chinese junks awaited the embassy. In this long and toilsome journey through Central India and the Dekhan, he describes, among other places through which he passed, the cities of Daulatabád, Goa, and Onor or Hanavar: and notes with special wonder the juggling performances of the Hindú yogis. His account of the country and natural productions of Malabar, its pepper, ginger, and spices, of the numerous sovereignties into which it was subdivided, and the singular custom of succession by the female line in preference to the male, is remarkably perspicuous and accurate; and he confirms the statements of Marco Polo as to the maritime and piratical habits of the people, alleging, however, that they captured only those vessels which attempted to pass their ports without the payment of toll. The embassy remained three months in Calicut, till the monsoon enabled them to sail for China; but every stage in this mission was doomed to misfortune. While the envoys and the suite, with the costly gifts of which they were the bearers, were in course of embarcation in the port, a violent tempest arose, by which part of the Chinese squadron was driven on shore and wrecked; while the remaining vessels, on board one of which Ibn Batuta's property and harem had already been embarked, were driven so far out to sea, that the captains, instead of returning to Calicut, made the best of their way to China. Batuta himself had accidentally delayed going on board; but his two colleagues perished in one of the stranded ships, and he was left with only his "prayer-carpet and ten dinars, which," he says, "I kept as a blessing, as they had been given me by some holy men." At length receiving intelligence that all his property had been confiscated on the arrival of the junk in China, he determined to resume his wanderings; and setting sail from Hanavar, arrived in ten days at the Zabiyah-Al-Mohli, or Maldive Islands.

"These islands," he says, "constitute one of the wonders of the world; for their number is about two thousand, nearly one hundred of which are so close together as to form a kind of ring" "The people are religious, chaste, and peaceable: they eat what is lawful, and their prayers are answered. Their bodies are weak, they make no war, and their weapons are prayers." Their chief subsistence was on fish, rice, and the fruit of the cocoa-tree; and the coir-rope, formed from the fibres of this tree, was their principal article of commerce: a sea shell, called wada, was current in lieu of coined money.

The arrival of Ibn Batuta in Ceylon had been the effect of accident; but once landed on the island, he determined not to quit it without visiting the mighty mountain of Serendib (Adam's Peak), which they had seen from the sea, "like a pillar of smoke," at the distance of nine days sail, and on the summit of which was the famous footstep attributed by tradition to "our forefather, Adam." The Cingalese name of this mountain is *Sumanakúta*, and of the footstep *Serapadà* or *Sripada*, the footstep of Buddha. The designation of Adam's Peak is derived from

Arab geographers only. For this venerated place of pilgrimage he accordingly set forward in a palanquin, attended by four yogis, whom the king Ayari provided as guides. The account of his route is interspersed, as usual, with notices of the mineral and vegetable riches, the rubies and carbuncles, the cinnamon and aloes, of the districts through which he passed. In his description of the monkeys, which abounded in the hills, it is not difficult to recognize the large species called the Wanderoo (*Macacus silenus*): "They are black and long-tailed, and the beard of the males is like that of a man."

His stay in the islands of the Indian Archipelago was not of long duration, and his notice of them relates principally to the spices, which then, as now, constituted their chief wealth. The camphor, the clove, the nutmeg, etc., with the plants which produce them, are described with minuteness and with tolerable accuracy: he also records the abundance and common use of elephants.

The only adventure which marked Ibn Batuta's voyage to Sumatra was the sight of a huge distant object in the air, which the sailors declared to be a rokh, the giant bird to which we have already alluded in adverting to the narrative of Sindbad. The fear of the mariners, who expected nothing less than instant destruction, was, however, removed by a change of wind, which carried them away from the monster, so that they could gain no clear notion of his shape, but reached their destination without mishap.

The political aspect of the eastern world, when visited by Ibn Batuta, was in a state of transition from the form which it had assumed in consequence of the Mogul conquests of the preceding century, to the general disorganization which paved the way for the establishment of a new empire by Tímúr. From the Euphrates eastward to the shores of the Northern Pacific, the whole surface of Asia, if we exclude the two peninsulas of Hither and Further India, was ruled by sovereign houses descended from Jenghíz; but of the four principal empires into which this enormous tract was subdivided,. the semi-European Khanate of Kapchak was the only one in which the symptoms of division and decay had not yet become apparent; the monarchies of Persia and Turkestán were virtually dissolved at the deaths of the respective monarchs Abú Saíd and Turmushrín, who were reigning when Ibn Batuta travelled; and he was himself an eyewitness in China of the commencement of the struggle in which the Mogul domination was overthrown. The Muhammedan empire in India, almost the only Asiatic power which had wholly escaped the Mogul tempest, was actually in the course of dismemberment, during his residence at Dehli, from the mad misgovernment of Muhammed-ben-Tughlak; and fell an easy prey, fifty years later, to the arms of Tímúr.

Of the voyages to India which fall within the period comprised by the present collective volume, that of Nicolò de' Conti takes the lead both in date and in importance.

Nicolò de' Conti, or as he was named in Latin De Comitibus, was a Venetian of noble family, who, when a young man, resided as a merchant in the city of Damascus, whence he started on his travels to the East, though in what year is not precisely known. He passed through Persia, sailed along the coast of Malabar, visited some parts of the interior of Hindustán, and also the islands of Ceylon, Sumatra, and Java. He afterwards went to the south of China, and on his return passed along the coasts of Ethiopia, sailed up the Red Sea, crossed the desert and reached Cairo, where he lost his wife and two children, and returned to Venice in 1444, after twenty-five years absence. As he had been compelled, in order to save his life, to renounce the Christian religion, he besought absolution for his apostasy from Pope Eugene IV. That pontiff granted his petition, merely requiring of him as a penance that he should relate his adventures to Poggio Bracciolini, the Pope's secretary. The latter wrote them in Latin, but this early translation was so scarce, that Ramusio, who, as he himself says, "made every exertion to find it, not only in the city of Venice, but in many other cities of Italy," failed in doing so, and "after much fruitless labour was informed that, in the city of Lisbon, it had been printed in Portuguese," and it was from this faulty Portuguese translation that his Italian version was made, as given in the first volume of his *Navigationi et Viaggi*. The original Latin, which Ramusio could not find, at length appeared in the fourth book of Poggio's treatise, *De Varietate*

Fortunæ libri quatuor, edited by the Abbé Oliva, Paris, 1723, 4to., and from this edition the present first translation into English is made.

The first Indian city which Conti reached was Cambaya, where he notices the number of the precious stones called sardonixes, and also the prevalence of the custom of Suttee. After twenty days sail from Cambaya he comes to two cities on the coast, the one named Pacamuria, the other Helly, which the editor has been unable to identify. In the districts around these cities he speaks of the growth and mode of drying of ginger. At a distance of three hundred miles inland, he comes to the great city of Bizenegalia (or Vijanagár), the capital of the mightiest kingdom at that time in India. A description of this vast city, which stood on the shore of the river Tungabudhra, is given in full in the narrative of Abd-er-razzak's voyage in the present collection. Eight days journey from Bizenegalia was the noble city of Pelagonda (Pennaconda?), subject to the same sovereign. Twenty days hence by land brought him to the seaport of Peudifetania, probably, judging from the itinerary of Odoardo Barbosa in the beginning of the next century, where the same name is mentioned, Durma-patnam, near Tellicherry. On the road he passed two cities, named Odeschiria and Cenderghiria, where the red sandal grows. These names respectively, Udayagiri, mountain of the sunrise, and Chandragiri, mountain of the moon, occur frequently in India; but it is difficult to detect those here referred here. His next point was Maliapúr, the burial place of St. Thomas, whose body was worshiped by the Nestorians. These Christians, he states, are scattered over all India, and in Maliapúr there were a thousand of them. Here there would seem to have been an irregularity in the narrative, probably from the confusion incidental to an oral description; as, after mentioning Maliapúr, he says, "All this province is called Malabar." This is the more apparent as he goes on to say, "Beyond this city is another, called Cahila, where pearls are found," which in all probability is the Colchos of the author of the *Periplus of the Erythœan Sea*, the modern pearl fishery of Kilkare, in the strait which separates the island of Ceylon from the continent. The very next place of which Conti speaks, moreover, is Ceylon, which he describes as three thousand miles in circumference. His account of the cinnamon tree, as growing in this island, is remarkably exact. The next point in his wanderings is Sumatra, which he calls Taprobana, but which he says is called by the natives Sciamuthera. This is the first printed instance within the editor's knowledge in which the name of Taprobana, which in earlier times unquestionably appertained to Ceylon, was given to Sumatra, although the same error occurs on the Catalan map of 1375, entitled *Image del Mon*. It is repeated in the Venetian map of the monk Fra Mauro, 1458, was maintained throughout the maps, almost all of them Italian, of the sixteenth century, and was continued by Mercator, in some of the editions of whose atlas it is preserved till the seventeenth century. Its first correction to Ceylon on the face of maps it is more difficult to speak of with certainty, but the earliest correction that the editor has met with in print is by Barros, who says: "Se verá o engaño que alguns presentes recebem em dizer que a Aurea Chersoneso a que nos chamamos Çamatra, he a Taprobana." On the maps of the seventeenth century, however, we find the two islands designated by their present names without reference to ancient nomenclature.

Conti remained one year in Sumatra. He remarks in strong terms on the cruelty and brutality of the inhabitants and their cannibalism. Amongst the natural productions he quotes pepper, long pepper, camphor, and gold in abundance. He describes the pepper tree and the *duriano* or *Durio Zibethinus* of Linnæus, one of the most highly esteemed fruits of the Malay Islands.

From Sumatra a stormy passage of sixteen days brings him to Tenasserim, which he describes as abounding in elephants and a species of thrush. From this point we find him again turning westward and arriving at the mouth of the Ganges, up which a sail of fifteen days brings him to the large and wealthy city of Cernove (Karunagar?). He speaks of the huge size of the bamboo tree, of which he found skiffs made for sailing on the river. He also alludes with wonder to the crocodiles and fishes *unknown to us* which were found in the Ganges, and to the bananas and cocoa-nut trees which adorned the villas on its banks. Sailing yet further up the river for the space of three months, in which course he passed four very famous cities, he at length landed at an extremely powerful city called Maarazia (Mathura?), where was great abundance of aloes, wood, gold, silver, precious stones, and pearls. From this city he diverged to some mountains lying to the east, for the purpose of procuring the carbuncles which were found there. After spending thirteen days in this expedition, he returned to the city of Cernove, and thence proceeded to Buffetania (Burdhwán). Sailing down the Ganges, he again turns eastward and visits Aracan, and thence crosses the Youmadoung mountains to the Irawadi, up which he sails till he reaches Ava, the circumference of which he describes to be fifteen miles. He gives an interesting description of the process of catching and rearing elephants, and speaks of the rhinoceros and of huge serpents of the python species. He also refers to the habit of tattooing and the use of the talepot leaves for the purpose of writing. After a passing allusion to Cathay, the name formerly given to the northern part of China, which he describes as beyond the country of Macinus (Siam), of which he is then speaking, his narrative brings us to a city called Panconia, probably Pegu, where he remained for four months. He here specifies the vines as being the only instances of that plant which occur in India, and there only in small quantities, and even then not used for the purpose of making wine. In this place he also mentions a variety of fruits, such as pineapples, oranges, and melons, together with white sandal wood and camphor, which latter disappears if they do not sacrifice to the gods before they cut the tree. Thence by a sudden transition he brings us to two islands called Java, distant from the continent one month's sail and within one hundred miles of each other. But for his former distinct mention of Sumatra under the name of Sciamuthera, it might have been supposed that he was here speaking of the islands of Sumatra and Java; but as he now describes one of these islands as three thousand miles in circumference and the other two thousand, and as he had in his description of Taprobana or Sciamuthera given to that island a circumference of six thousand miles, it is to be presumed that Java and Sumbava are here alluded to. This is the more probable, as it is tolerably certain that the southern coasts of neither of these two islands had been explored for nearly two centuries after the date of Conti's voyage. Hence their circumference could not be spoken of except from conjecture.

He remained in Java nine months with his wife and children, who accompanied him in all his journeys. He speaks of the cruelty of the people, and alludes to the practice of cock-fighting, so fashionable amongst them. He also makes reference to a bird without feet and with an oblong tail, the description of which would seem to agree with that of the bird of paradise, which, though not a native of Java, might have been imported from New Guinea; since the skins of these birds are wrapped round a stick and used as ornaments, the feet being previously removed, and it is to be observed that our traveller does not tell us that he saw the bird alive.

The islands referred to under the names of Sandai and Bandan, as lying at fifteen days sail from Java, would seem to be Bouro and Ceram, or Amboyna, from the statement that Bandan was "the only island in which cloves grow, which are exported hence to the Java Islands;" and from the further remark, that "the sea is not navigable beyond these islands, and the stormy atmosphere keeps navigators at a distance," it being well known how dangerous and rarely attempted at the present day is a passage through Torres' Straits, between New Guinea and Australia. It would appear that Conti did not visit these islands, but merely spoke from what he learned of them in Java, into which country their products were imported, and the more so as he states that, *having quitted Java*, he bent his course westward to a maritime city called Ciampa, which voyage occupied him one month. Departing thence, he in a like space of time reached Coloen, probably Quilon, on the coast of Travancore; for he calls the province Melibaria, which appears to be Malabar. Here he found the Galeopithecus or flying squirrel, which, though a native of the Molucca and Philippine Islands, is found in some parts of the west coast of India. He also accurately describes the Jack (*Artocarpus integrifolia*), and seems, from his allusion to fruits without kernels and with incised leaves to have met with the bread fruit tree. He also describes the mango under the name "amba." From Coloen, three days brought him to

Cocym, doubtless Cochin, where he relates a marvellous story of monsters in human form.

He then visited Colanguria (Kodungaloor), at the mouth of the Paliuria (Yellarapully), and then Meliancota. Thence he proceeded to Calicut, where he describes the habit of polygamy as practised, contrary to the usual fashion, by the women, who there "are allowed to take several husbands," so that some have ten and more. The husbands contribute among themselves to the maintenance of the wife, who lives apart from her husbands. The children are allotted to the husbands at the will of the wife, and "the inheritance of the father does not descend to the children, but to the grandchildren." Truly, it must, in that country, have been "a wise child who knew its own father." Departing from Calicut, he proceeded next westward to Cambay, which he reached in fifteen days. Hence returning by Calicut he visited the island of Socotra, where he spent two months. He found it for the most part inhabited by Nestorian Christians. From this point he makes his journey homeward in the manner we have already described.

Poggio here gives a summary of the answers given by Conti to his inquiries respecting the manners and customs of the Indians, for which we refer the reader to the text of this interesting narrative from page 21 to the close.

The next voyage in this collection, which, for the reasons we have assigned in the advertisement, stands first in the series, is that of Abd-er-Razzák, whose full designation is written thus,—Kamál-ad-dín Abd-er-

Razzák Ben Jalál-ad-dín Isḥák-as-Samarkandi. Abd-er-Razzák was born at Herát, in A.H. 816 (A.D. 1413). His father, Jalál-ad-dín Johák, was kázi in the time of Shah Rukh. In A.H. 841 (A.D. 1437), after his father's death, he was admitted into the service of Shah Rukh, and in A.H. 845 (A.D. 1441) he was sent on an important mission to one of the kings of India, namely, the king of the country of which Vijanagar was the capital. Of this embassy he gave an account in the Matla-as-Sá-dain, as here translated In A.H. 850 (A.D. 1446) Abd-er-Razzák was sent on an embassy into Ghilán, and had scarcely fulfilled his mission, when he was ordered to depart for Egypt with the title of ambassador. The death of his master, however, prevented his journey. After this, Abd-er-Razzák resided successively with Mirzá Abd-al-Latif, Mirzá Abd-Allah, Mirzá Bábur, and Mirzá Ibrahím; and in A.H. 856 (A.H. 1452) he made preparations for a journey into Irák. In that year the Sultan Abú al Kasim Babur, passing through the town of Taft Yazd, had an interview with the celebrated historian Sharaf-ad-dín Ali Yazdi, and our author was present at the conference. Two years afterwards he became attached to the person of the Sultan Abú Saíd, who treated him with the greatest honour; and in A.H. 863 (A.D. 1458), when Sultan Husain Bahádur undertook an expedition into Jurján, our author, who had been sent on a mission into that part of the country, had an opportunity of witnessing most of the events of the war. In A.H. 867 (A.D. 1462) Abd-er-Razzák was elected Shaikh of the monastery of Mirzá Shah

Rukh, at Herát, and held that office until his death, which happened in A.H. 887 (A.D. 1482).

The narrative of his voyage to India was introduced, not in a literal, but in a popular form, in the *Collection portative de Voyages*, published by Langlès, 1798-1820, six vols., 12mo. A very curious notice upon Langlès, by M. P. H. J. B. Audiffret, the keeper of the manuscripts in the Library at Paris, which was printed in the third volume of the *Biographie universelle et portative des cotemporains* (1854), is quoted by M. Quérard, in his *Supercheries Litteraires*, as proving that Langlès was not only undeserving of the literary reputation he enjoyed, but that he had been guilty of two literary frauds, one of which is connected with the document of which we now treat. It was for a long time believed by orientalists, says M. Audiffret, that the voyage from Persia into India by Abd-er-Razzák, a little work forming but the half of a small volume, was the only attempt made by M. Langlès in oriental literature. M. Audiffret says: "It is now proved beyond a doubt, that the voyage of Abd-er-Razzák was taken entirely from a French translation made by M. Galland (the celebrated translator of the *Arabian Nights' Entertainments*) from a history of Shah Rukh and the other descendants of Tímúr, written by the same Abd-er-Razzák, two copies of which are in the National Library at Paris. It is a painful task to have to show that the pretended translator has published M. Galland's work as his own, and in order to conceal his plagiarism, has stolen from one of the copies those paragraphs which related to the voyage of the Persian author, without recollecting that another copy existed upon which he himself had marked these paragraphs in brackets. Of the discovery of the "supercherie" consequent upon this first we do not here treat, as irrelevant to our subject.

The most satisfactory description of the work, however, will be found in the elaborate article by M. Quatremère, in the fourteenth volume of the *Notices et Extraits des Manuscrits*, which comprises a great portion of the life of Shah Rukh, and the text, accompanied by a version in French, of two other extracts from Abd-er-Razzák's history, relating respectively to the voyage of the ambassador of Shah Rukh to China, and to that of Abd-er-Razzák himself to India. From this latter the present translation has been made. M. Quatremère, whose high authority is unquestioned, passes the most favourable judgment as to the merits of the work, saying that it is incontestably one of the most curious and veracious histories that has been written in any of the Eastern languages.

Abd-er-Razzák set out from Herát in January 1442, and proceeded by way of Kohistán and Kirmán to Ormuz, of which emporium he speaks in terms of the highest admiration. From Ormuz he sailed for India, but being too late for the monsoon, he was compelled to pass several months at Muscat, where, as he drolly describes it, the heat was so intense, that the marrow boiled in the bones, and the metal of their swords melted like wax. The excessive heat threw him into a fever, which did not leave him till he got to sea, when, having a favourable voyage, he recovered his health. The port at which he arrives is Calicut, where he speaks in terms of commendation of the honesty of the people, and the facilities of commerce. He does not, however, equally admire the persons of the natives, who seem to him to resemble devils rather than men. These devils were all black and naked, having only a piece of cloth tied round their middle, and holding in one hand a shining javelin, and in the other a buckler of bullock's hide.

On being presented to the Sameri or King, whom he found, in a similar state of nudity, in a hall adorned with paintings, and surrounded by two or three thousand attendants, he delivered his presents, which consisted of a horse richly caparisoned, an embroidered pelisse, and a cap of ceremony. These did not seem to excite any warm admiration from the prince, and it is not impossible that, as the ambassador looked with considerable dislike on the people in spite of his commendations of their worthiness of conduct, his own manner may not have been remarkable for amiability. His stay at Calicut he describes as extremely painful, and in the midst of his trouble he has a vision, in which he sees his sovereign Shah Rukh, who assures him of deliverance. On the very next day, a message arrives from the King of Vijanagar, with a request that the Muhammedan ambassador might be permitted to repair to his court. The request of so powerful a prince was not refused, and Abd-er-Razzák left Calicut with feelings of great delight. From Calicut he proceeded to Mangalore, near which he saw a huge temple of cast bronze, containing an idol of human size, made of massive gold, with rubies for its eyes. From Mangalore he proceeds to Belloor, where the houses were like palaces and the women like celestial houris. Here also was a lofty temple surrounded by gardens, and surmounted by a cupola of polished blue stone, which was frequented by pilgrims from distant parts of India, whose presents formed the principal support of the place.

From Bellour he proceeded to Vijanagar, for the description of the splendour of which city, its vast extent, its palaces, bazaars and pretty women, we must refer the reader to the text. Abd-er-Razzák and his companions were better treated here than at Calicut. They had a handsome house assigned to them, and were admitted soon after their arrival to an audience of the king. That prince gave a gracious reception to the letter of Shah Rukh and to his ambassador; and as it was contrary to the custom of the country to give entertainments to ambassadors, he presented him daily with liberal supplies of provisions, gold and betel root.

During his stay he had an opportunity of witnessing the great yearly festival of Mahanadi, in which a thousand elephants, covered with armour and with castles filled with jugglers on their backs, were collected together, and performed a variety of gambols. But what pleased our ambassador the most was the loveliness of the female singers and dancers, which seems to have turned his head. At the close of the festival he was presented to the king, whom he found seated on a throne of gold bedecked with precious stones. The king conferred with him for a considerable time respecting the Shah of Persia and the great capitals of his kingdom, and made mention of a variety of costly presents which he proposed to send to the Shah by the hands of Abd-er-Razzák. This prosperous condition of the embassy, however, was doomed to meet with a reverse from the jealousy of some merchants of Ormuz, who declared that Abd-er-Razzák had come without any authority from Shah Rukh, and that he was merely a private adventurer. The result was a great change in the treatment shown to him by the courtiers during the absence of the king. On the king's return from an expedition that he had made into the south he sent for Abd-er-Razzák, and treating him with kindness, though with a marked diminution of consideration in his manner, gave him letters and some presents for the Shah, and promised him a better reception if he should ever return with more satisfactory proofs of the genuineness of his mission. The disgust of Abd-er-Razzâk is comically expressed in the following characteristic reply. "If, when once I have escaped from the desert of thy love I reach my own country, I will never again set out on another voyage, not even in the company of a king."

Abd-er-Razzák started from Vijanagar on the 5th November, 1443, and set sail on his return voyage from the port of Mangalore on 28th January, 1444.

After a stormy passage he arrived at Kalahat, in Arabia, in the month of March, 1444. We invite the reader's attention to the amusing description of his sea passage.

The next journey into India given in this volume is that of Athanasius Nikitin, a Russian, whose narrative was translated for the present work by the late amiable and highly accomplished Count Wielhorsky, Secretary to the Russian Legation at the court of St. James's, who has left us the following account of the narrative itself and of the document from which it has been translated.

"It will be remembered that during the middle ages, the monasteries in Western Europe were the only abodes of learning and science, and the only means through which records of times gone by were saved from oblivion and transmitted to posterity. The same may be said of the monastic orders of the Greek Russian Church with regard to the part they took in preserving the literary and historical monuments of remote ages. It was the task of many of those working and humble brethren, to commemorate in true but simple words, recollections of the past and occurrences of the present; to register periods of joy or of sorrow, and to describe in alternate succession events of the highest moment as well as trivial incidents of every-day life.

"A register of this description, the work of a successive number of chroniclers, was kept in the college of the Cathedral Church of St. Sophia at Novgorod. It first attracted the attention of M. P. Stroew, a gentleman formerly attached to the archives of the Ministry of Foreign Affairs at Moscow, and was published in 1821 under the title of *Sofiyski Premennik*, or *Sophian Chronicle*, in two volumes, 4to.

"It is in the second volume of this work, pp. 145-164, that Nikitin's journey to India was originally laid before the public *in extenso*.

"A few years before, the Russian historiographer, Karamzin, dicovered another codex of that curious manuscript, and acquainted the world with its existence in the following words (end of chapter vii, vol. vi):—

"'Hitherto, geographers have ignored the fact that the honour of one of the oldest voyages to India, undertaken and described by an European, belongs to the age and country of Ivan III. Athanasius Nikitin, a citizen of Tver, visited, about the year 1470, the kingdoms of the Deccan and of Golconda, for purposes of commerce. We possess his diary, which, although it does not evince any remarkable power of observation, or any great amount of knowledge, still must be considered a curiosity, the more so as the state of India at that time is but imperfectly known.'

"The manuscript alluded to by Karamsin, and of which he gives an abstract (notes to vol. vi, p. 629), was found in the archives of the monastery of Troitsk-Sergivsk, and has been used for the present translation. Although never printed, it is less defective than the one published by Stroew; in which several leaves are wanting. An authenticated copy of the former was obtained from the Archæological Commission at Moscow for the Hakluyt Society in London, at the request of Mr. R. H. Major, and through His Excellency Baron Brunnow, Russian Ambassador at the British Court.[1] The original bears all the marks of a manuscript written at the close of the fifteenth, and contains some additions made in the sixteenth century.

"A striking peculiarity of Nikitin's narrative, is the frequent recurrence of oriental words and sentences, spelt in Russian letters and embodied in the original text. Some of these have been translated, while others have been necessarily left without explanation. As to the Russian text itself, it is in some instances obscure, and in others utterly unintelligible; a circumstance which could not fail to be apparent in the translation. The reader will meet with more than one sentence of a doubtful meaning, and occasionally be at a loss for the sense of an entire passage. There is, besides, throughout the memorial a want of coherence, and a most painful absence of that minuteness of description which, in placing before the reader the objects depicted, can alone be considered as a source of interest or instruction.

"The date of Nikitin's journey may be inferred from a note of the chronicler given in Stroew's work. It states that the author accompanied Wessili Papin,

[1] It was transmitted to Baron Brunnow, with the following letter from Count Bloudolf, member of the Imperial Council, by whose orders it was transmitted.

'who was sent to the Shah of Shirván with a present of falcons from the Grand Duke Iwan III, one year before the war with Kuzan.' It therefore appears that our traveller set out in 1468. He must have returned to Russia in 1474; for, according to his own words, he spent "six great days," or Easter days, during his wandering through Persia, India, and part of Asia Minor.

"The following, in a few words, was his itinerary.

"Starting from Twer, and having performed his devotional duties at the shrine of the martyrs, Boris and Gleb, he proceeded down the Volga to the Caspian Sea. At Astracan he was robbed and made prisoner by the Tátars, who at the time were masters of that country. Released through the intercession of the Tátar ambassador Hassan-beg, under whose protection he had accomplished a part of his journey, he went to Bakoú, where the fire burns unextinguished. Thence he crossed the Caspian Sea and travelled on to Bokhára, at that time a vast emporium of eastern commerce. He then retraced his steps, and traversing the northern and western provinces of Persia, whose wealth and populous cities struck him with admiration, he reached Hormuz, the great commercial mart of the Persian Gulf, previously to its reduction by the Portuguese in 1515.

"He landed in India at Choul, a short distance south of Bombay, whence he proceeded through several places, rather difficult to trace on the map, to Beder, which he calls the chief city of the whole Muhammedan Hindustán. Having here taken up his residence, he gives a highly coloured account of the splendour and magnificence of the court of Beder, remarking that the youthful sultan and the country were ruled by the ambitious nobles, who delighted in wealth and luxury, while the people were wretched and miserable.

"He visited, in company with some natives, the Budhkhause at Perwattum, which he very properly calls the Jerusalem of the Hindús. There he witnessed the performance of various religious customs connected with the worship of Buddha, and on this occasion he enters upon a few details regarding domestic and devotional habits of the Hindús, as well as their relations to the Muhammedan invaders, who at that period were in possession of the greater part of the country.

"In the course of his account we find brief allusions to Calicut, Ceylon, Pegu, and also to some other places, the existence of which we have been utterly unable to ascertain. It appears, however, that he did not visit those places, but only speaks of them from hearsay.

"A staunch and zealous devotee, he never failed to keep the great festivals of the Greek-Russian Church, although he had no books of devotion to guide him. These, to his infinite distress, he had been robbed of in the affray above mentioned, a circumstance he constantly recurs to with the greatest sorrow and regret.

"At last, having spent about four years at Beder and in the adjoining countries, he bethought himself of returning to Russia, and set out one month before the Muhammedan Bairam. He embarked at Dabul, 'a port of the vast Indian Sea, the great meeting-place of all nations of the coast of India or Ethiopia,' and took his passage, for 'two golden coins,' to Hormuz.

"Proceeding thence through Shiráz, Ispahán, Kashán, Sultánieh, and Tabríz, he once more made his appearance at the Orda of Hassan-beg. Anxious to return to his native country, he embarked shortly after at Trebizond, and having experienced a great deal of bad weather and contrary winds, he ultimately reached in safety the port of Kaffa, the present Theodosia. Here he terminates his narrative by a long sentence in corrupt Turkish, expressive of his gratitude to heaven for his preservation and safe return to his native country.

"What became of him after this is not mentioned. The chronicler only remarks that, in the year he obtained the description of Nikitin's travels (1475), it was reported that he (Nikitin) had died before he reached Smolensk. The record of his voyage, written by himself, had been brought in the same year by some merchants to Moscow, and delivered to the diak, a kind of secretary of state, of the Grand-Duke.

"We have been anxious to depart as little as possible from the quaint idiom of our traveller, and should the reader be tempted occasionally to take exception at the uncouth style of an enterprising but uneducated man, he should remember that the chief attraction of a work of this kind consists in its antiquity and originality, and that the latter of these qualities might have been seriously impaired had we adopted a more polished and modern translation."

The last traveller whose account is given in this collective volume is Hieronimo de Santo Stefano, a Genoese merchant, who visited India on a mercantile speculation at the close of the fifteenth century. His voyage is a succession of sorrows, but was not a long one either in the performance or the recital. He first proceeded to Cairo, and thence up the Nile to Cane (Kenéh), thence to Cossier, and so down the Red Sea to Aden. Here he remained four months, and then sailed direct to Calicut. In this place he notices the extensive growth of ginger and of pepper, speaks of the idolatry of the people, who worship the sun and the ox, and moreover refers to the same peculiar kind of polygamy noticed by Conti, in which every lady has seven or eight husbands. From Calicut he sailed to Ceylon and the eastern coast of India, and thence to Pegu. At this latter place he was compelled to sell his merchandise to the king of the country, who agreed to give him two thousand ducats, but was so tardy in his payment, that a whole year was spent in daily solicitations, amidst great privations and annoyances. Santo Stefano's companion, Adorno, succumbed under the trial, and Santo Stefano himself nearly died with grief for his loss. Upon reflecting, however, that activity was better than idle mourning, he made fresh efforts for the recovery of his property, and at length succeeded. He then sailed to Sumatra, but had scarcely landed, when the king, who had heard of the death of his companion, asserted it to be the constant custom in Muhammedan countries, that the property of those who died childless should go to the king, and consequently seized the whole of the property for himself, on pretence that the whole belonged to Adorno. Fortunately, Santo Stefano was able to produce an invoice which had been made out at Cairo of all that belonged to him, and thus he was enabled, through the intervention of the Kázi, to recover a considerable portion of his property. Hence he set sail for Cambay. But his ill-luck still pursued him. Six months he was detained by stress of weather at the Maldives, and when eighty days after he resumed his voyage, there came on such a storm, that the ship and all his goods went to the bottom. By clinging to a plank for a whole day, he kept himself from drowning, and in the evening was picked up by a vessel bound, as his had been, for Cambay. Now utterly ruined, he was fortunately taken into the service of a merchant of Damascus, who sent him out as supercargo to Ormuz, from whence he made his way through Persia to Tripoli in Syria, at which place he wrote his narrative.

Although this is the last *personal narrative* with which we are acquainted, either of a voyage or overland journey to India in the fifteenth century, we must not pass without reference in this introduction the journey of a Portuguese to that country in 1487, subsequent to the memorable voyage of Bartholomew Diaz, in which he rounded the Cape of Good Hope (1486), but without any successful result. The ambition of John II had already, on a former occasion, led him to seek some information respecting India by means of a journey overland. Antonio de Lisboa, a Franciscan friar, had been dispatched for that purpose in company with a layman; but the attempt was rendered nugatory by their ignorance of Arabic, and after reaching Jerusalem they were obliged to return. This disappointment only rendered king John more determined on securing his object, and he now resolved on making a double effort to accomplish it. Bartholomew Diaz had a squadron fitted out for him, with which he set sail in August 1486, and first rounded that famous cape to which, from the storms he had encountered, he gave the name of Cabo dos Tormentos, or Cabo Tormentoso. In May of the next year, Pedro Covilham and Alfonso de Payva, both of them well versed in Arabic, received the following orders respecting a second journey overland. They were to discover the country of Prester John; to trace the Venetian commerce for drugs and spices to its source; to ascertain whether it were possible for ships to sail, round the southern extremity of Africa, to India; and to take particular information on every point relative to this important navigation. We learn from the missionary voyage by Francesco Alvarez, published in Lisbon, 1540, folio, an abridged translation of which was inserted in Purchas (vol. ii, page 1091), from "Master Hakluyt's papers," that Covilham "was borne in the towne of Covillan, in the kingdom of

Portugall, and being a boy, he went into Castile, and gat into the service of Don Alfonso, Duke of Sicile; and when the warre began betweene Portugall and Castile, hee returned home with Don John Gusman, brother to the said duke, which placed him in the house of Alfonso, king of Portugall; who for his valour presently made him a man at arms, and he was continually in that warre, and served also abroad in France. After the death of king Alfonso, he was one of the guard of the king Don John his sonne, untill the time of the treasons; when he sent him into Castile, because he spake the Castilian tongue very well, to spie out who were those gentlemen of his subjects which practised there against him. And returning out of Castile, he was sent into Barbarie, where he stayed a time, and learned the Arabian tongue, and was afterward sent to conclude a peace with the king of Tremizen; and being returned he was sent again to the king Amoli bela gegi, which restored the bones of the infant Don Fernando. At his returne he found that the king Don John, desiring by all meanes that his ships should find out the spiceries, had determined to send by land certaine men to discover as much as they might. And Alfonso de Paiva was chosen for this enterprise, a citizen of Castle Blanco, a very skilfull man, and very expert in the Arabian tongue.

"When Peter de Covillan was returned, king John called him and told him secretly, that having alwayes knowne him loyall and his faithfull servant, and readie to doe his majestie good service; seeing he understood the Arabian tongue; he purposed to send him with another companion to discover and learne where Prete Janni dwelt, and whether his territories reached unto the sea; and where the pepper and cinnamon grew, and other sorts of spicerie which were brought unto the citie of Venice from the countries of the Moores: seeing hee had sent for this purpose one of the house of Monterio, and one Frier Anthony, of Lisbon, prior of Porta de Ferro, which could not passe the citie of Jerusalem, saying that it was impossible to travell this way without understanding the Arabian tongue: and therefore seeing he understood the same well, hee prayed him to undertake this enterprize to doe him this so principall service; promising to reward him in such sort that he should be great in his kingdome, and all his posteritie should alwayes live contented. Peter answered him, 'That he kissed his majesties hands for the great favour which he had done him, but that he was sorry that his wisedome and sufficiencie was not answerable to the great desire he had to serve his highnesse; and yet, neverthelesse, as his faithful servant, he accepted this message with all his heart.'

"And so in the year 1487, the 7th of May, they were both despatched in Saint Arren, the king Don Emanuel alwayes there present, which at that time was but duke, and *they gave them a sea-card, taken out of a general map of the world*, at the making whereof was the licentiate Calzadilla, bishop of Viseo; and the doctor master, Roderigo, inhabitant of Pietre Nere; and the doctor master, Moyses, which at that time was a Jew; and all this worke was done very secretly in the house of Peter de Alcazova, and all the forenamed persons showed the uttermost of their knowledge, as though they should have beene commanders in the discoverie, of finding out the countries from whence the spices come, and as though one of them should have gone into Ethiopia to discover the country of Prete Janni, and as though *in those seas there had beene some knowledge of a passage into our westerne seas; because the said doctors said, they had found some memoriall of that matter.*"

These dark hints of earlier information existing with respect to the Cape of Good Hope are of the highest interest, but beyond our power to explain. It is true that Marco Polo described Zanguebar as an island of two thousand miles in circuit, but had he seriously believed that a passage round its southern coast would have laid open Asia to Europe, he would scarcely have passed over so great a fact in silence.

From whatever manuscripts the above map was compiled, we find from Castanheda, that Pedro de Covilham and Alfonso de Payva, with five hundred crowns in money and a letter of credit, left Lisbon for Naples in the month of May 1487; where, says Alvarez, their bills of exchange were paid by the son of Cosmo de Medicis; and from Naples they sailed to the Island of Rhodes. Then crossing over to Alexandria, they travelled to Cairo as merchants, and proceeding with the caravan to Tor, on the Red Sea at the foot of Mount Sinai, gained some information relative to the trade with Calicut.

Thence they sailed to Aden, where they parted; Covilham directing his course towards India, and Payva towards Suakem, in Abyssinia, appointing Cairo as the future place of their rendezvous. At Aden, Covilham embarked in a Moorish ship for Cananore, on the Malabar coast, and after some stay in that city, went to Calicut and Goa, being the first of his countrymen who had sailed on the Indian Ocean. He then passed over to Sofala, on the eastern coast of Africa, and examined its gold mines, where he procured some intelligence of the Island of St. Lawrence, called by the Moors the Island of the Moon.

Covilham had now, according to Alvarez, heard of cloves and cinnamon, and seen pepper and ginger; he therefore resolved to venture no farther until the valuable information he possessed was conveyed to Portugal. With this idea, he returned to Egypt; but found, on his arrival at Cairo, where he met with messengers from King John, that Payva had been murdered. The names of these messengers were Rabbi Abraham of Beja, and Joseph of Lamego; the latter immediately returned with letters from Covilham, containing, among other curious facts, the following remarkable report:—"*That the ships which sailed down the coast of Guinea might be sure of reaching the termination of the continent, by persisting in a course to the south; and that when they should arrive in the eastern ocean, their best direction must be to inquire for Sofala, and the Island of the Moon*" (Madagascar).

Rabbi Abraham and his companion, having visited

the city of Baghdad with the Isle of Ormuz previous to this event, had thus made themselves acquainted with many particulars respecting the spice trade. This alone was sufficient to recommend them to the patronage of John II, and they accordingly were employed by him to seek Covilham with Payva at Cairo, with additional directions to go to Ormuz and the coast of Persia, in order to improve their commercial information. Covilham eagerly embraced this opportunity to visit Ormuz, and having attended Abraham to the Gulf of Persia, they returned together to Aden, when the latter hastened to give John an account of their tour, and Covilham embarked for Abyssinia to complete that part of his voyage which the death of Payva had hitherto frustrated.

Crossing the straits of Babelmandeb, he landed in the dominions of the Negus. That prince took him with him to Shoa, where the court then resided, where he met with a very favourable reception. He at length became so necessary to the prince, that he was compelled to spend the remainder of his life in Abyssinia. He married in that country, and from occupying highly important posts, amassed a considerable fortune. It is stated by Alvarez, that when, in 1525, the Portuguese embassy, under Don Rodriguez de Lima, arrived in Abyssinia, Covilham shed tears of joy at the sight of his fellow countrymen. He passed thirty-three years of his life in Abyssinia, and died there. His original account is not now in existence, or is unknown; but from the third volume of *Bruce's Travels* we derive the following information, although from what authority he supplies it we are not told. He says: "Frequent despatches from him came to the King of Portugal, who, on his part, spared no expense to keep open the correspondence. In his journal, Covilham described the several ports in India which he had seen; the temper and disposition of the princes; the situation and riches of the mines of Sofala. He reported that the country was very populous, full of cities both powerful and rich; and he exhorted the king to pursue, with unremitting vigour, the passage round Africa, which he declared to be attended with very little danger, and that the Cape itself was well known in India. He accompanied this description with a chart or map, which he had received from the hands of a Moor in India, where the Cape, and cities all around the coast, were exactly represented."

Dr. Vincent's remarks on this passage from Bruce are important. He says: "Whence Bruce draws this account (see *Periplus*, p. 197) I cannot discover; and if there was such a map among the Moors it must be a fiction, for none of them had ever passed Corrientes by sea; and cities there are none for almost twenty degrees from Corrientes to the Cape, or from the Cape for twenty degrees to the northward on the western coast. That fictitious maps of this sort might exist, both in the Indies and Europe, among Muhammedans and Christians, is highly probable, for it was a prevailing notion in all ages, that Africa was circumnavigable.... We may allow even more than this, and say, that the natives had gone by land much farther to the south than the navigators by sea; and that their accounts were almost unanimous in maintaining the same assertion. The strongest evidence I have found of this, is that which the Portuguese afterwards report of Benomotapa, a great nation when they arrived in Africa, and the remnant of a much greater, which had possessed cities of great extent and regular buildings, and from which it was said there were public roads running far to the west and quite down to the Cape. Barbosa (Ramusio, v. i, p. 288, *et seq.*) mentions such a road: that it went far south may be true, but hardly to the Cape. We are not to believe these reports, perhaps, in their full extent." (*Periplus*, p. 206.) "Whenever I can discover the authority of Bruce it will deserve consideration; till then I shall think that if Covilham filled up the map he had received, or corrected it, or added to it such information as he could collect; it is a more probable account than the report of this Moorish map, which contained cities that never existed. Such a corrected map of Covilham's we read of in Castanheda, who seems to have seen it, as he says it was ill written and disfigured: this I take to be the map to which Bruce alludes."

In any case, it is the aforesaid letter of Covilham to King John, which, above all other information, assigns with equal justice and honour the theoretical discovery of the Cape to Covilham, as the practical is to be assigned to Diaz and De Gama; for Diaz returned without hearing anything of India, though he passed the Cape, and De Gama did not sail till after the intelligence of Covilham had ratified the discovery of Diaz.

In the valuable manuscript "Insularium Henrici Martelli Germani," in the British Museum, is a map which was made between the times of Diaz and De Gama's voyages, and which indicates the ultimatum of Diaz's adventure in the following legend: "Huc usque ad ilhe de' fonti ꝑvenit ultima navigatio portugalēsium. Ano. dm. 1489."

The reason of his return may possibly be that he had parted with one of his little fleet on his passage, and it may be supposed that the difficulty of obtaining information from the natives, may have contributed to his determination. He, however, erected a cross on a rocky islet in Algoa Bay, which rock still, in *perpetuam rei memoriam*, bears the name of De la Cruz. The great Cape itself, which he saw on his return, he styled the Cabo Tormentoso, from the tremendous storms he had encountered on his passage. A name of far more cheering omen was suggested by the hopeful foresight of the Portuguese monarch, who changed the "Stormy Cape" into the "Cape of Good Hope," a name which will in all probability, and as is to be desired, preserve the maritime glory of an enterprizing nation to the end of time.

The editor cannot close without expressing his great obligations to his friend, W. S. W. Vaux, Esq., for much valuable assistance in the course of this introduction.

NARRATIVE

OF THE

JOURNEY OF ABD-ER-RAZZAK,

AMBASSADOR FROM SHAH ROKH.

A.H. 845. A.D. 1442.

IN this year 845 (A.D. 1442), the author of this narrative, Abd-er-Razzak, the son of Ishak, in obedience to the orders of the sovereign of the world, set out on his journey towards the province of Ormuz and the shores of the ocean. In the hope that the author's friends, instead of finding fault, will take pleasure in reading this work, the narrative shall be given in its minutest details, and I shall insert in it all sorts of marvellous facts and wonderful matters worthy of notice. I shall set forth all the circumstances which have fallen under my notice in the space of three years; I shall recount, fully and in detail, all my adventures, and the dangers by which they have been rendered remarkable; and I shall also relate, in my usual manner, those events which affect the provinces of Khorassan, Ma-wara-amahar,[1] Irak, Fars, and Azerbijan. I venture to hope that my work will find credit amongst men of intelligence, and that the leading people of our age will allow the sun of their consideration to shine upon the recital.

[1] Better spelt in English Ma Wara-ee Alnahar. It is an Arabic designation, literally signifying—"beyond the river," and representing the Transoxiana of the ancients. Its limits are not easily defined, but the territory it comprehends is better recognized by Europeans as that occupied by the Uzbeck Tartars. The Arab geographers, Abulfeda and Nassir Eddin, have given long lists of places in the province, with their positions, as gathered from various authors. The three principal cities are Bokhara, Samarcand, and Osrushnah.

NARRATIVE OF THE JOURNEY OF ABD-ER-RAZZAK.

Narrative of my voyage into Hindoostan, and description of the wonders and remarkable peculiarities which this country presents.

Every man, the eyes of whose intelligence are illuminated by the light of truth, and whose soul, like a bird, soars with fixedness of vision into the regions of knowledge, observes with certainty, and brings home to his recognition the fact, that the revolution of the great bodies which people the heavens, as well as the progress of the smaller bodies which canopy the earth, are subject to the wisdom and the will of a Creator, Who is alike holy and powerful; that the intelligence of His omnipotence, and the characteristics of His omniscience, are manifested alike in the nature of those beings which resemble the atoms contained in creation, as well as in the movements and actions of man; that the bridle which guides all created beings is held by the hand of a Divine power, by the fingers of Providence; that the proudest existences are forced to bow the head beneath the commands of a God who does everything according to His pleasure.

"If Providence were not the mover of all the events of the world, how is it that the progress of those events is so frequently in opposition to our own will?"

"In every occurrence, whether fortunate or unfortunate, it is Providence who holds the reins, and guides His creatures; the proof of this is found in the fact that the measures adopted by men are all fallacious."

The events, the perils, which accompany a voyage by sea (and which in themselves constitute a shoreless and a boundless ocean), present the most marked indication of the Divine omnipotence, the grandest evidence of a wisdom which is sublime. Hence it is that the utility of such a voyage as this has been shown in the most perfect manner in the marvellous language of the king, who is the author of all knowledge, and also that the execution of so important an undertaking cannot be either accomplished or related, but by the help of that living and powerful Being, who makes easy that which is most difficult.

In pursuance of the orders of Providence, and of the decrees of that Divine prescience, the comprehension of which escapes all the calculations and reflections of man, I received orders to take my departure for India; and how shall I be able to set forth the events of my journey with clearness, seeing that I have wandered at hap-hazard into that country devoted to darkness. His majesty, the happy Khakan, condescended to allot to me my provisions and post horses. His humble slave, after having made the necessary preparations, started on his journey on the first day of the month of Ramazan (January 13th), by the route of Kohistan. In the middle of the desert of Kerman, he arrived at the ruins of a city, the wall of which and four bazaars could still be distinguished; but no inhabitant was to be found in all the country round.

(I passed in the desert near ancient dwellings, none of which presented signs of anything but ruin and decay.)

This desert extends to the frontier of Mekran and Seistan, as far as the environs of the city of Damghan, and all this space presents formidable dangers to travellers.

On the eighteenth day of Ramazan (Jan. 30th) I reached the city of Kerman; it is a pleasant place, as well as one of great importance. The *darogah* (governor), the Emir Hadji-Mohamed-Kaiaschirin, being then absent, I was compelled to sojourn in this city until the day of the feast. The illustrious Emir Borhan-Eddin-Seid-Khalil-Allah, son of the Emir Naim-Eddin-Seid-Nimet-Allah, who was the most distinguished personage of the city of Kerman, and even of the whole world, returned at this time from the countries of Hindoostan. He loaded me with attentions and proofs of his kindness. On the fifth day of Schewal (February 16th) I quitted the city of Kerman. On my road I met the Emir Hadji-Mohammed, on his return from an expedition which he had made into the province of Benboul. Continuing my journey, I arrived towards the middle of the month at the shore of the Sea of Oman, and at Bender-Ormuz. The prince of Ormuz, Melik-Fakhr-Eddin-Touranschah, having placed a vessel at my disposal, I went on board of it, and made my entry into the city of Ormuz. I had had assigned to me a house, with everything that I could require, and I was admitted to an audience of the prince.

Ormuz, which is also called Djerrun, is a port situated in the middle of the sea, and which has not its equal on the surface of the globe. The merchants of seven climates, from Egypt, Syria, the country of Roum,[1] Azerbijan, Irak-Arabi, and Irak-Adjemi, the provinces of Fars, Khorassan, Ma-wara-amahar, Turkistan, the kingdom of Deschti-Kaptchack,[2] the countries inhabited by the Kalmucks, the whole of the kingdoms of Tchin[3] and Matchin,[4] and the city of

[1] The Arabic name for Anatolia.

[2] Or rather Dasht-i-Kipchak, the desert of Kipchak in Tartary.

[3] China.

[4] The southern parts of China.

Khanbâlik,[1] all make their way to this port; the inhabitants of the sea coasts arrive here from the countries of Tchin, Java, Bengal, the cities of Zirbad,[2] Tenasserim, Sokotora, Schahrinou,[3] the islands of Dîwah-Mahall,[4] the countries of Malabar, Abyssinia, Zanguebar, the ports of Bidjanagar,[5] Kalbergah,[6] Gudjarat, Kanbaït,[7] the coasts of Arabia, which extend as far as Aden, Jiddah, and Yembo; they bring hither those rare and precious articles which the sun, the

[1] Pekin.

[2] This name in Indian language means, "the country under the wind," and is referred to India beyond the Ganges, comprising the whole South-East Peninsula.

[3] Query, Shahnoor or Sivanur, in the province of Bejapoor, fifty miles south south-east from Darwar.

[4] The Maldives.

[5] The author means the ports of the sovereignties so named, as the capital cities bearing the same name were not on the sea-coast. The city of Bijanagur, now in ruins, was once the metropolis of a mighty Hindoo empire. It was thither that our author, as the reader will hereafter see, ultimately directed his steps; and his narrative mainly consists of the description of this empire, its capital, and people. The remains of the city are situated on the south bank of the Toombuddra river, directly opposite to Annagoondy. It was begun to be built in A.D. 1336, and was finished in 1343. The incessant hostilities between the Mahommedan sovereigns of the Deccan and this Hindoo principality, resulted in the total defeat of Ram Rajah, the sovereign of Bijanagur, and the sacking of the metropolis in 1565, and its subsequent depopulation in 1567. The celebrated Italian traveller Cesare Federici, who was there in the latter year, speaks with enthusiasm of its extent and enormous wealth. An interesting account of this empire and its fall, is given in the commencing chapter of Colonel Wilks's "Historical Sketches of the South of India," London, 1810, 4to.

[6] The town now known as the capital of a district of the same name, is situated in the province of Beeder, one hundred and five miles west of Hyderabad. Though now of little note, it was formerly famous as the metropolis both of a Hindoo and Mahomedan sovereignty. Rajahs of Kalberga are mentioned by Ferishta as independent princes when the Deccan was invaded by Alla ud Deen in A.D. 1295, and on the establishment of Mahommedan independence in the Deccan in 1347, this city was made the capital of the new government.

[7] Cambay.

moon, and the rains have combined to bring to perfection, and which are capable of being transported by sea. Travellers from all countries resort hither, and, in exchange for the commodities which they bring, they can without trouble or difficulty obtain all that they desire. Bargains are made either by money or by exchange.

For all objects, with the exception of gold and silver, a tenth of their value is paid by way of duty.

Persons of all religions, and even idolators, are found in great numbers in this city, and no injustice is permitted towards any person whatever. This city is also named Dâr-alaman (the abode of security). The inhabitants unite the flattering character of the people of Irak with the profound cunning of the Indians.

I sojourned in this place for the space of two months; and the governors sought all kinds of pretexts to detain me; so that the favorable time for departing by sea, that is to say the beginning or middle of the monsoon, was allowed to pass, and we came to the end of the monsoon, which is the season when tempests and attacks from pirates are to be dreaded. Then they gave me permission to depart. As the men and horses could not all be contained in the same vessel, they were distributed among several ships. The sails were hoisted, and we commenced our voyage.

As soon as I caught the smell of the vessel, and all the terrors of the sea presented themselves before me, I fell into so deep a swoon, that for three days respiration alone indicated that life remained within me. When I came a little to myself, the merchants, who were my intimate friends, cried with one voice that the time for navigation was passed, and that every one who put to sea at this season was alone responsible for his death, since he voluntarily placed himself in peril. All, with one accord, having sacrificed the sum which they had paid for freight in the ships, abandoned their project, and after some difficulties disembarked at the port of Muscat. For myself, I quitted this city, escorted by the principal companions of my voyage, and went to a place called Kariat, where I established myself and fixed my tents, with the intention of there remaining. The merchants of the coasts designate by the word *telâhi* (loss) the condition in which they find themselves when, having undertaken a sea voyage, they cannot accomplish it, and are obliged to stop in some other place. In consequence of the severity of pitiless weather and the adverse manifestations of a treacherous fate, my heart was crushed like glass and my soul became weary of life, and my season of relaxation became excessively trying to me.

At the moment when, through the effect of so many vicissitudes, the mirror of my understanding had become covered with rust, and the hurricane of so many painful circumstances had extinguished the lamp of my mind, so that I might say in one word I had fallen into a condition of apathetic stupidity, on a sudden I one evening met a merchant who was on his return from the shores of Hindoostan. I asked him whither he was going? he replied: "My only object is to reach the city of Herat." When I heard him utter the name of that august city I went very nearly distracted. The merchant having consented at my request to tarry awhile, I threw off the following verses upon paper.

When in the midst of strangers, at the hour of the evening prayer I set me down to weep,

I recall my adventures, the recital of which is accompanied with unusual sighs.

At the remembrance of my mistress and of my country I weep so bitterly,

That I should deprive the whole world of the taste and habit of travelling.

I am a native of the country of the Arabs, and not of a strange region.

O mighty God, whom I invoke! vouchsafe to bring me back to the companionship of my friends.

Everything which relates to my condition, and to the tediousness and dangers against which I have had to contend, has been set forth in full detail in this narrative. As far as regards a certain number of men and horses, which were embarked at Ormuz upon a separate vessel, I have been unable hitherto to ascertain what has been their fate. It may be that some day I shall be able to put their adventures into writing.

Description of what occurred during the time that I was involuntarily detained upon the sea shore, and of what happened to me in the encampment of Kariat, and in the city of Kalahat.

At the time that I was perforce sojourning in the place called Kariat, and upon the shores of the ocean, the new moon, of the month of Moharrem of the year 846 [May 1442], showed me in this abode of weariness the beauty of her disk. Although it was at that time spring, in the season in which the nights and days are of equal length, the heat of the sun was so intense that it burned the ruby in the mine and the marrow in the bones; the sword in its scabbard melted like wax, and the gems which adorned the handle of the khandjar were reduced to coal.

Soon as the sun shone forth from the height of heaven,
The heart of stone grew hot beneath its orb;
The horizon was so much scorched up by its rays,
That the heart of stone became soft like wax;
The bodies of the fishes, at the bottom of the fish-ponds,
Burned like the silk which is exposed to the fire;
Both the water and the air gave out so burning a heat,
That the fish went away to seek refuge in the fire;

In the plains the chase became a matter of perfect ease,
For the desert was filled with roasted gazelles.

The extreme heat of the atmosphere gave one the idea of the fire of hell. As the climate of this country is naturally opposed to human health, my elder brother, a respectable and learned man, Maulana-Afif-Eddin-Abd-el-Wahhâb, the rest of my companions, and myself, fell sick, in consequence of the excessive heat, and we resigned our fate into the hands of Divine goodness.

Since the power of doing our own will has escaped from our hands, we surrender ourselves to God, waiting to see what His munificence will work for us.

The constitution of each one of us had undergone so sad a change; trouble, fatigue, sickness, and the burning of the fever, went on increasing every day. This cruel condition was prolonged for the space of four months; our strength gave way by degrees, and the malady increased.

I am reduced to such a state of weakness, O my friend, that the zephyr carries me each instant from one climate to another, like the smell of the rose.

I continue no longer in my gay position, for the action of fate has made me rise and fall like the cord of a hydraulic machine.

No one has seen the pain withdraw from my body, any more than cause and effect have been seen to separate themselves the one from the other.

In the meanwhile I was informed that, in the environs of the city of Kalahat, there was a place called Sour, which offered a salubrious temperature and agreeable waters. In spite of my extreme weakness I went on board the vessel, and departed from Kalahat. No sooner had I arrived than my malady increased; in the daytime I was consumed by the fire of a burning fever, and in the night I was devoured by the anguish of chagrin. The unwholesomeness of the disease disordered my bodily frame, much as the earthly globe is disordered by an excess of smoky vapours; the tyrannical hand of the fever, aided by the tempest of my misfortunes, overturned the tent of my bodily health, which the conjunction of the four elements, like so many religious guardians, tended to support. I was torn to pieces by the torments of absence, by the sorrows of exile. During the day my heart was bedrenched with blood in consequence of the injuries of a treacherous fate, and my lips were powerless to utter a word; during the night my eyes remained constantly open, and my soul was on the point of quitting the asylum of my body. That feeble body, beaten to the ground by chagrin and the sorrows of exile, was content to bid adieu to my soul; and my soul, having lost all hope of prolonging its existence, gave welcome to death, and abandoned its fate to the goodness of the living and merciful God.

My respectable brother, Maulana-Afif-eddin-Abd-Wahhâb, in obedience to that maxim, "Man knows not in what country he must die," and in obedience to that other sentence, "Wherever thou mayst be death shall reach thee", committed his soul into the hands of the Deity, and was buried in the neighbourhood of that place of pilgrimage where some of the illustrious companions of the prophet repose.

The grief of this loss, and the pain of this separation, produced a deep impression upon me, which it is impossible to describe or to represent by words.

Alas! how much beauty would there be in the flower of youth, if only it bore with it the characteristic of eternal duration!

But we must separate from relations and friends; such is the irrevocable decree of heaven.

Unhappy me! detaching myself from life, and regarding the past as having never occurred, I determined to continue my voyage in a vessel which was leaving for Hindoostan. A few strong men carried me on board the ship.

On that sea which fate renders terrible take resignation for thy barque.

Set foot upon this vessel, for it is God Himself who directs thy course.

If men of eminence will look upon matters with discriminating attention, this occurrence offers a sort of analogy with the history of Moses, who was placed in an ark and committed to the water. Everything externally spoke of death, but the interior was the enclosure of safety. In like manner Khidr[1] showed Moses a fact perfectly analogous in the sinking of a vessel, for externally it seemed that it must lead to the loss of men, while in the interior it offered deliverance from the hand of a tyrant.

In short, the air of the sea having become more salubrious, gave me the hope of a perfect cure: the morning of health began to dawn upon the longing of my hopes; the wounds caused by the sharp arrows of my malady began to heal, and the water of life, hitherto so troubled, recovered its purity and transparency. Before long a favourable

[1] The prophet Alkhedr, whom the Mahometans usually confound with Phineas, Elias, and St. George, saying that his soul passed by a metempsychosis successively through all three. In Sale's "Koran", we find the following incidents described as occurring between him and Moses, and to which doubtless our author here refers. We give it verbatim. "Moses said unto him, Shall I follow thee that thou mayst teach me part of that which thou hast been taught for a direction unto me? He answered, Verily thou canst not bear with me; for how canst thou patiently suffer those things the knowledge whereof thou dost not comprehend? Moses replied, Thou shalt find me patient if God please, neither will I be disobedient unto thee in anything. He said, If thou follow me therefore, ask me not concerning anything until I shall declare the meaning thereof unto thee. So they both went on by the sea shore until they went up into a ship; and he made a hole therein. And Moses said unto, Hast thou made a hole therein, that thou mightest drown those who are on board? Now hast thou done a strange thing. He answered, Did I not tell thee that thou couldest not bear with me? Moses said, Rebuke me not, because I did forget, and impose not on me a difficulty in what I am commanded."

breeze began to blow, and the vessel floated over the surface of the water with the rapidity of the wind.[1]

During several days the realization of this sentence, "*They have progressed by the help of a favorable wind*," carried joy and gladness to the heart of my companions; and this maxim: "*Hast thou not seen the ships ride over the sea by the goodness of God*," opened the gate of joy in the hearts of my friends. Finally, after a voyage of eighteen days and as many nights, by the aid of the supreme king and ruler, we cast anchor in the port of Calicut; and the detail of the marvels of this country, and the narrative of the voyage of his humble slave, will here be found described to the life.

Narrative of our arrival in Hindoostan, and description of the customs and institutions of that country, and of the marvels and astonishing facts which it presents.

Calicut is a perfectly secure harbour, which, like that of Ormuz, brings together merchants from every city and from every country; in it are to be found abundance of precious articles brought thither from maritime countries, and especially from Abyssinia, Zirbad, and Zanguebar; from time to time ships arrive there from the shores of the House of God[2] and other parts of the Hedjaz, and abide at will, for a greater or longer space, in this harbour; the town is inhabited by Infidels, and situated on a hostile shore. It contains a considerable number of Mussulmauns, who are

[1] Here begins a long and emphatic description of a vessel; I should have translated this portion, but I felt that these curious details interrupted the narrative in a disagreeable manner.—*Note by M. Quatremère.*

[2] Mecca.

constant residents, and have built two mosques, in which they meet every Friday to offer up prayer. They have one Kadi, a priest, and for the most part they belong to the sect of Schafei.[1] Security and justice are so firmly established in this city, that the most wealthy merchants bring thither from maritime countries considerable cargoes, which they unload, and unhesitatingly send into the markets and the bazaars, without thinking in the meantime of any necessity of checking the account or of keeping watch over the goods. The officers of the custom-house take upon themselves the charge of looking after the merchandise, over which they keep watch day and night. When a sale is effected, they levy a duty on the goods of one-fortieth part; if they are not sold, they make no charge on them whatsoever.

In other ports a strange practice is adopted. When a vessel sets sail for a certain point, and suddenly is driven by a decree of Divine Providence into another roadstead, the inhabitants, under the pretext that the wind has driven it there, plunder the ship. But at Calicut, every ship, whatever place it may come from, or wherever it may be bound, when it puts into this port is treated like other vessels, and has no trouble of any kind to put up with.

His majesty, the happy Khakan, had sent as a present for the prince of Calicut, some horses, some pelisses, some robes of cloth of gold, and some caps, similar to those distributed at the time of the Nauruz;[2] and the motive which had induced him to do so was as follows. Some ambassadors deputed by this monarch, returning from Bengal in com-

[1] Abu Abdallah Mohammed Ben Edris, surnamed Schafei from one of his ancestors, who was descended from the grandfather of Mahomet, was the first writer on jurisprudence among the Mahometans. He wrote a book on the "Principles of Islamism," in which the whole civil and canonical law of the Mahometans is contained. With him originated one of the four sects of Islamism regarded as orthodox.

[2] New Year's day, celebrated with feasts, liberation of prisoners, etc.

pany with the ambassadors of the latter country, having been obliged to put into Calicut, the description which they gave of the greatness and power of the Khakan reached the ears of the sovereign of that city. He learned from authentic testimony, that the kings of all the habitable globe, of the East as well as of the West, of the land and of the sea, had sent rival ambassadors and messages, showing that they regarded the august court of that monarch as the Kiblah, to which they should pay their homage,—as the Kabah, the object to which they should direct their aspirations.

A short time afterwards, the king of Bengal, complaining of the invasion of Ibrahim, Sultan of Djounah-pour, had laid his cause before the court, which is the asylum of kings, and asked for succour. The emperor despatched to the country of Djounah-pour the Scheikh-alislam Kerim-eddin-Abu'l-makarim-Djami, bearer of peremptory orders addressed to the king. His message was to the effect that the king must refrain from interfering with the kingdom of Bengal, in default of which he might take the responsibility to himself of whatever the consequence should be. The prince of Djounah-pour having received this summary ultimatum, gave up all idea of an attack upon the country of Bengal.

As soon as the sovereign of Calicut was informed of these occurrences, he prepared some presents, consisting of objects of value of different kinds, and sent an ambassador charged with a despatch, in which he said: "In this port, on every Friday and every solemn feast day, the Khotbah[1] is celebrated, according to the prescribed rule of Islamism. With your majesty's permission, these prayers shall be adorned and honoured by the addition of your name and of your illustrious titles."

The sound of his Khotbah is become so acceptable to the

[1] A sermon preached every Friday afternoon after the service in the principal mosques, in which they praise God, bless Mohammed, and pray for the Khalif.

world, that all the infidels have shown themselves willing to adopt it.

These deputies, setting out in company with the ambassadors from Bengal, reached the noble court of the emperor, and the Emirs laid before that monarch the letter and the presents by which it was accompanied. The messenger was a Mussulmaun, distinguished for his eloquence; in the course of his address he said to the prince, "If your majesty will be pleased to favour my master, by despatching an ambassador sent especially to him, and who, in literal pursuance of the precept expressed in that verse, '*By thy wisdom and by thy good counsels engage men to enter on the ways of thy Lord,*' shall invite that prince to embrace the religion of Islamism, and draw from his beclouded heart the bolt of darkness and error, and cause the flame of the light of faith, and the brightness of the sun of knowledge to shine into the window of his heart, it will be, beyond all doubt, a perfectly righteous and meritorious deed." The emperor acceded to this request, and gave instructions to the Emirs that the ambassador should make his preparations for setting out on his journey. The choice fell upon the humble author of this work. Certain individuals, however, hazarded their denunciations against his success, imagining in their own minds that it was likely he would never return from so long a voyage. He arrived, nevertheless, in good health after three years of absence, and by that time his calumniators were no longer in the land of the living.

As soon as I landed at Calicut I saw beings such as my imagination had never depicted the like of.

Extraordinary beings, who are neither men nor devils,
At sight of whom the mind takes alarm;
If I were to see such in my dreams
My heart would be in a tremble for many years.

I have had love passages with a beauty, whose face was like the moon; but I could never fall in love with a negress.

The blacks of this country have the body nearly naked; they wear only bandages round the middle, called *lankoutah*, which descend from the navel to above the knee. In one hand they hold an Indian poignard, which has the brilliance of a drop of water, and in the other a buckler of ox-hide, which might be taken for a piece of mist. This costume is common to the king and to the beggar. As to the Mussulmauns, they dress themselves in magnificent apparel after the manner of the Arabs, and manifest luxury in every particular. After I had had an opportunity of seeing a considerable number of Mussulmauns and Infidels, I had a comfortable lodging assigned to me, and after the lapse of three days was conducted to an audience with the king. I saw a man with his body naked, like the rest of the Hindus. The sovereign of this city bears the title of *Sameri*. When he dies it is his sister's son who succeeds him, and his inheritance does not belong to his son, or his brother, or any other of his relations. No one reaches the throne by means of the strong hand.

The Infidels are divided into a great number of classes, such as the Bramins, the Djoghis,[1] and others. Although they are all agreed upon the fundamental principles of polytheism and idolatry, each sect has its peculiar customs. Amongst them there is a class of men, with whom it is the practice for one woman to have a great number of husbands, each of whom undertakes a special duty and fulfils it. The hours of the day and of the night are divided between them; each of them for a certain period takes up his abode in the house, and while he remains there no other is allowed to enter. The *Sameri* belongs to this sect.

When I obtained my audience of this prince, the hall was

[1] "Hindu ascetics; a caste of Hindus, who are commonly weavers. The people of this cast do not burn, but bury their dead, and the women are sometimes buried alive with their husband's corpse."—Forbes's "Hindustani Dictionary."

filled with two or three thousand Hindus, who wore the costume above described; the principal personages amongst the Mussulmauns were also present. After they had made me take a seat, the letter of his majesty, the happy Khakan, was read, and they caused to pass in procession before the throne, the horse, the pelisse, the garment of cloth of gold, and the cap to be worn at the ceremony of Nauruz. The Sameri showed me but little consideration. On leaving the audience I returned to my house. Several individuals, who brought with them a certain number of horses, and all sorts of things beside, had been shipped on board another vessel by order of the king of Ormuz; but being captured on the road by some cruel pirates, they were plundered of all their wealth, and narrowly escaped with their lives. Meeting them at Calicut, we had the honour to see some distinguished friends.

Thanks be to God we are not dead, and we have seen our very dear friends; we have also attained the object of our desires.

From the close of the month of the second Djoumada [beginning of November 1442], to the first days of Zou'lhidjah [middle of April 1443], I remained in this disagreeable place, where everything became a source of trouble and weariness. During this period, on a certain night of profound darkness and unusual length, in which sleep, like an imperious tyrant, had imprisoned my senses and closed the door of my eyelids, after every sort of disquietude, I was at length asleep upon my bed of rest, and in a dream I saw his majesty, the happy Khakan, who came towards me with all the pomp of sovereignty, and when he came up to me said: "Afflict thyself no longer." The following morning, at the hour of prayer, this dream recurred to my mind and filled me with joy.

Although, in general, dreams are but the simple wanderings of the imagination, which are seldom realized in our waking hours, yet it does sometimes occur that the facts which are shown in sleep are afterwards accomplished; and such dreams have been regarded by the most distinguished men as intimations from God. Every one has heard of the dream of Joseph, and that of the minister of Egypt.

My reflections led me to the hope, that perhaps the morning beam of happiness was about to dawn upon me from the bosom of Divine goodness, and that the night of chagrin and weariness had nearly reached its close. Having communicated my dream to some skilful men, I asked them its interpretation. On a sudden a man arrived, who brought me the intelligence that the king of Bidjanagar, who holds a powerful empire and a mighty dominion under his sway, had sent to the Sameri a delegate charged with a letter, in which he desired that he would send on to him the ambassador of his majesty, the happy Khakan. Although the Sameri is not subject to the laws of the king of Bidjanagar, he nevertheless pays him respect, and stands extremely in fear of him; since, if what is said is true, this latter prince has in his dominions three hundred ports, each of which is equal to Calicut, and on *terra firma* his territories comprise a space of three months' journey. The coast, which includes Calicut with some other neighbouring ports, and which extends as far as Kabel, a place situated opposite the Island of Serendib, otherwise called Ceylon, bears the general name of Melibar. From Calicut are vessels continually sailing for Mecca, which are for the most part laden with pepper. The inhabitants of Calicut are adventurous sailors: they are known by the name of Tchini-betchegan (son of the Chinese), and pirates do not dare to attack the vessels of Calicut. In this harbour one may find everything that can be desired. One thing alone is forbidden, namely, to kill a cow, or to eat its flesh: whosoever should be discovered slaughtering or eating one of these animals, would be immediately punished with death. So respected is the cow in these parts, that the inhabitants take its dung when dry and rub their foreheads with it.

The humble author of this narrative having received his audience of dismissal, departed from Calicut by sea. After having passed the port of Bendinaneh,[1] situated on the coast of Melibar, reached the port of Mangalor, which forms the frontier of the kingdom of Bidjanagar. After staying there two or three days he continued his route by land. At a distance of three parasangs from Mangalor he saw a temple of idols, which has not its equal in the universe. It is an equilateral square, of about ten ghez[2] in length, ten in breadth, and five in height. It is entirely formed of cast bronze. It has four *estrades*. Upon that in the front stands a human figure, of great size, made of gold; its eyes are formed of two rubies, placed so artistically that the statue seems to look at you. The whole is worked with wonderful delicacy and perfection. After passing this temple, I came each day to some city or populous town. At length I came to a mountain whose summit reached the skies, and the foot of which was covered with so great a quantity of trees and thorny underwood, that the rays of the sun could never penetrate the obscurity, nor could the beneficial rains at any time reach the soil to moisten it. Having left this mountain and this forest behind me, I reached a town called Belour, the houses of which were like palaces, and its women reminded one of the beauty of the Houris. In it there is a temple of idols, so lofty as to be visible at a distance of many parasangs. It would be impossible to describe such a building without being suspected of exaggeration. I can only give a general idea of it. In the middle of the town is an

[1] Langles, in annotating this word in the version of this journey inserted in his "Collection portative de Voyages," conjectures it to be a corruption of Cananor.

[2] Cubits.

open space, of about ten ghez in extent, and which, if one may use a comparison, rivals the garden of Irem.[1] The roses of all kinds are as numerous as the leaves of the trees, on the borders of the streams rise a great number of cypresses, whose towering height is reflected in the waters, plantain trees shoot out their tufted branches, and it would seem as if heaven itself looks down upon this beautiful spot with pleasure and admiration. All the ground of this parterre, all the environs of this place of delight, are paved with polished stones, joined together with so much delicacy and skill, that they seem to form but one single slab of stone, and look like a fragment of the sky which might be supposed to have been brought down to the earth. In the middle of this platform rises a building composed of a cupola formed of blue stones, and terminating in a point. The stone presents three rows of figures.

What can I say of this cupola, which, as regards the delicacy of the work, offered to the world an idea of paradise?

Its vault, rounded and lofty, resembled a new moon; its elevation vied with that of the heavens.

So great a number of pictures and figures had been drawn by the pen and the pencil, that it would be impossible, in the space of a month, to sketch it all upon damask or taffeta. From the bottom of the building to the top there is not a hand's breadth to be found uncovered with paintings, after the manner of the Franks and the people of Khata.[2] The temple consists of a structure of four estrades; this structure is thirty ghez in length, twenty in breadth, fifty in height.

[1] Irem is the name given by orientals to the earthly Paradise, which Chedad ben Ad, a fabulous monarch of Arabia, made an attempt at constructing in imitation of the celestial Paradise, of which he had heard. He brought together there all sorts of delights, but on the day of its completion he and his subjects were destroyed by a powerful tempest, and the Paradise became invisible.

[2] China.

Since that its head shot up towards the skies, that vault, previously without stones in it, now seems formed of them.

Since that its stones have rubbed themselves against the sun, the gold of that orb has taken a purer alloy.

All the other buildings, great and small, are covered with paintings and sculptures of extreme delicacy. In this temple morning and evening, after devotional exercises, which have nothing in them which can be agreeable to God, they play on musical instruments, perform concerts, and give feasts. All the inhabitants of the town have rents and pensions assigned to them on this temple. The most distant cities send hither their alms. In the opinion of these men without religion, this place is the Kabah of the Guèbres.

After having sojourned in this town for the space of two or three days we continued our route, and at the end of the month of Zou'lhidjah [end of April] we arrived at the city of Bidjanagar. The king sent a numerous cortège to meet us, and appointed us a very handsome house for our residence.

The preceding details, forming a close narrative of events, have shown to readers and writers that the chances of a maritime voyage had led Abd-er-Razzak, the author of this work, to the city of Bidjanagar. He saw a place extremely large and thickly peopled, and a king possessing greatness and sovereignty to the highest degree, whose dominion extends from the frontier of Serendib to the extremities of the country of Kalbergah. From the frontiers of Bengal to the environs of Belinar (Melibar), the distance is more than a thousand parasangs. The country is for the most part well cultivated, very fertile, and contains about three hundred harbours. One sees there more than a thousand elephants, in their size resembling mountains, and in their forms resembling devils. The troops amount in number to eleven lak (1,100,000).

One might seek in vain throughout the whole of Hindoostan to find a more absolute *raï* (king); for the monarchs of this country bear the title of *raï*. Next to him the Brahmins hold a rank superior to that of all other men. The book of Kalilah and Dimna, the most beautiful work existing in the Persian language, and which presents us with the stories of a *raï* and a Brahmin, is probably a production of the talent of the literati of this country.

The city of Bidjanagar is such that the pupil of the eye has never seen a place like it, and the ear of intelligence has never been informed that there existed anything to equal it in the world. It is built in such a manner that seven citadels and the same number of walls enclose each other. Around the first citadel are stones of the height of a man, one half of which is sunk in the ground while the other rises above it. These are fixed one beside the other, in such a manner that no horse or foot soldier could boldly or with ease approach the citadel. If any one would wish to find what point of resemblance this fortress and rampart present with that which exists in the city of Herat, let him picture to himself that the first citadel corresponds with that which extends from the mountain of Mokhtar and Direh dou Buraderim (the Valley of the Two Brothers) as far as the banks of the river and the bridge of Mâlan, situated east of the town of Ghinan, and west of the village of Saïban.

It is a fortress of a round shape, built on the summit of a mountain, and constructed of stones and lime. It has very solid gates, the guards of which are constantly at their post, and examine everything with a severe inspection.

The second fortress represents the space which extends from the bridge of the new river, to the bridge of the Karav, lying to the east of the bridge of Renghineh and Djakan, and to the west of the garden of Zibendeh and of the village of Hasan.

The third citadel comprises as much space as lies between

the mausoleum of the Imaum Fakhr-eddin-Râzi and the dome-shaped monument of Mohammed-Sultan-Śchah.

The fourth corresponds to the space which separates the bridge Andjil from the bridge of Kâred.

The fifth comprises a space equal to that which extends from the garden of Zagaṇ to the bridge of Andjegan.

The sixth is equivalent to the space contained between the King's gate and the gate of Firouz-abad.

The seventh fortress, which is placed in the centre of the others, occupies an area ten times larger than the market-place of the city of Herat. It is the palace which is used as the residence of the king. The distance from the gate of the first fortress, which lies on the north, to the first gate, which is situated in the south, is calculated to be two parasangs. It is the same distance from the east to the west. The space which separates the first fortress from the second, and up to the third fortress, is filled with cultivated fields, and with houses and gardens. In the space from the third to the seventh one meets a numberless crowd of people, many shops, and a bazaar. At the gate of the king's palace are four bazaars, placed opposite each other. On the north is the portico of the palace of the *raï*. Above each bazaar is a lofty arcade with a magnificent gallery, but the audience hall of the king's palace is elevated above all the rest. The bazaars are extremely long and broad. The rose merchants place before their shops high *estrades*, on each side of which they expose their flowers for sale. In this place one sees a constant succession of sweet smelling and fresh looking roses. These people could not live without roses, and they look upon them as quite as necessary as food.

Each class of men belonging to each profession has shops contiguous the one to the other; the jewellers sell publicly in the bazaar pearls, rubies, emeralds, and diamonds. In this agreeable locality, as well as in the king's palace, one sees numerous running streams and canals formed of chiselled stone, polished and smooth. On the left of the Sultan's portico rises the divan-khaneh (the council-house), which is extremely large and looks like a palace. In front of it is a hall, the height of which is above the stature of a man, its length thirty ghez, and its breadth ten. In it is placed the defter-khaneh (the archives), and here sit the scribes. The writing of this people is of two kinds: in one they write their letters with a kalam of iron upon a leaf of the Indian nut (the cocoa-nut tree), which is two ghez in length and two fingers in breadth. These characters have no colour, and the writing lasts but a short time. In the second kind of writing they blacken a white surface, they then take a soft stone, which they cut like a kalam,[1] and which they use to form the letters; this stone leaves on the black surface a white colour, which lasts a very long time, and this kind of writing is held in high estimation.

In the middle of this palace, upon an high estrade, is seated an eunuch, called Daiang, who alone presides over the divan. At the end of the hall stand tchobdar (hussars) drawn up in line. Every man who comes upon any business, passes between the tchobdar, offers a small present, prostrates himself with his face to the ground, then rising up explains the business which brought him there, and the Daiang pronounces his opinion, according to the principles of justice adopted in this kingdom, and no one thereafter is allowed to make any appeal.

When the Daiang leaves the divan they carry before him several parasols of different colours, and sound a trumpet. On each side of him walk panegyrists, who pronounce complimentary expressions in his honour. Before reaching the king's apartment there are seven doors to be passed, each of which is guarded by a janitor. When the Daiang arrives at each door a parasol is unfolded. He passes through the seventh door alone, gives the prince an account of what

[1] The reed they use for writing.

matters are going on, and after the lapse of a few minutes retires. Behind the king's palace are the house and hall allotted to the Daiang. To the left of the said palace is the *darab-khâneh* (the mint). In this country they have three kinds of money, made of gold mixed with alloy: one called *varahah* weighs about one *mithkal*, equivalent to two dinars, *kopeki*; the second, which is called *pertab*, is the half of the first; the third, called *fanom*, is equivalent in value to the tenth part of the last-mentioned coin. Of these different coins the *fanom* is the most useful. They cast in pure silver a coin which is the sixth of the *fanom*, which they call *tar*. This latter is also a very useful coin in currency. A copper coin worth the third of a *tar*, is called *djitel*. According to the practice adopted in this empire, all the provinces, at a fixed period, bring their gold to the mint. If any man receive from the divan an allowance in gold, he has to be paid by the *darab-khâneh*. The soldiers receive their pay every four months, and no payment is ever made by a draft upon the revenues of any province.

This empire contains so great a population that it would be impossible to give an idea of it without entering into the most extensive details. In the king's palace are several cells, like basins, filled with bullion, forming one mass. All the inhabitants of this country, both those of exalted rank and of an inferior class, down to the artizans of the bazaar, wear pearls, or rings adorned with precious stones, in their ears, on their necks, on their arms, on the upper part of the hand, and on the fingers. Opposite the Divan-Khâneh (the palace of the council) is the Fil-Khâneh (the house of the elephants).

Although the king possesses a considerable number of elephants in his dominions, the largest of these animals are kept near the palace, in the interior of the first and second fortress, between the north and the west. These elephants copulate, and bring forth young. The king possesses one white elephant of an extremely great size, on whose body are scattered here and there grey spots like freckles. Every morning this animal is led out before the monarch, and the sight of him seems to act as a happy omen. The elephants of the palace are fed upon *kitchri*.[1] This substance is cooked, and it is taken out of the copper in the elephant's presence; salt is thrown on it, and fresh sugar is sprinkled over it, and the whole is then mixed well together. They then make balls of it, weighing about two *man*, and, after steeping them in butter, they put them into the elephant's mouth. If one of these ingredients has been forgotten, the elephant attacks his keeper, and the king punishes this negligence severely. These animals take this food twice a day.

Each elephant has a separate compartment, the walls of which are extremely solid, and the roof composed of strong pieces of wood. The neck and the back of these animals are bound with chains, the end of which is strongly fastened to the top of the roof. If they were fixed otherwise, the elephant would easily undo them: the fore feet also are held by chains.

The mode of catching the elephant is as follows. On the road which the animal takes when he goes to drink, they dig a trench, and cover the mouth of it over, but very lightly. When an elephant falls into it, two or three days are allowed to elapse before any one goes near him. At the end of that time a man comes and strikes the animal with several blows of a stick well applied: upon this another man shows himself, and violently drives away the man who struck the blows, and, seizing his stick, hurls it a great way off; after which he throws some food to the elephant, and goes away. For several days the first of these men comes to beat the elephant, and the second prevents him from continuing to do so. Before long the animal becomes very friendly with this latter individual, who by degrees approaches the elephant, and

[1] A kind of food made of pulse, rice, and butter, eaten in Hindoostan.

offers him fruits, for which this animal is known to have a liking. He then scratches him and rubs him, and the elephant, won over by this manœuvre, submits without resistance, and allows a chain to be passed round his neck.

The story goes, that an elephant having escaped, fled into the desert and into the jungles. His keeper, who went in pursuit of him, dug a trench on his road. The animal, who dreaded the contrivances of this man (like a gazelle which has escaped from the net of the hunter), took up with his trunk a block of wood like a beam, placed it before him at short distances, on the surface of the ground, as he proceeded; and thus testing the road, he reached the watering place. The keepers of the elephant had lost all hope of retaking him, and yet the king had a very strong desire to gain possession of this animal again. One of the keepers hid himself in the branches of a tree under which the elephant had to pass. At the moment when the elephant came up, this man threw himself upon the back of the animal, who still had about his body and chest one of the thick cords with which the elephants are bound. This cord he laid strong hold of. Do what the elephant would to shake himself and twist about, and to strike blows with his trunk both right and left, he could not get free. He rolled himself on his side, but every time he did so the man leapt cleverly to the opposite side, and at the same time gave him some heavy blows upon the head. At length the animal, worn out, gave up the contest, and surrendered his body to the chains and his neck to the fetters. The keeper led the elephant into the presence of the king, who rewarded him with a noble generosity.

Even the sovereigns of Hindoostan take part in hunting the elephant. They remain a whole month, or even more, in the desert or in the jungles, and when they have taken any of these animals they are very proud of it. Sometimes they cause criminals to be cast under the feet of an elephant, that the animal may crush them to pieces with his knees, his trunk, and his tusks. The merchants who trade in elephants go to seek them in the island of Ceylon, and export them to different countries, where they sell them according to the tariff, which varies by the *ghez*.

Opposite the *darab-khaneh* (the mint) is the house of the Governor, where are stationed twelve thousand soldiers as a guard, who receive every day a payment of twelve thousand *fanom*, levied on the receipts of the houses of prostitution. The magnificence of the places of this kind, the beauty of the young girls collected therein, their allurements, and their coquetry, surpass all description. I will confine myself to the description of some particulars. Behind the *darab-khaneh* is a sort of bazaar, which is more than three hundred *ghez* in length, and more than twenty in breadth. On two sides are ranged chambers and *estrades;* in front of them are erected, in the form of thrones, several platforms constructed of beautiful stones. On the two sides of the avenue formed by the chambers are represented figures of lions, panthers, tigers, and other animals. All are so well drawn, and their movements have so natural an appearance, that you would think these animals were alive. Immediately after mid-day prayer they place before the doors of the chambers, which are decorated with extreme magnificence, thrones and chairs, on which the courtezans seat themselves. Each of these women is bedecked with pearls and gems of great value, and is dressed in costly raiment. They are all extremely young, and of perfect beauty. Each one of them has by her two young slaves, who give the signal of pleasure, and have the charge of attending to everything which can contribute to amusement. Any man may enter into this locality, and select any girl that pleases him, and take his pleasure with her. Anything that he carries about with him is delivered into the keeping of those engaged in the service of the houses of prostitution; and if anything is lost, these latter are responsible for it.

Each of the seven fortresses alike contains a great number of places of prostitution, and their general proceeds amount to twelve thousand *fanom,* which forms the pay allotted to the guards. These latter have it assigned to them as a duty to make themselves acquainted with every event which occurs within the fortresses; if any article is lost or stolen by thieves it is their place to report it; if not they are bound to make it good. Some slaves which had been bought by my companions, had run away. Information was given of the circumstance to the governor, who gave orders to the superintendents of the quarter in which we lived to bring back the fugitives or to make good the loss. These guards, on being informed of the value of the slaves, paid up the amount.

Such are the details which relate to the city of Bidjanagar and its sovereign.

The author of this narrative, having arrived in this city at the end of the month of *Zou'lhidjah* [the end of April 1443] took up his abode in an extremely lofty house, which had been assigned to him, and which resembled that which one sees in the city of Herat, over the King's gate, which gate serves as a passage for the entire population. He rested himself for several days from the fatigues of his journey. It was on the first day of *Moharrem* [May 1st, 1443], that I took up my abode in this great city. One day some messengers sent from the palace of the king came to seek me, and at the close of that same day I presented myself at court, and offered for the monarch's acceptance five beautiful horses, and some *tokouz* of damask and satin. The prince was seated in a hall, surrounded by the most imposing attributes of state. Right and left of him stood a numerous crowd of men ranged in a circle. The king was dressed in a robe of green satin, around his neck he wore a collar, composed of pearls of beautiful water and other splendid gems. He had an olive complexion, his frame was thin, and he was rather tall; on his cheeks might be seen a slight down, but there was no beard on his chin. The expression of his countenance was extremely pleasing. On being led into the presence of this prince I bowed my head three times. The monarch received me with interest, and made me take a seat very near him. When he took the august letter of the emperor, he handed it to the interpreter and said: "My heart is truly delighted to see that a great king has been pleased to send me an ambassador." As the humble author of this narrative, in consequence of the heat, and the great number of robes in which he was dressed, was drowned in perspiration, the monarch took pity upon him, and sent him a fan, similar to the khata which he held in his hand. After this a salver was brought, and they presented to the humble author two packets of betel, a purse containing five hundred *fanoms*, and twenty *mithkals*[1] of camphor. Then, receiving permission to depart, he returned to his house. Hitherto his provisions had been brought him daily, consisting of two sheep, four pair of fowls, five *man*[2] of rice, one of butter, one of sugar, and two *varahahs* of gold; and they continued supplying him regularly with the same articles. Twice in the week, at the close of day, the king sent for him, and put questions to him respecting his majesty, the happy Khakan. On each occasion the author received a packet of betel, a purse of *fanoms*, and some *mithkal* of camphor.

The king said to him by his interpreter: "Your monarchs invite an ambassador, and receive him to their table; as you and we may not eat together, this purse full of gold is the feast we give to an ambassador."

[1] The name both of a weight and a coin, the value of which has much changed. Its present weight is about three pennyweights.

[2] M. Langlès, in his note on this passage says, that as the author has not specified the mann to which he refers, it is impossible to fix its value. There are more than ten sorts in Persia and India. If the market "mann" is meant, it weighs about seven pounds and a half.

The betel is a leaf like that of the orange, but longer. In Hindoostan, the greater part of the country of the Arabs, and the kingdom of Ormuz, an extreme fondness prevails for this leaf, which in fact deserves its reputation. The manner of eating it is as follows. They bruise a portion of *faufel* (areca), otherwise called *sipari*, and put it in the mouth. Moistening a leaf of the betel, together with a grain of chalk, they rub the one upon the other, roll them together, and then place them in the mouth. They thus take as many as four leaves of betel at a time, and chew them. Sometimes they add camphor to it, and sometimes they spit out the saliva, which becomes of a red colour.

This substance gives a colour to and brightens the countenance, causes an intoxication similar to that produced by wine, appeases hunger, and excites appetite in those who are satiated; it removes the disagreeable smell from the mouth, and strengthens the teeth. It is impossible to express how strengthening it is, and how much it excites to pleasure. It is probable that the properties of this plant may account for the numerous harem of women that the king of this country maintains. If report speaks truly, the number of the *khatoun* [princesses] and concubines amounts to seven hundred. In each of these harems, a child who has reached the age of ten is no longer free of admission. Two women never inhabit the same house, and each has a separate maintenance. As soon as a beautiful girl is found in any part of the kingdom, when the consent of her father and mother is obtained, she is conducted with great pomp to the harem. From that moment nobody sees her, but she enjoys the highest consideration.

ACCOUNT OF AN EVENT RELATING TO THE KING OF BIDJANAGAR, WITH THE DETAILS OF THAT OCCURRENCE.

DURING the time that the author of this narrative was still sojourning in the city of Calicut, there happened in the city of Bidjanagar an extraordinary and most singular occurrence, the circumstances of which we shall now relate.

The king's brother, who had had a new house built for himself, invited thither the monarch and the principal personages of the empire. Now it is the established usage of the infidels never to eat in presence of each other. The men who were invited were assembled together in one grand hall. At short intervals the prince either came in person, or sent some messenger to say, that such or such great personage should come and eat his part of the banquet. Care had been taken to bring together all the drums, kettle-drums, trumpets, and flutes that could be found in the city, and these instruments playing all at the same time, made a tremendous uproar. As soon as the individual who had been sent for entered the above-mentioned house, two assassins, placed in ambush, sprang out upon him, pierced him with a poignard, and cut him in pieces. After having removed his limbs, or rather the fragments of his body, they sent for another guest, who, once having entered this place of carnage, disappeared, like those who have set out upon the journey of the life to come, never to return; and the language of fate seemed to address to these unfortunate ones the words of this verse:

Thou shalt not return any more. When thou hast taken thy departure, it is for ever.

In consequence of the noise of the drums, the clamour, and the tumult, no one, with the exception of a small number to whom the secret was entrusted, was aware of what was going on. In this manner all those who had any name or rank in the state were slaughtered. The prince, leaving his house all reeking with the blood of his victims, betook himself to the king's palace, and addressing himself to the guards who were stationed in that royal residence, invited them with flattering words to go to his house, and caused them to follow the steps of the other victims. So that the palace was thus deprived of all its defenders. This villain then entered into the king's presence, holding in his hand a dish covered with betel-nut, under which was concealed a brilliant poignard. He said to the monarch: "The hall is ready, and they only wait your august presence." The king, following the maxim which declares, that eminent men receive an inspiration from Heaven, said to him: "I am not in good health to day." This unnatural brother, thus losing the hope of enticing the king to his house, drew his poignard, and struck him therewith several violent blows, so that the prince fell at the back of his throne. The traitor thus believing that the king was dead, left there one of his confidants to cut off the monarch's head, then going out of the hall, he ascended to the portico of the palace, and thus addressed the people: "I have slain the king, his brothers, and such and such emirs, Brahmins, and viziers; now I am king."

Meanwhile his emissary had approached the throne with the intention of cutting off the king's head, but that prince seizing the seat behind which he had fallen, struck the wretch with it with so much violence on the chest that he fell upon his back. The king then, with the help of one of his *djandar* [guards], who at the sight of this horrible transaction had hidden himself in a corner, slew this assassin, and went out of the palace by the way of the harem.

His brother, still standing on the top of the steps of the hall of council, invited the multitude to recognize him as their king. At that moment the monarch cried out: "I am alive. I am well and safe. Seize that wretch." The whole crowd assembled together threw themselves upon the guilty prince, and put him to death. The only one who escaped was Daiang, the vizier, who previously to this sad event had gone on a voyage to the frontier of Ceylon. The king sent a courier to him to invite him to return, and informed him of what had just occurred. All those who had in any way aided in the conspiracy were put to death. Men in great numbers were slain, flayed, burnt alive, and their families entirely exterminated. The man who had brought the letters of invitation, was put to the last degree of torture. Daiang, who was on his road home from his journey, when he heard all the details of this affair, was perfectly stupified. On being admitted to the honour of kissing the feet of the monarch, he offered to God his fervent thanksgivings for the preservation of the life of the prince, and devoted himself more earnestly than he had ever done before to the celebration of the festival known by the name of *Mahanadi.*

Description of the festival called Mahanadi, which is celebrated with extreme devotion amongst the Infidels.

The idolators, who exercise an imposing authority in this country, with a view of displaying their pride, their power, their tyranny, and their glory, prepare every year a royal feast, a banquet worthy of a sovereign. This solemnity bears the name of Mahanadi. The manner in which it is celebrated is as follows. In pursuance of orders issued by the king of Bidjanagar, the generals and principal personages from all parts of his empire, which extends over a space of three months' journey, presented themselves at the palace.

They brought with them a thousand elephants, resembling the waves of a troubled sea, or a stormy cloud, which were covered with brilliant armour, and with castles magnificently adorned, in which were jugglers and artificers. On the trunks and ears of these animals had been drawn, with cinnabar and other substances, extraordinary pictures and figures of wonderful beauty. When the chiefs of the army, with the eminent personages and learned Brahmins from each province, as well as the elephants, were collected at the appointed time in the palace, during three consecutive days, in the month of *Redjeb*, the vast space of land magnificently decorated, in which the enormous elephants were congregated together, presented the appearance of the waves of the sea, or of that compact mass of men which will be assembled together at the day of the resurrection. Over this magnificent space were erected numerous pavilions, to the height of three, four, and five stories, covered from top to bottom with figures in relief. They represented everything that the imagination can picture, men, wild beasts, birds, and animals of every kind, down to flies and gnats: everything was drawn with extraordinary skill and delicacy. Some of these pavilions were arranged in such a manner, that they could turn rapidly round and present a new face. At each moment a new chamber or a new hall presented itself to the view.

In the front of this place rose a palace with nine pavilions, magnificently ornamented. In the ninth the king's throne was set up. In the seventh was allotted a place to the humble author of this narrative, from which every one was excluded excepting the author's friends. Between the palace and the pavilions, in an extremely beautiful situation, were musicians and storytellers, who sang and invented tales. The part of musicians is generally filled by women. Some young girls, with cheeks as full as the moon, and with faces more lovely than the spring, clothed in magnificent dresses, and showing features which, like the freshest rose, charmed every heart, were placed behind a pretty curtain opposite the king. On a sudden the curtain was raised and again fell, and the damsels arranged themselves for the dance, with a grace calculated to seduce every sense and captivate every mind. The jugglers execute some feats of skill which are quite wonderful: they place on the ground three pieces of wood, which touch each other, each of which is one cubit in length, half a cubit in breadth, and three quarters of a cubit in height; on the top of the two first they place two other pieces, of nearly the same length and breadth, and above the second piece, which lies on the top of the first, they place another, a little smaller, so that the first and second pieces of wood form as it were steps by which to reach the third piece, which crowns the whole. A large elephant, trained to this exercise, stepping upon the first and second pieces of wood ascends the third, the surface of which is scarcely broader than the sole of one of the feet of this animal. While the elephant supports himself with his four feet upon this beam, they raise behind him the other pieces of wood. The animal once placed on the top of this beam, follows with his trunk all the airs which the musicians play, and moving in cadence with the time, raises and lowers his trunk alternately.

After this they erect a column of ten *ghez* in height, on the top of which they fix a long piece of wood, like the beam of a pair of scales, and which has a hole in the middle. At one end of this beam they attach a stone, the weight of which is equivalent to that of the elephant, and at the other end, at the distance of one *ghez* they place a broad plank, which is of one *ghez* in length; by means of a cord they lower the end to which the plank is fastened, and on this the elephant mounts. His keeper then lets go the cord by little and little, until the two extremities of the piece of wood are exactly balanced, like the beams of a pair of scales, and at a height of ten *ghez*. This piece of wood, one end of which bears the elephant and the other a stone of corresponding weight, turns, after the fashion of a semicircle, making a half rotation from right to left, in presence of the king; and in this elevated position the elephant follows all the airs of the musicians, and makes the movements in cadence.

All the musicians, orators, and jugglers, receive from the king gold and suits of apparel. During three consecutive days, from the moment when the burning sun like a peacock of enchanting plumage displayed himself proudly in the midst of the heavens, until that in which the raven of darkness unfolded its wings, the royal festival was prolonged in a style of the greatest magnificence.

It would be impossible, without entering into details of too great a length, to describe in this place the picture of the different kinds of fireworks, sports in which fireworks were employed, and games and amusements which this fête presented. On the third day, at the moment when the king arose, the humble author of this narrative was conducted into the presence of the monarch. The throne, which was of an extraordinary size, was made of gold, and enriched with precious stones of extreme value; the whole workmanship was perfect in its delicacy and ingenuity. It is probable, that in all the kingdoms of the world, the art of inlaying precious stones is no where better understood than in this country.

Before the throne was a square cushion, on the edges of which were sewn three rows of pearls of the most beautiful water. During the three days the king remained seated on this cushion behind the throne. When the fête of Mahanadi was ended, at the hour of evening prayer, the monarch sent to summon me. On my arrival at the palace I was introduced in the midst of four *estrades*, which were about ten ghez both in length and in breadth. The roof and the walls were entirely formed of plates of gold, enriched with precious stones.

Each of these plates was as thick as the blade of a sword, and was fastened with golden nails. Upon the *estrade*, in the front, is placed the throne of the king, and the throne itself is of very great size. The pomp of the king when seated thereon was most imposing. He questioned me on particular points respecting his majesty the happy Khakan, his emirs, his troops, the numbers of his horses, and also respecting his great cities, such as Samarcand, Herat, and Shirez. He expressed towards the emperor sentiments of the greatest friendship, and said to me: "I shall send, together with an able ambassador, some rows of elephants, two *tokouz* [twice nine] of eunuchs, and other presents."

During this audience one of the king's favorites put a question to me, through the medium of an interpreter, upon the subject of the magnificent *estrades* enriched with precious stones. He said to me: "In your country they could not execute work like that." I replied: "Certainly in my country they are able to produce workmanship of equal beauty, but it is not the custom." The monarch highly approved of what I had said. He ordered to be given me some purses of *fanoms*, some betel, and some fruits reserved for his own use.

Certain inhabitants of Ormuz, who have become established in this country, having been informed of the favour which was shown me by the king, and of the design which he had entertained of sending an embassy to the court, which is the asylum of princes, were extremely troubled thereat, and resorted to every expedient to overthrow to its very foundations this edifice of peace and friendship. In pursuance of their wickedness and malignity, they spread abroad a rumour that the author of this work was not really sent by the happy Khakan. This assertion reached the ears of the emir and of the vizier.

But why speak of the emir and the vizier? It came even to the king.

As will be seen in what followed.

At this period Daiang, the vizier, who manifested towards the author of this work the most lively interest, set out on an expedition into the kingdom of Kalberga. The reasons which had led to this invasion were as follows. The king of Kalberga, Sultan Ala-eddin-Ahmed-schah, having heard of the conspiracy formed against the life of Diou-rai, and of the assassination of the principal personages attached to the government of this prince, had received the intelligence with extreme delight. He sent to this monarch an eloquent messenger, charged with the following message: "Send me a sum of seven *laks* of *verahahs*, or else I will march into your country a formidable army, and I will overturn from its foundations the empire of idolatry." Diou-rai, the king of Bidjanagar, was equally troubled and irritated by the receipt of such a message. On receiving it he said: "Since I am alive, what cause of alarm can there be because certain of my servants are killed?"

"*Why should I fear though a thousand of my servants should die? In the space of a day or two I can bring together a hundred times as many.*"

"While the sun shines, atoms without number are to be seen."

"If my enemies flatter themselves that they will find in me weakness, negligence, idleness, or apathy, it goes for nothing. I am protected by a powerful and happy star. Fortune watches over me with affection. Meanwhile, whatever my enemies may find themselves able to take from my kingdom, will be in their eyes a booty for them to distribute among their *seids* and their learned men. Whereas, for my part, whatever shall fall into my power out of the territories of my enemy, shall be given by me to the *bazdars* [falconers] and to the Brahmins."

Troops were sent out on both sides, which made great ravages on the frontiers of the two kingdoms.

The king had admitted into his council, to supply the

place of Daiang, a Christian, named Nimeh-pezir. This man thought himself equal to a vizier; he was a creature of small stature, malicious, ill-born, mean, and stern. All the most odious vices were united in him, without one finding in him any counterbalancing estimable quality. This wretch, as soon as he had defiled by his presence the seat of authority, suppressed, without any reason, the daily allowance which had been assigned to us. Soon after, the inhabitants of Ormuz, having found a favourable occasion, manifested without reservation that diabolical malignity which was stamped upon their character, and the conformity of their perverse inclinations having united them intimately with the vizier Mineh-pezir, they said to that man: "Abd-er-Razzak is not an ambassador sent by his majesty the happy Khakan; he is but a merchant who has been charged with the conveyance of a letter from that monarch. They also circulated amongst the idolators a variety of falsehoods, which produced a deep impression upon their minds. For a considerable time the author, placed as he was in the midst of a country inhabited by infidels, remained in a painful position, and doubtful as to what course he ought to follow. While all these perplexities, however, were hanging over me, the king, on several occasions when he met me on his road, turned towards me with kindness and asked after my welfare. He is in truth a prince who possesses eminent qualities.

If we say that he is just in everything, such an eulogium is sufficient.

Daiang, after having made an invasion upon the frontiers of the country of Kalberga, and taken several unfortunate prisoners, had retraced his steps. He expressed to Nimeh-pezir some keen reproaches for the neglect he had shown in the author's affairs, to whom, on the very day of his arrival, he caused to be paid a sum of seven thousand *varahahs*, for which he delivered him an order upon the mint. Two persons, Kojah-Masood and Kojah Mohammed, both natives of Khorassan, who had fixed their abode in the kingdom of Bidjanagar, were appointed to undertake the duties of ambassadors, and various presents and stuffs were accordingly sent to them. Fatah-Khakan, the one of the descendants of the Sultan Firouz-Schah, who had filled the throne of Delhi, also dispatched a delegate named Kojah-Djemal-eddin, charged with a present and a letter.

On the day of the audience of dismissal the king said to the humble author of this work: "It has been asserted that thou wast not really sent by his majesty Mirza-Schah-Rokh, otherwise we should have shown thee greater attentions; if thou comest back on a future occasion into my territories, thou shalt meet with a reception worthy of a king such as we are." But the author said to himself mentally:

If, when once I have escaped from the desert of thy love, I reach my own country, I will never again set out on another voyage, not even in the company of a king.

In a letter addressed to his majesty, the monarch inserted those statements so full of malignity which had been invented by the inhabitants of Ormuz, and expressed himself in the following terms: "We had had the intention of seeking the good will of the emperor by some gifts and presents worthy of a sovereign. Certain persons, however, have assured us that Abd-er-Razzak was not in any way attached to the court of your majesty." In detailing the titles which are assumed by the august Khakan, he said: "This prince unites in his person the qualities of a king, and that which constitutes the glory of a sovereign, with the purity of the prophets, and the virtues of the saints." So that the tongue of great and small, the writing of every able man, and the pen of every secretary ought to express (with respect to this monarch) the following sentiment.

Thou art a Noah, who, like Abraham, possesses the love of God; a Khidr, who holds the rank of Moses.

Thou art Ahmed, who encircles the majesty of the throne of God; thou art Jesus, whose aspect expresses the Divine Spirit.

Henceforth the habitable globe shall be regarded as forming part of thine empire; it is therefore that thou holdest the equinoctial line under the line of thy authority.

As, according to the ideas of these people, the country of Bidjanagar is placed under the equinoctial line, the expression to "hold the equinoctial line under the line of his authority," is perfectly correct.

The humble author of this work, after having completed his negociations, set forth on his journey, and directed his homeward course towards the shores of the sea of Oman.

Account of the Author's voyage on his return from the countries of Hindoostan. Description of a storm. History of the Deluge.

The sun of the Divine Mercy displayed itself above the horizon of happiness. The star of fortune arose to the east of my hopes. The bright glimmer of joy and satisfaction showed itself in the midst of the darkness of night, in conformity to this maxim:

"*God is the friend of those who hold the true faith: He will bring them forth from the darkness, and will lead them forth into the light.*"

Those nights of affliction and weariness, passed in the sad abode of idolatry and error, were succeeded by the breaking of the dawn of happiness, and the brilliant out-shining of the sun of prosperity; and the evening, which was full of the anxieties of weakness, became changed into days of gladness and confidence.

The duration of the night was longer than that of the day, but now the face of everything is changed. The latter has been constantly on the increase, and the former on the decrease.

As the city from which I was returning was situated at the extremity of the regions of Hindoostan, and as the whole country which I had traversed was inhabited by idolators, my travelling resources had been entirely absorbed by the troubles I had undergone. But why speak of what does not deserve to be recalled? at all events in spite of my grievous position—

In place of hope I have but this maxim as my sole provision for my voyage:

"Despair not of the mercy of God."

With a heart full of energy, and with vast hopes, I set out on my journey, or rather, I committed myself to the goodness and compassion of God. On the twelfth day of the month of *Schaban* [Nov. 5th, 1443], accompanied by the ambassadors, I left the city of Bidjanagar to commence my journey. After travelling eighteen days, on the first day of the month of *Ramazan* [Nov. 23rd, 1443], I reached the shores of the sea of Oman and the port of Maganor. There I had the honour of being admitted to the society of the Sheriff-Emir Seid-Ala-eddin-Meskhedi, who was a hundred and twenty years old. For many years he had been an object of veneration both to Mussulmans and idolators. Throughout the country his words were regarded as oracles, and no one ventured to object to his decisions.

One of the ambassadors of Bidjanagar, Kojah-Masud, had just died in this city.

Under this vault, the dwelling of evil, who knows in what spot our head will rest beneath the brink of the tomb!

After having celebrated in the port of Maganor the festival which follows the fast, I made my way to the port of Manor [Honawer] to procure a vessel, and I laid in all the provisions necessary for twenty persons during a voyage of forty days. One day, at the moment that I was on the point of embarking, I opened the *Book of Fates*, the author of which was the Iman Djafar-Sadek, and which is composed from verses of the *Alcoran*. There I found a presage of joy and happiness, for I lighted upon this verse:

"*Fear nothing, for thou hast been preserved from the hand of unjust men.*"

Struck with the coincidence of this passage with my situation, I felt all those anxieties disappear from my heart, which had caused me alarm in the prospect of encountering the sea. Abandoning myself entirely to the hope of a happy deliverance, I embarked on the eighth day of the month of Zu'lkadah [Jan. 28th, 1444] and put to sea. While the vision *of those ships which float over the mountain-like waves of the sea,* presented to my thoughts the traces of the Divine power, at the same time, in the conversation of the companions of my voyage, I collected observations respecting remarkable names and facts worthy of note, and throughout our little company peace and contentment prevailed.

The eye of sad events and of misfortunes was gone to sleep, Fortune appeared to have given herself up to indolence, and we were surrounded with happiness.

The ship, after a million of shocks, reached the open sea.

On a sudden there arose a violent wind on the surface of the sea, and on all sides were heard groaning and cries.

The night, the vessel, the wind, and the gulf, presented to our minds all the forebodings of a catastrophe. On a sudden, through the effect of the contrary winds, which resembled men in their drink, the wine which produced[1] this change penetrated even to the vessel. The planks of which it was composed, and which by their conformation seemed to form a continuous line, were on the point of becoming

[1] Poetically speaking.

divided like the separate letters of the alphabet. To our thoughts was strikingly presented the truth of that passage:

"*The waves cover it, the billow rises beneath it, and above it is the cloud.*"

The sailor who, with respect to his skill in swimming, might be compared to a fish, was anxious to throw himself into the water like an anchor. The captain, although familiarized with the navigation of all the seas, shed bitter tears, and had forgotten all his science. The sails were torn, the mast was entirely bent by the shock of the wind. The different grades of passengers who inhabited this floating house threw out upon the waves riches of great value, and, after the manner of the Sofis, voluntarily stripped themselves of their worldly goods. Who could give a thought to the jeopardy in which their money and their stuffs were placed, when life itself, which is so dear to man, was in danger? For myself, in this situation, which brought before my eyes all the threatening terrors which the ocean had in its power to present, with tears in my eyes I gave myself up for lost. Through the effect of the stupor, and of the profound sadness to which I became a prey, I remained, like the sea, with my lips dry and my eyes moist, and resigned myself entirely to the Divine Will. At one time, through the driving of the waves, which resembled mountains, the vessel was lifted up to the skies; at another, under the impulse of the violent winds, it descended like divers to the bottom of the waters.[1]

The agitation of the waters of the sea caused my body to melt like salt which is dissolved in water; the violence of the deluge annihilated and utterly dispersed the firmness which sustained me, and my mind, hitherto so strong, was like the ice which is suddenly exposed to the heat of the month of

[1] M. Quatremère here states that he has omitted two verses, which, from the strangeness of their style, are utterly unintelligible.

Tamouz; even now my heart is troubled and agitated, as is the fish which is taken out of fresh water.

May the torrent of destruction overturn the edifice of fate, which thus brings in successive waves the waters of misfortune upon my head.

Many times I said to myself, and it was in language dictated by my situation that I repeated, this verse:

A dismal night! the fear of the waves, and so frightful an abyss? What judgment can they who are so peaceful on shore form of our situation?

The pure water of my life was troubled by the agitation of the sea; and the brilliant mirror of my ideas, in consequence of the dampness of the water, and the putrefaction of the air, was covered with rust. Each moment that the pupils of my eyes contemplated that muddy water, it resembled, through the effect of my extreme alarm, a flaming sword. At the sight of the agitated sea, overset by the tempestuous winds, I drew from my breast an icy sigh; it was a sharp weapon, which tore my very soul.

Overwhelmed at every point, and seeing the gate of hope shut on every side against me, with an eye full of tears and a heart full of burning chagrin, I addressed myself to God with the expression of this verse:

Oh, our Lord, place not upon us a burden which is too heavy for our strength to bear?

I prayed to the Being, who is supremely merciful, and who never upbraideth with his benefits, to be pleased, from the immense sea of His goodness, to bedew and to bestow fresh verdure upon the little shrub of my existence; and to deign, in the distribution of the water of His kindness, to wash completely and disperse from the face of my situation the dust which rendered my life a grievance to me. In the midst of this sad position, I reflected and put the question to myself: "What, then, is this catastrophe, which has made fortune in her revolution fall so heavily upon me?

"What, then, is this shame, which, through the hostility of a perfidious fate, of a base and contemptible destiny, has caused the serenity of my face to disappear? On the one side, I have been unable to snatch my precious life from the fury of the waves of death, nor have I been able, in carrying out the business of my sovereign, to bring to the surface of the water the pearl of my exertions. For a generous soul neglects nothing which can tend to the fulfilment of the obligations which it has contracted towards its benefactor, and when it becomes a question of executing the business of its master, it regards life itself, which is ordinarily so precious, as utterly valueless. If the man of sincerity casts [his loyalty to] his king into the fire of events, his nature, like that of a gem, must show no alteration in the smallest atom; or rather the gold of his loyalty, after the manner of pure gold, becomes still more refined."

I was in the midst of these reflections, and everything about me spoke of dejection and trouble, when at length, by virtue of that Divine promise: "*Who is He who hears the prayers of the afflicted, and drives away his misery?*"[1] on a sudden, the zephyr of God's infinite mercy began to blow upon me from that point which is indicated by these words: "*Despair not of the mercy of the Most High.*" The morning of joy began to dawn from the East of happiness, and the messenger of a propitious fate brought to the ears of my soul these consolatory words: "Since on your behalf we have divided the sea, we have saved you." The impetuous hurricane was changed to a favourable wind, the tossing of the waves ceased, and the sea, in conformity with my desires, became completely calm. My fellow-passengers, after having celebrated at sea the feast of victims, gained sight, at the close of the month of Zu'lhidjah [middle of March, 1444] of the mountain of Kalahat, and found themselves at length in safety from all the perils of the deep. At this period, the

[1] Koran, surate 27, verse 63.

new moon of the month of Moharrem, of the year 848 [middle of March 1444], like a beneficent spirit looked on us with a friendly eye.

THE CLOSING EVENTS OF THE AUTHOR'S VOYAGE BY SEA. HIS ARRIVAL AT ORMUZ, UNDER THE PROTECTION OF GOD MOST HIGH.

IN retracing the story of my voyage, I had reached the point at which the new moon of Moharrem shewed us her shining face on the sea. The vessel still remained at sea for several days. On our arrival at the port of Muscat we cast anchor.

After having repaired the damages which the vessel had suffered through the effect of the storms, we re-embarked, and continued our voyage.

After leaving Muscat, the vessel arrived at the port of Jurufgan, where it put in for a day or two. On this occasion we felt during one night such excessive heat, that at day-break one would have said that the heavens had set the earth on fire. So intense was the heat which scorched up the atmosphere, that even the bird of rapid flight was burnt up in the heights of heaven, as well as the fish in the depths of the sea. I re-embarked and set sail from the port of Jurufgan, and reached Ormuz on the forenoon of Friday, the eighth day of the month of Safar [April 22nd, 1444]. Our voyage from the port of Honawer[1] to Ormuz had lasted sixty-*five days*.

[1] Onore.

THE TRAVELS

OF

NICOLÒ CONTI, IN THE EAST,

IN THE

EARLY PART OF THE FIFTEENTH CENTURY.

THE TRAVELS

OF

NICOLÒ CONTI, IN THE EAST,

IN THE

EARLY PART OF THE FIFTEENTH CENTURY,

AS RELATED BY POGGIO BRACCIOLINI, IN HIS WORK ENTITLED "HISTORIA DE VARIETATE FORTUNÆ." LIB. IV.

A CERTAIN Venetian named Nicolò, who had penetrated to the interior of India, came to pope Eugenius (he being then for the second time at Florence) for the purpose of craving absolution, inasmuch as, when, on his return from India, he had arrived at the confines of Egypt, on the Red Sea, he was compelled to renounce his faith, not so much from the fear of death to himself, as from the danger which threatened his wife and children who accompanied him. I being very desirous of his conversation (for I had heard of many things related by him which were well worth knowing), questioned him diligently, both in the meetings of learned men and at my own house, upon many matters which seemed very deserving to be committed to memory and also to writing. He discoursed learnedly and gravely concerning his journey to such remote nations, of the situation and different manners and customs of the Indians, also of their animals and trees and spices, and in what place each thing is produced. His accounts bore all the appearance of being true, and not fabrications. He went farther than any former traveller ever penetrated, so far as our records inform us. For he crossed the Ganges and travelled far beyond the island of Taprobana, a point which there is no evidence that any European had previously reached, with the exception of a commander of the fleet of Alexander the Great, and a Roman citizen[1] in the time of Tiberius Claudius Cæsar, both of whom were driven there by tempests.

Nicolò, being a young man, resided as a merchant in the city of Damascus in Syria. Having learnt the Arabic language, he departed thence with his merchandise in company with six hundred other merchants (who formed what is commonly called a caravan), with whom he passed over the deserts of Arabia Petræa, and thence through Chaldæa until he arrived at the Euphrates. He says that on reaching the border of these deserts, which are situated in the midst of the province, there happened to them a very marvellous adventure; that about midnight, while they were resting, they heard a great noise, and thinking that it might be Arabs who were coming to rob them, they all got up, through fear of what might be about to happen. And while they stood thus they saw a great multitude of people on horseback, like travellers, pass in silence near their tents without offering them any molestation. Several merchants who had seen the same thing

[1] This refers to a story related by Pliny (*Hist. Nat.*, lib. vi, cap. 22), to the effect that a freedman of one Annius Plocamus, being overtaken by a tempest when off the coast of Arabia, was, after being tossed about for a fortnight, driven on shore at Hypuros, in the island of Taprobana. The king of this island, having questioned the freedman respecting the Romans, was so much struck by his answers that he became desirous of their friendship, and forthwith despatched ambassadors to Rome. The description given by these ambassadors of their island of Taprobana is inserted by Pliny in his history, and forms the twenty-second chapter of the sixth book.

before, asserted that they were demons, who were in the habit of passing in this manner through these deserts.

On the river Euphrates there is a noble city, a part of the ancient city of Babylon, the circumference of which is fourteen miles, and which is called by the inhabitants thereof by the new name of Baldochia.[1] The river Euphrates flows through the centre of the city, the two parts of which are connected together by a single bridge of fourteen arches, with strong towers at both ends. Many monuments and foundations of buildings of the ancient city are still to be seen. In the upper part of the city there is a very strong fortress, and also the royal palace.

Sailing hence for the space of twenty days down the river, in which he saw many noble and cultivated islands, and then travelling for eight days through the country, he arrived at a city called Balsera,[2] and in four days' journey beyond at the Persian Gulf, where the sea rises and falls in the manner of the Atlantic Ocean. Sailing through this gulf for the space of five days he came to the port of Colcus, and afterwards to Ormuz (which is a small island in the said gulf), distant from the mainland twelve miles. Leaving this island and turning towards India for the space of one hundred miles, he arrived at the city of Calacatia, a very noble emporium of the Persians. Here, having remained for some time, he learned the Persian language, of which he afterwards made great use, and also adopted the dress of the country, which he continued to wear during the whole period of his travels. Subsequently he and some Persian merchants freighted a ship, having first taken a solemn oath to be faithful and loyal companions one to another.

Sailing in this wise together, he arrived in the course of a month at the very noble city of Cambay, situated in the second gulf[3] after having passed the mouth of the river Indus. In this country are found those precious stones

[1] Baghdad. [2] Bussorah. [3] The Gulf of Cambay.

called sardonixes. It is the custom when husbands die, for one or more of their wives to burn themselves with them, in order to add to the pomp of the funeral. She who was the most dear to the deceased, places herself by his side with her arm round his neck, and burns herself with him; the other wives, when the funeral pile is lighted, cast themselves into the flames. These ceremonies will be described more at length hereafter.

Proceeding onwards he sailed for the space of twenty days, and arrived at two cities situated on the sea shore, one named Pacamuria, and the other Helly. In these districts grows ginger, called in the language of the country *beledi*, *gebeli*, and *neli*. It is the root of a shrub, which grows to the height of two cubits, with great leaves, similar to those of the blue lilies called *Iris*, with a hard bark. They grow like the roots of reeds, which cover the fruit. From these the ginger is obtained, on which they cast ashes and place it in the sun for three days, in which time it is dried.

Departing hence, and travelling about three hundred miles inland, he arrived at the great city of Bizenegalia, situated near very steep mountains. The circumference of the city is sixty miles: its walls are carried up to the mountains and enclose the valleys at their foot, so that its extent is thereby encreased. In this city there are estimated to be ninety thousand men fit to bear arms. The inhabitants of this region marry as many wives as they please, who are burnt with their dead husbands. Their king is more powerful than all the other kings of India. He takes to himself twelve thousand wives, of whom four thousand follow him on foot wherever he may go, and are employed solely in the service of the kitchen. A like number, more handsomely equipped, ride on horseback. The remainder are carried by men in litters, of whom two thousand or three thousand are selected as his wives on condition that at his death they should voluntarily burn themselves with him, which is considered to be a great honour for them.

The very noble city of Pelagonda is subject to the same king; it is ten miles in circumference, and is distant eight days' journey from Bizenegalia. Travelling afterwards hence by land for twenty days he arrived at a city and seaport called Peudifetania, on the road to which he passed two cities, viz., Odeschiria and Cendergiria, where the red sandal wood grows. Proceeding onwards the said Nicolò arrived at a maritime city which is named Malepur, situated in the Second Gulf beyond the Indus.[1] Here the body of Saint Thomas lies honourably buried in a very large and beautiful church: it is worshiped by heretics, who are called Nestorians, and inhabit this city to the number of a thousand. These Nestorians are scattered over all India, in like manner as are the Jews among us. All this province is called Malabar. Beyond this city there is another, which is called Cahila, where pearls are found. Here also there grows a tree which does not bear fruit, but the leaf of which is six cubits in length and almost as many broad, and so thin that when pressed together it can be held in the closed hand.[2] These leaves are used in this country for writing upon instead of paper, and in rainy weather are carried on the head as a covering to keep off the wet. Three or four persons travelling together can be covered by one of these leaves stretched out. In the middle of the gulf there is a very noble island called Zeilam,[3] which is three thousand miles in circumference, and in which they find, by digging, rubies, saffires, garnets, and those stones which are called cats' eyes. Here also cinnamon grows in great abundance. It is a tree which very much resembles our thick willows, excepting that the branches do not grow upwards, but are spread out horizontally: the leaves are very like those

[1] The Bay of Bengal.

[2] The Fan Palm, or Palmyra tree (*Borassus flabelliformis*, L.): but the thinness of the leaves is enormously exaggerated.

[3] Ceylon.

of the laurel, but are somewhat larger. The bark of the branches is the thinnest and best, that of the trunk of the tree is thicker and inferior in flavour. The fruit resembles the berries of the laurel: an odoriferous oil is extracted from it adapted for ointments, which are much used by the Indians. When the bark is stripped off the wood is used for fuel.[1]

In this island there is a lake, in the middle of which is a city three miles in circumference. The islands are governed by persons who are of the race of bramins, and who are reputed to be wiser than other people. The bramins are great philosophers, devoting the whole of their life to the study of astrology, and cultivating the virtues and refinements of life.

He afterwards went to a fine city of the island Taprobana, which island is called by the natives Sciamuthera.[3] He remained one year in this city (which is six miles in circumference and a very noble emporium of that island), and then sailed for the space of twenty days with a favourable wind, leaving on his right hand an island called Andamania,[4] which means the island of gold, the circumference of which is eight hundred miles. The inhabitants are cannibals. No travellers touch here unless driven so to do by bad weather, for when taken they are torn to pieces and devoured by these cruel savages. He affirms that the island of Taprobana is six thousand miles in circumference. The men are cruel and their customs brutal. The ears both of the men and women are very large, in which they wear earrings ornamented with precious stones. Their garments are made of linen and silk, and hang down to their knees. The men marry as many wives as they please. Their houses are extremely low, in order to

[1] This account of the cinnamon is remarkably exact.

[2] There are no longer any traces of a lake in the centre of Ceylon of sufficient magnitude to contain a city three miles in circumference.

[3] Sumatra.

[4] The Andaman Isles. The three principal islands lying in close contiguity with each other may have been mistaken by Nicolò for one island.

protect them against the excessive heat of the sun. They are all idolators. In this island pepper, larger than the ordinary pepper, also long pepper, camphor, and also gold are produced in great abundance. The tree which produces the pepper is similar to the ivy, the seeds are green and resemble in form those of the juniper tree: they dry them in the sun, spreading a few ashes over them. In this island there also grows a green fruit, which they call *duriano*,[1] of the size of a cucumber. When opened five fruits are found within, resembling oblong oranges. The taste varies, like that of cheese.

In one part of the island called Batech, the inhabitants eat human flesh, and are in a state of constant warfare with their neighbours.[2] They keep human heads as valuable property, for when they have captured an enemy they cut off his head, and having eaten the flesh, store up the skull and use it for money. When they desire to purchase any article, they give one or more heads in exchange for it according to its value, and he who has most heads in his house is considered to be the most wealthy.

Having departed from the island of Taprobana he arrived, after a stormy passage of sixteen days, at the city of Ternassari,[3] which is situated on the mouth of a river of the same name. This district abounds in elephants and a species of thrush.

Afterwards, having made many journeys both by land and sea, he entered the mouth of the river Ganges, and, sailing

[1] *Durio Zibethinus*, L., one of the most highly esteemed fruits of the Malay Islands, but extremely offensive to those who are unaccustomed to it, on account of its nauseous odour.

[2] Batta; a district extending from the river Singkell to the Tabooyong, and inland to the back of Ayer Bañgis. Marsden, in his "History of Sumatra" (p. 390, 3rd edit.), gives instances of canibalism among this people as late as the year 1780.

[3] Tenasserim, the capital of a district of the same name in the Birman empire.

up it, at the end of fifteen days he came to a large and wealthy city, called Cernove. This river is so large that, being in the middle of it, you cannot see land on either side. He asserts that in some places it is fifteen miles in width. On the banks of this river there grow reeds extremely high, and of such surprising thickness that one man alone cannot encompass them with his arms:[1] they make of these fishing boats, for which purpose one alone is sufficient, and of the wood or bark, which is more than a palm's breadth in thickness, skiffs adapted to the navigation of the river. The distance between the knots is about the height of a man. Crocodiles and various kinds of fishes unknown to us are found in the river. On both banks of the stream there are most charming villas and plantations and gardens, wherein grow vast varieties of fruits, and above all those called *musa*,[2] which are more sweet than honey, resembling figs, and also the nuts which we call nuts of India.[3]

Having departed hence he sailed up the river Ganges for the space of three months, leaving behind him four very famous cities, and landed at an extremely powerful city called Maarazia, where there is a great abundance of aloe wood, gold, silver, precious stones, and pearls. From thence he took the route towards some mountains situated towards the east, for the purpose of procuring those precious stones called carbuncles, which are found there. Having spent thirteen days on this expedition, he returned to the city of Cernove, and thence proceeded to Buffetania. Departing thence he arrived, at the end of a month's voyage, at the mouth of the river Racha,[4] and navigating up the said river, he came in the space of six days to a very large city called by the same name as the river, and situated upon the bank thereof.

Quitting this city he travelled through mountains void of

[1] Bamboos. [2] Bananas. *Musa Paradisiaca*, L.

[3] Cocoa nuts, formerly called *Nuces Indicæ*. [4] Aracan.

all habitations[1] for the space of seventeen days, and then through open plains for fifteen days more, at the end of which time he arrived at a river larger than the Ganges, which is called by the inhabitants Dava.[2] Having sailed up this river for the space of a month he arrived at a city more noble than all the others, called Ava, and the circumference of which is fifteen miles.

Hac sola in civitate plurimas tabernas rei, quam joci gratia scripsi, ridiculæ lascivæque esse affirmat; vendi in his a solis feminis ea que nos *sonalia*, a sono, ut puto, dicta appellamus, aurea, argentea æreaque, in modum parvulæ avellanæ; ad has virum, antequam uxorem capiat, proficisci (aliter enim rejicitur a conjugio:) execta atque elevata paulum membri virilis cute, trudi inter pellem et carnem ex his sonaliis usque ad duodecimum, et amplius, prout libuit variis circum circa locis; inde consuta cute intra paucos sanari dies; hoc ad explendum mulierum libidinem fieri; his enim tanquam internodiis, membrique tumore, feminas summa voluptate affici. Multorum dum ambulant membra tibiis repercussa resonant, ita ut audiantur. Ad hoc Nicolaus sæpius a mulieribus, quæ eum a parvitate Priapi deridebant, invitatus, noluit dolorem suum aliis voluptati esse.

This province, which is called by the inhabitants Macinus,[3] abounds in elephants. The king keeps ten thousand of these animals, and uses them in his wars. They fix castles on their backs, from which eight or ten men fight with javelins, bows, and those weapons which we call crossbows. Their manner of capturing these elephants is said to be generally as follows, and it agrees with the mode stated by Pliny [lib. 8, c. 8]: In the rutting season they drive tame female ele-

[1] The Youmadoung mountains, forming the western boundary of Burmah Proper.

[2] The Irrawaddy.

[3] This province cannot be Mangi, as supposed by Ramusio, but is most probably Siam, formerly called Sian.

phants into the woods, where they are left until the wild male elephants seek them; the female then gradually withdraws, feeding, into a place set apart for this purpose, surrounded by a wall and furnished with two large doors, one for the entrance and another for exit. When the elephant perceives the female to be there and enters by the first door to come to her, she, as soon as she sees him, runs out through the other, and the doors are then immediately closed. As many as a thousand men then enter, through apertures made for that purpose in the walls, with very strong ropes with running nooses; a man then presents himself to the beast in the forepart of the enclosure. As soon as the elephant sees him he runs furiously at him to kill him, while the men behind throw the nooses over his hind feet as he raises them, and then drawing the cords tight fasten them to a pole fixed into the ground, and leave the elephant there for three or four days, giving him only a little grass daily. In the course of fifteen days he becomes quiet. They afterwards tie him between two tame elephants and lead him through the city, and thus in ten days he is rendered as tame as the others.

It is also related by Nicolò, that in other parts they tame them thus. They drive the elephants into a small valley enclosed on all sides, and having removed the females they leave the males shut up there, and tame them by hunger. At the end of four days they drive them thence and conduct them to narrow places constructed for the purpose, and there make them gentle. The kings purchase these for their own use. The tame elephants are fed upon rice and butter, and the wild ones eat branches of trees and grass. The tame elephants are governed by one man, who guides them with an iron hook, which is applied to the head. This animal is so intelligent, that when he is in battle he frequently receives the javelins of the enemy on the sole of his foot, in order that those whom he carries on his back may not be injured.

The king of this province rides on a white elephant, round the neck of which is fastened a chain of gold ornamented with precious stones, which reaches to its feet.

The men of this country are satisfied with one wife; and all the inhabitants, as well men as women, puncture their flesh with pins of iron, and rub into these punctures pigments which cannot be obliterated, and so they remain painted for ever. All worship idols: nevertheless when they rise in the morning from their beds they turn towards the east, and with their hands joined together say, "God in Trinity and His law defend us."

In this country there is a kind of apple, very similar to a pomegranate, full of juice and sweet.[1] There is also a tree called *tal*,[2] the leaves of which are extremely large, and upon which they write, for throughout all India they do not use paper excepting in the city of Cambay. This tree bears fruit like large turnips, the juice contained under the bark becoming solid, forms very agreeable sweet food.

This country produces frightful serpents[3] without feet, as thick as a man, and six cubits in length. The inhabitants eat them roasted, and hold them in great esteem as food. They also eat a kind of red ant, of the size of a small crab, which they consider a great delicacy seasoned with pepper.

There is here also an animal which has a head resembling that of a pig, a tail like that of an ox, and on his forehead a horn similar to that of the unicorn, but shorter, being about a cubit in length.[4] It resembles the elephant in size and colour, with which it is constantly at war. It is said that its horn is an antidote against poisons, and is on that account much esteemed.

In the upper part of this country, towards Cathay, there

[1] Probably the Jamboo apple: *Eugenia Jambos*. L.

[2] The Fan Palm. See *ante*, p. 7.

[3] A species of python.

[4] The rhinoceros.

are found white and black bulls, and those are most prized which have hair and a tail like that of a horse, but the tail more full of hair and reaching to their feet. The hair of the tail, which is very fine and as light as a feather, is valued at its weight in silver. Of this kind of hair they make fans, which are used for the service of their idols and of their kings. They also place them over the crupper of their horses in a gold or silver cone, so that they may completely cover the hinder parts of the animal: they also fasten them to the neck, so that, hanging down, they may form an ornament to the breast. This is considered a distinguished kind of embellishment. The cavalry also carry the hair at the head of their lances as a mark of high nobility.

Beyond this province of Macinus is one which is superior to all others in the world, and is named Cathay.[1] The lord of this country is called the Great Khan, which in the language of the inhabitants means emperor. The principal city is called Cambaleschia.[2] It is built in the form of a quadrangle, and is twenty-eight miles in circumference. In the centre is a very handsome and strong fortress, in which is situated the king's palace. In each of the four angles there is constructed a circular fortress for defence, and the circuit of each of these is four miles. In these fortresses are deposited military arms of all sorts, and machines for war and the storming of cities. From the royal palace a vaulted wall extends through the city to each of the said four fortresses, by which, in the event of the people rising against the king, he can retire into the fortresses at his pleasure. Fifteen days distant from this city there is another, very large, called

[1] Cathay embraces the northern part of China, but its limits cannot now be defined.

[2] Kanbalu, the ancient name for Peking. See "The Travels of Marco Polo," by Marsden, p. 287, for a full description of "the great and admirable palace of the Grand Khan, near to the city of Kanbalu," as it was about one hundred and fifty years before the time when Conti visited the East.

Nemptai,[1] which has been built by this king. It is thirty miles in circumference, and more populous than the others. In these two cities, according to the statement of Nicolò, the houses and palaces and other ornaments are similar to those in Italy: the men, gentle and discreet, wise, and more wealthy than any that have been before mentioned.

Afterwards he departed from Ava and proceeded towards the sea, and at the expiration of seventeen days he arrived at the mouth of a moderately sized river,[2] where there is a port called Xeythona; and having entered the river, at the end of ten days he arrived at a very populous city called Panconia, the circumference of which is twelve miles.[3] He remained here for the space of four months. This is the only place in which vines are found, and here in very small quantity: for throughout all India there are no vines, neither is there any wine. And in this place they do not use the grape for the purpose of making wine. They have pine apples, oranges, chesnuts, melons, but small and green, white sandal wood, and camphor. The camphor is found within the tree, and if they do not sacrifice to the gods before they cut the bark, it disappears and is no more seen.

In central India there are two islands towards the extreme confines of the world, both of which are called Java. One of these islands is three thousand miles in circumference, the other two thousand. Both are situated towards the east, and are distinguished from each other by the names of the Greater and the Less. These islands lay in his route to the ocean. They are distant from the continent one month's sail, and lie within one hundred miles of each other.[4] He

[1] Nemptai is supposed to be the same as the city called, in the time of Marco Polo, Hăng-chow-Keun-che, and in common parlance Keun-che, whence the corruption Quin-sai. Its present name is Hăng-chow-foo.

[2] Most probably the river Pegu.

[3] Pegu is the city which corresponds most nearly with this description.

[4] La Martinière, in his "Dictionnaire Géographique," says that Little Java was the island now called Bally, while Odoardo Barbosa, in his

remained here for the space of nine months with his wife and children, who accompanied him in all his journeys.

The inhabitants of these islands are more inhuman and cruel than any other nation, and they eat mice, dogs, cats, and all other kinds of unclean animals. They exceed every other people in cruelty. They regard killing a man as a mere jest, nor is any punishment allotted for such a deed. Debtors are given up to their creditors to be their slaves. But he who, rather than be a slave, prefers death, seizing a naked sword issues into the street and kills all he meets, until he is slain by some one more powerful than himself: then comes the creditor of the dead man and cites him by whom he was killed, demanding of him his debt, which he is constrained by the judges to satisfy.

If any one purchase a new scimiter or sword and wish to try it, he will thrust it into the breast of the first person he meets, neither is any punishment awarded for the death of that man. The passers by examine the wound, and praise the skill of the person who inflicted it if he thrust the weapon in direct. Every person may satisfy his desires by taking as many wives as he pleases.

The amusement most in vogue amongst them is cock-fighting. Several persons will produce their birds for fighting, each maintaining that his will be the conqueror. Those who are present to witness the sport make bets amongst themselves upon these combatants, and the cock that remains conqueror decides the winning bet.

In Great Java a very remarkable bird is found, resembling a wood pigeon, without feet, of slight plumage, and with an oblong tail; it always frequents trees. The flesh of this bird

account of his travels in India, states that it was called by the natives Ambaba, probably the modern Sumbawa. The circumference, however, as given by Conti (two thousand miles), does not correspond with either of these islands, which are extremely small. There can be little doubt but that Sumatra was sometimes called Java.

is not eaten, but the skin and tail are highly prized, being used as ornaments for the head.[1]

At fifteen days' sail beyond these islands eastward, two others are found: the one is called Sandai, in which nutmegs and maces grow; the other is named Bandan; this is the only island in which cloves grow, which are exported hence to the Java islands. In Bandan three kinds of parrots are found, some with red feathers and a yellow beak, and some party-coloured, which are called *nori*,[2] that is *brilliant*, both kinds of the size of doves: also some white of the size of hens. These last are called *cachi*,[3] which means the more excellent: they excel in talking, imitating human speech in a wonderful manner, and even answering questions. The inhabitants of both islands are black. The sea is not navigable beyond these islands, and the stormy atmosphere keeps navigators at a distance.

Having quitted Java, and taken with him such articles as were useful for commerce, he bent his course westward to a maritime city called Ciampa, abounding in aloes wood, camphor, and gold. In that journey he occupied one month; and departing thence, he, in the same space of time, arrived at a noble city called Coloen,[4] the circumference of which is twelve miles. This province is called Melibaria,[5] and they collect in it ginger, called by the natives *colobi*, pepper,

[1] It is not easy to conjecture what bird is here alluded to. Nicolò does not tell us that he saw the bird alive, and it is therefore possible that it may be one of the *Paradisea*, or birds of paradise, the skins of which are wrapped round a stick and used as ornaments, *the feet being previously removed*. It is true that the bird of paradise is not a native of Java but of New Guinea, but these places are sufficiently near to admit of the skin having been imported into Java.

[2] A species of Lorius: so called from the Javanese word *loerri* or *noerri* (the *l* and *n* are convertible letters in the Javanese language), which means a parrot with bright coloured plumage.

[3] A species of *cacatua*,—the cockatoo: called in the Javanese language *kokilo*.

[4] Quilon?

[5] Malabar.

brazil wood, and cinnamon, which is known there by the name of *crassa*. There are also serpents without feet, six ells in length, wild, but harmless unless irritated. They are pleased with the sight of little children, and by this means are enticed into the presence of men.[1] In the same province, and also in another called Susinaria, there is found another kind of serpent with four feet, and an oblong tail like that of large dogs, which are hunted for food. It is as harmless as kids or goats, and the flesh is prized as the best kind of food.

This region also produces other serpents of a remarkable form, one cubit in length and winged like bats. They have seven heads arranged along the body, and live in trees. They are extremely rapid in flight, and the most venomous of all, destroying men by their breath alone. There are also flying cats, for they have a pellicle extending from the fore to the hinder feet and attached to the body, which is drawn up when they are at rest.[2] They fly from tree to tree by extending their feet and shaking their wings. When pursued by hunters they fall to the earth when fatigued by flying, and so are taken. A tree grows here in great abundance, the trunk of which produces fruit resembling the pineapple, but so large as to be lifted with difficulty by one man; the rind is green and hard, but yields nevertheless to the pressure of the finger. Within are from two hundred and fifty to three hundred apples, resembling figs, very sweet to the taste, and which are separated from each other by follicles. They have a kernel within, resembling the chesnut in hardness and flavour, flatulent, and which is cooked in the same manner as the chesnut; when thrown upon live embers, unless previously incised somewhat, it bounces up with a crackling noise. The external bark is used as provender for cattle.[3] The

[1] The python.

[2] The Galeopithecus.

[3] The tree here described is clearly the Jack (*Artocarpus integrifolia*, L). The subsequent mention of fruits without kernels, and of incised

fruit of this tree is sometimes found under the earth in its roots; these excel the others in flavour, and for this reason it is the custom to set these apart for royal use. This fruit has no kernel. The tree is like a large fig tree, the leaves being intercised like those of the palm: the wood is equal to boxwood, and is therefore much prized for its applicability to many purposes. The name of this tree is *cachi*. There is also another fruit, called *amba*,[1] green and resembling very much a nut, but larger than the nectarine; the outer rind is bitter, but within it is sweet like honey: before they are ripe they steep them in water to remove the acidity, in the same manner as we are in the habit of steeping green olives.

Having quitted Coloen he arrived, after a journey of three days, at the city Cocym.[2] This city is five miles in circumference, and stands at the mouth of a river, from which it derives its name. Sailing for some time in this river he saw many fires lighted along the banks, and thought that they were made by fishermen. But those who were with him in the ship exclaimed, smiling, "Icepe, Icepe." These have the human form, but may be called either fishes or monsters, which, issuing from the water at night, collect wood, and procuring fire by striking one stone against another, ignite it and burn it near the water; the fishes, attracted by the light, swim towards it in great numbers, when these monsters, who lie hid in the water, seize them and devour them. They said that some which they had taken, both male and female, differed in no respect as to their form from human beings. In this district the same fruits are found as in Coloen.

He then visited in succession Colanguria, which is placed at the mouth of another river, Paliuria, and then Meliancota, which name in the language of the country signifies great city. This last city is eight miles in circumference. He next

leaves, leads to the supposition that the author had also met with the bread fruit (*Artocarpus incisa*, L.).

[1] The Mango (*Mangifera Indica*, L.).

[2] Cochin?

proceeded to Calicut, a maritime city, eight miles in circumference, a noble emporium for all India, abounding in pepper, lac, ginger, a larger kind of cinnamon, myrobalans, and zedoary. In this district alone the women are allowed to take several husbands, so that some have ten and more. The husbands contribute amongst themselves to the maintenance of the wife, who lives apart from her husbands. When one visits her he leaves a mark at the door of the house, which being seen by another coming afterwards, he goes away without entering. The children are allotted to the husbands at the will of the wife. The inheritance of the father does not descend to the children, but to the grandchildren. Departing from Calicut, he proceeded next westward to Cambay, which he reached in fifteen days. Cambay is situated near to the sea, and is twelve miles in circuit; it abounds in spikenard, lac, indigo, myrobalans, and silks. There are priests here who are called bachari, who only marry one wife. The wife is, by law, burnt with the body of her husband. These priests do not eat any animal food, but live upon rice, milk, and vegetables. Wild cattle are found in great abundance, with manes like those of horses, but with longer hair, and with horns so long that when the head is turned back they touch the tail. These horns being extremely large, are used like barrels for carrying water on journeys.

Returning to Calicut, he spent two months on the island of Sechutera, which trends westward, and is distant one hundred miles from the continent.[1] This island produces Socotrine aloes, is six hundred miles in circumference, and is for the most part inhabited by Nestorian Christians.

Opposite to this island, and at a distance of not more than five miles, there are two other islands, distant from each other one hundred miles, one of which is inhabited by men

[1] This must be the island of Socotra, and the continent mentioned in the text the African continent; but the size of the island is much exaggerated.

and the other by women. Sometimes the men pass over to the women, and sometimes the women pass over to the men, and each return to their own respective islands before the expiration of six months. Those who remain on the island of the others beyond this fatal period die immediately. Departing hence, he sailed in five days to Aden, an opulent city, remarkable for its buildings. He then sailed over to Æthiopia, where he arrived in seven days, and anchored in a port named Barbora. He then, after sailing for a month, landed at a port in the Red Sea called Gidda,[1] and subsequently near Mount Sinai, having spent two months in reaching this place from the Red Sea, on account of the difficulty of the navigation. He afterwards travelled through the desert to Carras,[2] a city of Egypt, with his wife and four children and as many servants. In this city he lost his wife, and two of his children, and all his servants by the plague. At length, after so many journeys by sea and land, he arrived in safety at his native country, Venice, with his two children.

In answer to my inquiries respecting the manner and customs of the Indians, he spoke as follows :—

All India is divided into three parts : one, extending from Persia to the Indus ; the second, comprising the district from the Indus to the Ganges ; and the third, all that is beyond. This third part excels the others in riches, politeness, and magnificence, and is equal to our own country in the style of life and in civilization. For the inhabitants have most sumptuous buildings, elegant habitations, and handsome furniture ; they lead a more refined life, removed from all barbarity and coarseness. The men are extremely humane, and the merchants very rich, so much so that some will carry on their business in forty of their own ships, each of which is valued at fifty thousand gold pieces. These alone use tables at their meals, in the manner of Europeans, with

[1] Jiddah or Ziden, in Arabia.

[2] Cairo ?

silver vessels upon them; whilst the inhabitants of the rest of India eat upon carpets spread upon the ground. There are no vines, nor is the use of wine known among the Indians; but they make a drink similar to wine of pounded rice mixed with water, the juice of certain trees, of a red colour, being added to it. In Taprobana they cut off the branches of a tree called *thal,* and hang them up on high: these branches give out a sweet juice, which is a favourite drink with them. There is also a lake lying between the Indus and the Ganges, the water of which possesses a remarkable flavour, and is drunk with great pleasure. All the inhabitants of that district, and even those living at a great distance, flock to this lake for the purpose of procuring the water. By means of relays of carriers mounted on horseback, they draw the water fresh every day. They have no corn or bread, but live upon a certain kind of meal, rice, flesh, milk, and cheese. They have a great quantity of poultry, capons, partridges, pheasants, and other wild birds. They are much addicted to fowling and hunting. They have no beards, but very long hair. Some tie their hair at the back of their head with a silken cord, and let it flow over their shoulders, and in this way go to war. They have barbers like ourselves. The men resemble Europeans in stature and the duration of their lives. They sleep upon silken mattrasses, on beds ornamented with gold. The style of dress is different in different regions. Wool is very little used. There is great abundance of flax and silk, and of these they make their garments. Almost all, both men and women, wear a linen cloth bound round the body, so as to cover the front of the person, and descending as low as the knees, and over this a garment of linen or silk, which, with the men, descends to just below the knees, and with the women to the ankles. They cannot wear more clothing on account of the great heat, and for the same reason they only wear sandals, with purple and golden ties, as we see in ancient statues. In some places the women have shoes made of thin leather, ornamented with gold and silk. By way of ornament they wear rings of gold on their arms and on their hands; also around their necks and legs, of the weight of three pounds, and studded with gems. Public women are everywhere to be had, residing in particular houses of their own in all parts of the cities, who attract the men by sweet perfumes and ointments, by their blandishments, beauty, and youth; for the Indians are much addicted to licentiousness; but unnatural crimes are unknown among them. The manner of adorning the head is various, but for the most part the head is covered with a cloth embroidered with gold, the hair being bound up with a silken cord. In some places they twist up the hair upon the top of the head, like a pyramid, sticking a golden bodkin in the centre, from which golden threads, with pieces of cloth of various colours interwoven with gold, hang suspended over the hair. Some wear false hair, of a black colour, for that is the colour held in highest estimation. Some cover the head with the leaves of trees painted, but none paint their faces, with the exception of those who dwell near Cathay.

The inhabitants of central India are only allowed to marry one wife; in the other parts of India polygamy prevails very generally, excepting among those Christians who have adopted the Nestorian heresy, who are spread over the whole of India, and confine themselves to one solitary mate. The funeral rites are not the same in all parts of India. Anterior India excels all others in the care and magnificence displayed in the burial of the dead. The sepulchre is a cave dug in the earth, strengthened by a wall and ornamented. The dead are placed herein on a handsome bier, with golden pillars as supports. Around are placed baskets containing very rich vestments and rings, as though for the use of the deceased in the other world. The entrance to the cave is walled up, in order to prevent all approach to it. Over the whole an arch is constructed at great cost, by means of which the grave is kept protected from all moisture and preserved for a very long period. In central India the dead are burned, and the living wives, for the most part, are consumed in the same funeral pyre with their husband, one or more, according to the agreement at the time the marriage was contracted. The first wife is compelled by the law to be burnt, even though she should be the only wife. But others are married under the express agreement that they should add to the splendour of the funeral ceremony by their death, and this is considered a great honour for them. The deceased husband is laid on a couch, dressed in his best garments. A vast funeral pyre is erected over him in the form of a pyramid, constructed of odoriferous woods. The pile being ignited, the wife, habited in her richest garments, walks gaily around it, singing, accompanied by a great concourse of people, and amid the sounds of trumpets, flutes, and songs. In the meantime one of the priests, called Bachali, standing on some elevated spot, exhorts her to a contempt of life and death, promising her all kinds of enjoyment with her husband, much wealth, and abundance of ornaments. When she has walked round the fire several times, she stands near the elevation on which is the priest, and taking off her dress puts on a white linen garment, her body having first been washed according to custom. In obedience to the exhortation of the priest she then springs into the fire. If some show more timidity (for it frequently happens that they become stupified by terror at the sight of the struggles of the others, or of their sufferings in the fire), they are thrown into the fire by the bystanders, whether consenting or not. Their ashes are afterwards collected and placed in urns, which form an ornament for the sepulchres.

The dead are mourned for in various ways. The natives of central India cover up even their heads. Some set up poles in the highways, with painted and cut paper hanging from the top to the ground. They sound gongs for three days, and give food to the poor for the love of God. Others mourn for three days, the members of the family and all the neighbours assembling together in the house of the deceased, where no meat is dressed, but all the food required is brought from without. During this period the friends carry a bitter leaf in their mouths. Those who have lost their father or mother do not change their dress for a whole year, and only take food once in the day, neither do they cut their nails or their hair, or shave their beards. In many cases the dead are mourned for by women, who stand round the body, naked to the waist, and beat their breasts, exclaiming, "Alas! alas!" One recites in a song the praises of the dead, to which the others answer at certain places, beating their breasts the while. Many place the ashes of their princes in golden or silver vases, and command them to be thrown into some lake sacred to the gods, as they assert, and through which they say lies the road to their divinities.

Their priests, the Bachali, abstain from all animal food, particularly the ox, which they consider it a great crime to kill or to eat, as being of all the most useful to man: the Indians use the ox as a beast of burthen. These priests live upon rice, herbs, fruit, and vegetables: they have only one wife, who is burnt with her dead husband. Lying by the side of the corpse, with her arm under its neck, she submits herself to the flames, without giving way to any expression of pain.

There is a class of philosophers found throughout all India, called Brahmins, who devote themselves much to astronomy and the prediction of future events. They are men of superior cultivation, and are distinguished by a greater sanctity of life and manners. Nicolò asserts that he saw among them one who was three hundred years old, an instance of longevity which they regard as miraculous; so much so, that wherever he went he was followed by the children. An art which they call geomantia, is practised by many of them, by means of which they frequently predict future events with as much accuracy as though they were present. They also make use of incantations, by means of which they are frequently able to excite tempests and also to allay them. On this account many eat in secret, fearing lest they should be fascinated by the eyes of lookers on. Nicolò told me with all seriousness, that on one occasion, when he was commander of a ship, they were becalmed for seven days in the midst of the ocean. The sailors, fearing that the calm might continue, assembled together at a table placed by the mast, and having performed various sacred rites over it, danced round it, calling frequently on their god, Muthia, by name. In the meantime one of the Arabs, being possessed by the demon, began to sing in a marvellous manner, and to run all about the ship like an insane person. He then approached the table, and eating some coal placed there, demanded the blood of a cock as a drink, and which Nicolò says he sucked from a fowl, which was placed to his mouth after having its throat cut. Then he demanded what they wanted, and they replied a wind. Then having promised that he would give them in three days a prosperous wind, which should carry them into port, and showing, by casting his hands behind his back, what wind he would give, and having, moreover, cautioned them that they should be well prepared to meet the force of the wind, he shortly afterwards was thrown to the ground as one half dead, having utterly forgotten all that he had just done and said. As he had predicted, a wind sprung up, and they arrived in port in the course of a few days. The natives of India steer their vessels for the most part by the stars of the southern hemisphere, as they rarely see those of the north.

They are not acquainted with the use of the compass, but measure their courses and the distances of places by the elevation and depression of the pole. They find out where they are by this mode of measurement. They build some ships much larger than ours, capable of containing two thousand butts, and with five sails and as many masts. The lower part is constructed with triple planks, in order to withstand the force of the tempests to which they are much exposed. But some ships are so built in compartments, that should one part be shattered, the other portion remaining entire may accomplish the voyage.

Gods are worshipped throughout all India, for whom they erect temples very similar to our own, the interior being painted with figures of different kinds. On solemn days these temples are adorned with flowers. Within they place their idols, some made of stone, some of gold, some of silver, and others of ivory. These idols are sometimes of the height of sixty feet. The modes of praying and of sacrificing among them are various. They enter the temple morning and evening, having first washed themselves in pure water; and sometimes prostrating themselves upon the ground with hands and feet held up, repeat their prayers and kiss the ground, at others offer incense to their gods by burning spices and the wood of the aloe. The Indians situate on this side of the Ganges do not possess bells, but produce sound by striking together small brazen vessels. They also present feasts to their gods, after the manner of the ancient heathens, which are afterwards distributed among the poor to be eaten. In the city of Cambaita the priests, standing before the idols of their gods, deliver a discourse to the people, in which they exhort them to the performance of their religious duties, and particularly urge upon them how acceptable it is to the gods that they should quit this life for their sake. Many present themselves who have determined upon self immolation, having on their neck a broad circular piece of iron, the fore part of which is round and the hinder part extremely sharp. A chain attached to the fore part hangs suspended upon the breast, into which the victims, sitting down with their legs drawn up and their neck bent, insert their feet. Then, on the speaker pronouncing certain words, they suddenly stretch out their legs, and at the same time drawing up their neck, cut off their own head, yielding up their lives as a sacrifice to their idols. These men are regarded as saints. In Bizenegalia also, at a certain time of the year, their idol is carried through the city, placed between two chariots, in which are young women richly adorned, who sing hymns to the god, and accompanied by a great concourse of people. Many, carried away by the fervour of their faith, cast themselves on the ground before the wheels, in order that they may be crushed to death,—a mode of death which they say is very acceptable to their god. Others, making an incision in their side, and inserting a rope thus through their body, hang themselves to the chariot by way of ornament, and thus suspended and half dead accompany their idol. This kind of sacrifice they consider the best and most acceptable of all.

Thrice in the year they keep festivals of especial solemnity. On one of these occasions the males and females of all ages, having bathed in the rivers or the sea, clad themselves in new garments, and spend three entire days in singing, dancing, and feasting. On another of these festivals they fix up within their temples, and on the outside on the roofs, an innumerable number of lamps of oil of Susimanni, which are kept burning day and night. On the third, which lasts nine days, they set up in all the highways large beams, like the masts of small ships, to the upper part of which are attached pieces of very beautiful cloth of various kinds, interwoven with gold. On the summit of each of these beams is each day placed a man of pious aspect, dedicated to religion, capable of enduring all things with equanimity, who is to pray for the favour of God. These men are assailed by the people, who pelt them with oranges, lemons, and other odoriferous fruits, all which they bear most patiently. There are also three other festival days, during which they sprinkle all passers by, even the king and queen themselves, with saffron-water, placed for that purpose by the wayside. This is received by all with much laughter.

Their weddings are celebrated with singing, feasting, and the sound of trumpets and flutes, for, with the exception of organs, all the other instruments in use among them for singing and playing are similar to our own. They make sumptuous feasts both day and night, at which there is both singing and instrumental music. Some sing, dancing in a circle, after our manner; while others sing forming a line in single file, one after the other, and exchanging little painted rods, of which each person carries two, with those whom they meet on turning; the effect of which he describes as being extremely pretty. Warm baths are not used amongst them, excepting by Indians of the superior classes to the north of the Ganges. The others wash themselves many times in the day with cold water. Oil is not produced here: our fruits also, such as peaches, pears, cherries, and apples, are not found amongst them. The vine is rare, and, as we have said before, only found in one place. In the province of Pudifetania there grows a tree about three cubits in height, which bears no fruit, and which is called by a name signifying "modesty". If a man approach it, it contracts and draws up all its branches, and expands again when he departs.[1]

At fifteen days' journey beyond Bizenegalia, towards the north, there is a mountain called Albenigaras, surrounded by pools of water which swarm with venomous animals, and the mountain itself is infested with serpents. This mountain produces diamonds. The ingenuity of man, not having been able to find any mode of approaching the mountain, has, however, discovered a way of getting at the diamonds produced on it. There is another mountain near it, a little higher. Here, at a certain period of the year, men bring

[1] The sensitive plant, *Mimosa pudica*, L., which is not, however, a native of India, although common in gardens.

oxen, which they drive to the top, and having cut them into pieces, cast the warm and bleeding fragments upon the summit of the other mountain, by means of machines which they construct for that purpose. The diamonds stick to these pieces of flesh. Then come vultures and eagles flying to the spot, which, seizing the meat for their food, fly away with it to places where they may be safe from the serpents. To these places the men afterwards come, and collect the diamonds which have fallen from the flesh. Other stones, which are considered precious, are procured with less difficulty. They dig holes near sandy mountains in places where the stones are found, and continue their excavations until they come to sand mixed with water. This sand they collect and wash with water, through sieves made for the purpose. The sand passes away through the sieve, and the stones, if any, are left behind: this mode of digging for stones of this description prevails universally. Great care is exercised by the masters to prevent theft by the workmen or servants,—overseers being appointed, who not only shake the clothes of the operators, but even examine every part of their persons.

They divide the year into twelve months, which they name after the signs of the zodiac. The æra is computed variously. The greater part date its commencement from Octavian, in whose time there was peace all over the world. But they call 1,400, 1,490. Some regions have no money, but use instead stones which we call cats' eyes. In other parts their money consists of pieces of iron, worked into the form of large needles. In others the medium of exchange consists of cards inscribed with the name of the king. In some parts again of anterior India, Venetian ducats are in circulation. Some have golden coins, weighing more than the double of our florin, and also less, and, moreover, silver and brass money. In some places pieces of gold worked to a certain weight are used as money. The natives of this part of India, when engaged in war, use javelins, swords, arm-pieces, round shields, and also bows. The inhabitants of the other parts of India wear also the helmet and corslet. The natives of central India make use of balistæ, and those machines which we call bombardas, also other warlike implements adapted for besieging cities. They call us Franks, and say: "While they call other nations blind, that they themselves have two eyes and that we have but one, because they consider that they excel all others in prudence." The inhabitants of Cambay alone use paper; all other Indians write on the leaves of trees, of which they make very beautiful books. But they do not write as we or the Jews do, from left to right or right to left, but perpendicularly, carrying the line from the top to the bottom of the page. There are many languages and dialects in use among the Indians. They have a vast number of slaves, and the debtor who is insolvent is everywhere adjudged to be the property of his creditor.

In criminal charges oaths are allowed, where there is no witness to prove the offence. There are three modes of swearing. In one, the person to whom the oath is administered stands before the idol, and swears by the idol that he is innocent. Having taken the oath, he then licks with his tongue a piece of iron, such as a mattock, red hot; if he escape uninjured he is declared innocent. Others again, having first taken the oath, carry the same piece of iron, or a red hot iron plate for several paces before the idol; if burnt in any part he is punished as guilty, if he escape unhurt he is exempt from the punishment awarded for the offence. There is a third manner of swearing, and this is the most common of all. A vessel is placed before the idol filled with boiling butter. He who swears that he is innocent of the offence charged against him, plunges two fingers into the butter, which are immediately wrapped up in linen and a seal impressed upon it, to prevent the covering being removed. On the third day the bandage is taken off. If any injury appear upon the fingers the accused is punished, if no injury present itself he is released.

Pestilence is unknown among the Indians; neither are they exposed to those diseases which carry off the population in our own countries: the consequence is that the number of these people and nations exceeds belief. Their armies consist of a million of men and upwards. Nicolò mentions a certain battle, the victors of which brought home, by way of triumph, twelve chariots laden with cords of gold and silk, to which were attached the hair from the backs of the heads of the dead. He added, moreover, that he was sometimes present at their battles, as a spectator, but without taking any part in them, and being recognized by both parties as a stranger escaped unhurt.

The island of Java, called *Major*, produces a tree of great rarity, in the middle of which there is found an iron rod, very thin and as long as the trunk of a tree. He who carries about him a small piece of this iron rod, so that it may touch his flesh, is invulnerable by iron, and for this reason many persons open their skin and insert it in their bodies. This is esteemed of the highest importance by them.

He says that on the boundaries of central India there is an unique bird called semenda, in the beak of which there are, as it were, several distinct pipes with many openings. When death approaches, this bird collects a quantity of dry wood in its nest, and, sitting upon it, sings so sweetly with all its pipes that it attracts and soothes the hearers to a marvellous degree; then igniting the wood by flapping its wings, it allows itself to be burnt to death. In a short time a worm is produced from the ashes, and from this worm the same kind of bird is again produced. The inhabitants have made a pipe of admirable sweetness for singing, in imitation of the bill of this bird; and as Nicolò admired it very much, they told him the origin of it in the manner in which I have narrated it.

There is also a river in anterior India, in the island of Ceylon, called Arotani, in which the fishes are so abundant that they can be taken by the hand. But if any one hold the captured fish for a short time in his hand, he is forthwith attacked by fever. On laying down the fish, his health returns to him. The cause of this phenomenon is referred by the natives to a certain legend, which Nicolò related to me, respecting their gods. But it appears to me that the cause is natural; for, among ourselves, if any one hold in his hand the fish called the torpedo, he is immediately benumbed, and his hand is affected by a particular kind of pain.

While preparing to insert in this work, for the information of my readers, the various accounts respecting the Indians related to me by Nicolò, having carefully preserved the truth of the narrative, there arrived another person from upper India, towards the north. He stated that he was sent to the pontiff for the purpose of obtaining information in another globe, as it were, respecting Christians, whom fame reported to exist towards the western sun. He says that there is a kingdom twenty days journey from Cathay, of which the king and all the inhabitants are Christians, but heretics, being said to be Nestorians; that the patriarch of that people had delegated him to collect more precise information respecting us. He asserted that their churches were larger and more ornamented than ours, and were constructed entirely of tortoise-shell. That their patriarch possessed great wealth in gold and silver, receiving, at the annual census, one ounce of silver from each head of a family. I conversed with him through the medium of an Armenian interpreter, who understood the Turkish and Latin languages; but only obtained information about the extent of the roads, and about localities; for the interpreter and the Indian not using their own language, it became very difficult to learn anything respecting their manners and customs, and all those other matters which afford so much pleasure in the narrating. He asserted, however, that the power of him whom they call the Great Khan (that is to say, the emperor of all) is very vast, for he has dominion over nine very potent kings. Travelling through the country of the northern Scythians, who are called at the present day Tartars, and of the Parthians, for the space of several months, he arrived at length at the Euphrates; then, having embarked at Tripoli, he proceeded to Venice, and afterwards to Florence. He said that he had seen many cities finer than this of ours, both in their private and public edifices: many of them occupying an extent of ten or twenty miles in circumference. He appeared to be a truthful person. Having visited Rome, as an act of pious devotion, and conversed with the pope, he departed, asking neither gold nor silver, his visit appearing to be that of one who came in obedience to the command he had received so to do, and not for the sake of gain, as is the wont of many who come with lying pretences.

About the same time some men came to the pope from Æthiopia upon matters regarding the faith. When I questioned them, by means of an interpreter, respecting the position and source of the Nile, and whether it was known to them, two of them asserted that, in their country, they were near to its sources. Then was I seized with a great desire of learning those things which appear to have been unknown to ancient writers and philosophers, and also to Ptolemy, who was the first that wrote upon this subject; all of whom indulged in much vain conjecture respecting the source and inundations of the Nile. But when assured that those things which they told me were true, and as I learnt from them many other things which appeared to be worthy to be made known, I determined to commit them to writing.

They asserted that the Nile took its rise near the equinoctial region, from three small sources at the feet of very high mountains, the summits of which were always capped with clouds. The waters of two of them, distant about forty paces from each other, unite at a distance of less than half a mile, and form a river which cannot be passed on foot. The third, which is the largest, is a mile distant from the others, and unites with them at a distance of ten miles from its source. They further testify that the Nile is augmented by the waters of more than a thousand rivers, which flow into it on each side; that the rains fall very heavily in the months of March, April, and May, only, by which the swollen rivers cause the Nile to rise and overflow; that the water of the Nile, before it is mingled with that of other rivers, is extremely sweet and palatable. They assert also that those who wash in it are cleansed from the itch and leprosy.

At a distance of fifteen days journey beyond the sources of the Nile, there are fertile regions, inhabited and cultivated, and containing many fine cities; and beyond these places a sea, but my informants had never seen it. These people also told me that near the sources of the Nile there was a city, of which they were natives, called Varvaria, twenty-five miles in circumference, and extremely populous; that every night a thousand horsemen kept watch, in order to repress the tumults of the multitude; that the climate of this district was very agreeable, from its mildness, and that the soil excelled all others in fertility, bearing herbage three times in the year, and fruit twice. This region abounds in corn and wine, the greater part of the Ethiopians using as wine, a liquor prepared from barley. Figs, nectarines, oranges, a vegetable resembling our cucumbers, lemons also, and cedars, and all our fruits, with the exception of the almond, are, as they report, to be found there. They spoke of a vast number of trees of which we know nothing, and had never before heard: but it was not easy to commit what was said to writing, on account of the difficulty experienced with the interpreter, who only knew Arabic. I have written down the description of one only. It is of the height of a man, and, in girth, as much as a man can embrace with his arms, with many layers of bark one over the other. Between these layers the fruit is deposited, in character resembling our chesnuts; from which, when pounded, they make a white bread, very sweet to the taste, which they use on festival occasions. The leaves of the tree are from one to two cubits in length.

The Nile is unnavigable as far as the island of Meroe, on account of the frequent falls through masses of rugged rock. Beyond Meroe, it is navigable as far as Egypt, but they say that the journey occupies six months, in consequence of the numerous sinuosities of the river. Those who inhabit the regions in which the Nile takes its source see the sun towards the north, but in the month of March it is beheld directly over their heads. In all Ethiopia there is but one written alphabet, but, owing to the size of the provinces, there are different languages. Some of them reported that the maritime region towards India produced ginger, cloves, sugar, and nuts, which are called *muscatæ*.[1] There are deserts between Ethiopia and Egypt fifty days' journey in extent, over which food and drink are carried by camels. The road across is infested in many places by wild Arabs, who are scattered about and wander through the desert naked like wild beasts, riding on camels, the flesh and milk of which they use for food. They rob travellers of their camels, food, and drink; and this is the reason why so many perish of hunger, and the number of those who succeed in reaching us so few.

The Ethiopians are much longer lived than we are, for they live to be more than a hundred and twenty years old, many even reach the age of one hundred and fifty years. The whole country is extremely populous, like one which

[1] Nutmegs and maces.

never suffers from pestilence; so that the numbers increase from the freedom from disease and the longevity of the people. Their customs also vary according to the difference of region. All however, both men and women, wear linen and silken garments (for they have no wool): in some places the women wear long trains, which they bear after them fastened by girdles of the width of a palm, adorned with gold and gems. Some cover the head with pieces of cloth, interwoven with gold; some wear the hair at the back of the head flowing, others tie it up. They abound much more in gold and silver than we do; the men wear rings, the women wear armlets enriched with various precious stones. The period from Christmas to Lent is kept by them as a festival, being devoted to feasting and dancing. They use small tables so that two or three may eat together, using table-cloths and napkins after the European manner. They have one king, who calls himself, after God, the king of kings. They say that there are many kings subject to him.

They report that they have amongst them many kinds of animals. Their cattle have a hump on the shoulder, in the manner of camels, with horns extending backwards three cubits in length, and so large that one of them can contain an amphora of wine.[1] They have some dogs, which are as large as our asses, and which will hunt down lions. Their elephants are large in size and very numerous. Some keep them for the purpose of display and pleasure, some as animals useful in war. They are captured when young and brought up tame, the larger ones when taken are killed. Their tusks grow to the length of six cubits. They also rear lions for display, rendering them so tame that they can be introduced into their theatres. There is a kind of beast of various colours, very like to an elephant, excepting that it has no proboscis

[1] Sanga or Galla oxen, described and figured by Salt in his "Voyage to Abyssinia," pp. 258, 259. The horns mentioned by him as being in the collection of Lord Valentia, are now in the British Museum.

and that its feet resemble those of the camel: it has two horns, very sharp at the extremity, one cubit in length, one of which is situate on the forehead and the other on the nose.[1] They have another animal called *zebed*, rather longer than a hare, and resembling it in other respects;[2] possessing such a peculiar odour, that if it lean against a tree for the purpose of scratching itself, it imparts to it a smell so extremely sweet, that persons passing near shortly afterwards and guided by the scent, cut out the part against which it had supported itself, and dividing it into minute portions sell them dearer than gold. They informed me that there was also another animal,[3] nine cubits long and six in height, with cloven hoofs like those of an ox, the body not more than a cubit in thickness, with hair very like to that of a leopard and a head resembling that of the camel, with a neck four cubits long and a hairy tail: the hairs are purchased at a high price, and worn by the women suspended from their arms, and ornamented with various sorts of gems. Another wild animal is hunted by them for food. It is as large as an ass, with stripes of a red and green colour, and has horns three cubits in length and spiral from the top.[4] Another also, resembling a hare, has small horns, is of a red colour, and can surpass a horse in leaping.[5] There is yet another, similar to a goat, with horns more than two cubits in length extending over the back, which are sold for more than forty gold pieces, because their smoke is beneficial in cases of fever.[6] Another, like the last, without horns but with red hair, and the neck more than two cubits in length. They also mentioned another of the size of a camel and of the

[1] The rhinoceros.

[2] Doubtless the zibett (viverra civetta), the well-known producer of the "civet."

[3] The giraffe.

[4] Probably the koodoo (Strepsiceros Kudu).

[5] Perhaps the Modoqua antelope (neotragus Saltianus), a small Abyssinian species named in compliment to the late Mr. Salt.

[6] Ibex.

colour of the leopard, with a neck six cubits in length, and having a head like that of a roebuck.[1] To these they added an account of a bird standing six cubits in height from the ground, with slender legs, feet resembling those of a goose, the neck and head small, and the beak like that of a hen. It flies but little, but in running surpasses the swiftness of the horse.[2]

Many other things which they told me I have omitted, in order that I might not weary the reader; for they stated that there were some desert places which were inhabited by serpents, some of which were fifty cubits long, without feet and with a scorpion's tail, and which would swallow a whole calf at once.[3] As almost all of them agreed in these statements, and they appeared to be worthy men, who could have no object in deceiving me, I have thought it good that the information they gave me should be handed down for the common advantage of posterity.[4]

[1] Another description of the giraffe.

[2] The ostrich.

[3] Boa constrictor.

[4] These references to animals are particularly valuable, as they seem to indicate that our travellers had penetrated farther south than even Abyssinia. The "Mountains of the Moon" have wonderfully disappeared or diminished, and it almost seems as if our travellers may have reached the lands within the Mozambique Coast, or further south towards Latterkoo, or the country between the N'gami and Natal, where the fine Koodoo antelope and the rarer striped *Inagelaphus Angasii*, figured and described by Dr. Gray, is found. The rhinoceros seems to be found in Darfur, but rarely, whereas the *R. Keitloa*, *R. Simus*, and another species, abound in some parts of the more southern lands.

THE TRAVELS

OF

ATHANASIUS NIKITIN.

THE TRAVELS

OF

ATHANASIUS NIKITIN,

OF TWER.

VOYAGE TO INDIA.

By the prayer of our holy fathers, O Lord Jesus Christ, Son of God, have mercy upon me, Thy sinful servant, Athanasius, son of Nikita.

This is, as I wrote it, my sinful wandering beyond the three seas: the first, the sea of Derbend—Doria Khvalitskaia;[1] the second, the India Sea—Doria Hondustanskaia; the third, the Black Sea—Doria Stembolskaia.[2]

I started from the church of our holy Saviour of Zlatoverkh, with the kind permission of the Grand-Duke Michael Borissowich and the bishop Gennadius of Twer;[3] went

[1] The Caspian Sea, called at that time *More Chvalisskoie*, and still called by the people "More Chvalynskoie." Doria, according to the author, is the Persian word for sea.

[2] Sea of Stamboul.

[3] Conforming to the Russian custom, which still prevails with all classes of the Russian community, our traveller, before setting out on a long voyage, went to hear prayers at one of the principal churches in Twer at that period. Michael Borissowich, or son of Boris, named here Grand-Duke of Twer, was brother-in-law to Iwan III, who reigned as Grand-Duke of Russia from 1462 to 1505. In consideration of his rela-

down the Volga, came to the convent of the holy life-giving Trinity, and the holy shrines of Boris and Gleb the martyrs; and received the blessing of the hegumen Macarius and the brethren.[1] From Koliazin I went to Ooglich; thence to Kostromah, to the Kniaz Alexander, with an epistle. And the Grand-Duke of all Russia allowed me to leave the country unhindered,[2] and I went on by Plesso to Nijni-Novgorod, to the namestnik Michael Kisseleff, and to Iwan Saraeff, the collector of duties, both of whom let me pass freely.[3]

Vassili Papin merely passed through that town;[4] but I stopped a fortnight to wait for the Tartar ambassador of Shirvanshah—Assanbek, who was coming with falcons from the Grand-Duke Ivan, ninety in number.[5]

tionship he retained the title of *Grand-Duke*, which had already been abolished for most of the smaller states until 1486, when his dominions were annexed to the Grand Duchy of Muscow. Yempteobr, i, 206.

[1] This convent, still in existence at Koliasin, on the Volga, enclosing within its precincts the remains of Boris and Gleb the martyrs, was a spot much resorted to for devotional purposes. A. Nikitin, as we shall frequently have occasion to see in the sequel, was a man of a religious turn of mind, who would not forego an opportunity, as the one offered to him at Koliazin, without seizing it eagerly. Boris and Gleb, both sons of St. Wladimir, on the death of their father in 1014, being called upon to succeed to part of his domains, was treacherously put to death by their elder brother, the ambitious Wiatopalk. Assailed by the assassins when they were saying their prayers, and thus destroyed at the very prime of life, their melancholy death inspired the people with a profound devotion for the youthful martyrs, who from that time were ranged among the saints of the Greek Church.

[2] At that remote period post-horses, turnpike-roads, and bridge-tolls were already established on the high roads, but it required an order of the Grand-Duke, in which the number of horses and the quantity of refreshment the traveller was entitled to exact, were distinctly specified.

[3] The namestniks, or lieutenants, were the chief authorities in the different provinces—the poshlimuk, the person entrusted with the collection of tolls, duties, and customs, which were numerous and oppressive during the dominion of the Tartars.

[4] Probably a traveller of some distinction, but whose character is not disclosed.

[5] This was the ambassador of Shirvanshah, whose dominions extended

With him I descended the Volga. We passed unmolested through Kazan,[1] the Orda,[2] Ooslan, Sarai,[3] and Berekezany, and we entered the river Buzan.[4] Here we fell in with three godless Tartars, who told us false tidings: —"The sultan Kaissim watches foreign merchants in the Buzan, and three thousand Tartars are with him."

Assanbek, the ambassador of Shirvanshah, gave to each of them a coat and a piece of linen, that they might guide him around Astrakhan, avoiding the town. They took the coat, but informed the zar of Astrakhan.

I abandoned my boat and crept into the ambassador's with my companions, and we sailed by Astrakhan at moonlight. The zar perceived us, and at once the Tartars cried: "Do not fly;" and the zar ordered the whole orda to chase us.

on the western shores of the Caspian Sea, forming the present Shirvan. Those princes, in the reign of Iwan III, ceased to be the oppressors of Russia, and, in many instances, appeared as affectionate allies of that sovereign. Hence the present of ninety falcons, which may be considered as a mark of courtesy, which Ivan III not only paid to his Tartar allies, but also to the Roman emperor Maximilian. Karamsin iii, 333-34.

[1] Kazan, until 1552, was the capital of an independent Tartar kingdom, a fragment of Baty's dismembered empire.

[2] This is the name formerly given to the seats of the Tartar kings that ruled over Russia; subsequently it was also applied to the different kingdoms that sprung up from the immense empire of Baty in the beginning of the fifteenth century; as the Zolotaia Orda (golden or great orda), Krimskaia Orda, the Ordea of Crimea, etc. etc.

[3] Sarai, now a heap of stones and the abode of loathsome reptiles, still observable on the borders of the Akhtouba, an arm of the Volga, forty-six miles from the sea, was at that time the capital of the great or Golden Orda, the famous residence of the great conqueror Baty, the place where, during two centuries, the Grand-Dukes of Russia had to pay their allegiance and their tribute to the tyrannical khans, and to endure the greatest hardships and humiliations ever inflicted upon a conquered people. In 1462 Achmat was khan of Saray. After a succession of wars with Ivan III he fell in 1480, and was succeeded by his sons, who, however, lost all power over Russia.

[4] Buzan is one of the many streams through which the Volga empties its waters into the Caspian Sea, it runs north to the main arm of the river.

For our sins we were overtaken on the Bogoon (Buzan). One of our men was shot; but we shot two of theirs.

The smaller of our boats ran foul of some fishing-stakes, was seized, and instantly plundered with all my things in her. In the larger we reached the sea, but having grounded at the mouth of the Volga we were taken, and the boat was hauled up again to the fishing-stakes. There they took her and four head Russians, dismissing us bare and naked beyond the sea, and forbidding us to return home because of the news.

And so we went on to Derbend in two boats: in one, the ambassador Assanbek, some *Teziks,* and ten head Russaks; in the other, six Muscovites and six Tweritians. A storm having arisen at sea, the smaller boat was wrecked on shore. Then came the Kaitaks[1] and made the whole party prisoners, and we came to Derbend, where Vassily Papin had arrived safe and well, but we robbed. I prayed him and also Assanbek, the ambassador of Shirwanshah, as we had travelled together, to take pity on the men that had been plundered by the Kaitaks near Tarki.[2] And this he did, and went up the hill to Boolat-bek; and Boolat-bek sent immediately to Shirvanshah-bek, to say that a Russian craft had been wrecked near Sarai, and that the Kaitaks coming up had taken the people and plundered their goods. Shirvanshah-bek at once dispatched a messenger to Alil-bek, the Kaitakian Kniaz, his brother-in-law, saying, "A ship of mine was wrecked near Tarki, and thy people arriving seized my people and plundered their goods. Now, for the sake of me, thou shouldest send them to me and recover their goods, for these people are sent in my name. And shouldest thou ever want any thing of me, do thou name it, and I will not refuse it to my brother; but for the sake of me let them go in liberty." Alil-bek complied willingly,

[1] The Kaitaks, or Tartar tribe that occupied the present Daghestan.

[2] Tarki, a town of Daghestan, not far from the Caspian Sea.

and immediately sent the prisoners to Derbend, whence they were directed to Shirvanshah in *Koytul*, his own orda. We all proceeded there, and prayed that he would give us the means to return to Russia; but he gave us nothing, as we were too many. So we wept and dispersed to wherever it was;[1] whoever had anything in Russia returned home; whoever was in debt went where his eyes looked; some stayed at Shamakha; others sought work at Bakou.

As for me, I went to Derbend and then to Bakou, where the fire burns unextinguished,[2] and thence across the sea to Chebokhara (Bokhara). Here I lived six months, and one month I lived at Sareh, in the land of Mazanderan, and one month at Amyl (Amol). Then I went to Dimovand (Demowend), and from Demowend to Orey[3] (here were killed the

[1] Wherever each chose to go.

[2] By this unextinguished fire the author means the naphtha springs and the mud volcanoes, for which the peninsula of Abscharon is famous. Before the Mahommedan conquest it was a favourite resort of the Ghebers or fire-worshippers. "The quantity of naphtha procured in this plain to the south-east of Baku is enormous. It is drawn from wells, some of which have been found to yield from 1000 to 1,500 lbs. a day. Near the naphtha springs still stands the Atash Kudda, or fire temple of the Ghebers, a remarkable spot, something less than a mile in circumference, from the centre of which a bluish flame is seen to arise. This fire does not consume, and if a person finds himself in the middle of it, he is not sensible of any warmth."—(Kinneir's Persia, p. 359.)

[3] Orey or Rhey, a city now in ruins, at a short distance south from Teheran, is generally supposed to be identical with the ancient *Rhages*, the capital of the Parthian kings, where Alexander halted for five days in his pursuit of Darius. The ruins cover a great extent of ground, having in their centre a modern village with a noble mosque and mausoleum,—an oasis in the midst of the surrounding desert (Macculloch, *Geogr. Dict.*, *Teheran*). With regard to the curse alluded to, we find in Olearius, Voyages, etc., liv. iv, p. 678 (translated by De Wicquefort, two vols., folio, Leide, 1718), who visited that country in 1637, the following passage, which thoroughly confirms Nikitin's statement. Speaking of the ruins of Rhey, he says:—"The soil there is reddish, and produces neither herb nor fruit. The Persians ascribe the cause of it to the curse which befel that land on account of Omar Saad, who was one of the first military chiefs in the time of Hossein (Shaussen), son of Haly, their

children of Shaussen Aley, the grandchildren of Mahmet, and he cursed the Assassins, and seventy cities fell to ruins), and from Orey (or Drey?) to Kashan, where I remained one month. I also spent a month at Nain, and another at Yezd. From Yezd I proceeded to Sirjan (or Kirwan) and to Tarom (Tarem), where the cattle are fed with dates at four *altyn* the *batman*;[1] and from Tarem to Lar, and from Lar to Bender (Bunder-Abbas); and here there is a seaport, Hormyz (Hormuz), and the Indian Sea, called in the Persian tongue *Doria of Hondustan.*

Hormuz is four miles across the water and stands on an island. Twice a day the sea flows around it, and here I celebrated the first great day, having reached Hormuz four weeks before the great day. I have not named the many and large cities through which I passed.

At Hormuz the sun is scorching and burns man. I stopped there a month. On the first week after the great day,[2] I shipped my horses in a *tava*,[3] and sailed across the Indian Sea in ten dayes to Moshkat (Muscat). Thence in four days to *Degh*(?); and farther to Kuzrat (Gujrat) and Kanbat (Cambay), where the indigo grows; and lastly to Chivil.[4] We sailed six weeks in the tava till we reached Chivil, and left Chivil on the seventh week after the great day.

great prophet. This Omar, who first had made professions of friendship towards Hossein, was the only man who consented to serve Fesid-Peser against him; for Hossein being of the blood of Mahomet, and in great renown for his sanctity, there was no general found at Medina who would take up arms against him, except Omar, who was persuaded to undertake the war, by the promise of receiving possession of the city of Rhey and its territory, which he had been coveting for a long time. But the death of Hossein, who fell during the war, brought upon that land the curse, which, by the common belief, still appeared in the tint and barrenness of the soil."

[1] A batman is a measure of weight still used in Turkey, Persia, Bokhara, and in Caucasus, equal to 26 pouds, or 936 lbs. (about 8 1-9th cwt.) avoirdupois. An altyn is three copecs, or one penny.

[2] Easter Sunday.

[3] A vessel.

[4] Chaoul, a flourishing seaport before the Portuguese conquest, thirty

This is an Indian country. People go about naked, with their heads uncovered and bare breasts; the hair tressed into one tail, and thick bellies. They bring forth children every year and the children are many; and men and women are black. When I go out many people follow me, and stare at the white man.

Their kniaz[1] wears a *fata*[2] on the head; and another on the loins; the boyars wear it on the shoulders and on the loins; the *kniaginies* wear it also round the shoulders and the loins. The servants of the kniaz and of the boyars attach the fata round the loins, carrying in the hand a shield and a sword, or a scimitar, or knives, or a sabre, or a bow and arrows—but all naked and barefooted. Women walk about with their heads uncovered and their breasts bare. Boys and girls go naked till seven years, and do not hide their shame.

We left Chivil, and went by land in eight days to Pilee(?), to the Indian mountains; thence in ten days to Oomri,[3] and from that Indian town to Jooneer(?) in six days.

Here resides Asat, khan of Indian Jooneer, a tributary of Meliktuchar. I hear he holds seven *tmas* of Meliktuchar, while Meliktuchar himself presides over twenty tmas. He has been fighting the *Kofars* for twenty years, being sometimes beaten, but mostly beating them.

The khan rides on men, although he has many good elephants and horses. Among his attendants are many Khorassanians, some of whom come from the countries of

miles south south-east of Bombay. This was a place of considerable note during the Bhamenee dynasty of the Deccan.—Hamilton's *Indian Gaz.*

1 "Kniaz" is the Russian word for prince or chief, and "kniaginia" for princess; "boyars" means noblemen.

2 *Fata* is a large silken garment, still worn in some countries of Russia by the women of the lower classes, round the head or over the upper part of the body.

3 Perhaps Umrut (Omrita), a town in the province of Aurungabad, forty miles south by east from Surat.

Khorassan, Oroban, Surkmesk, and Chegotan. They all are brought over by sea in *tavas* or Indian ships.

And I, poor sinner, brought a stallion to the land of India; with God's help I reached Jooneer all well, but it cost me a hundred roubles.

The winter began from Trinity day,[1] and we wintered at Jooneer and lived there two months; but day and night for four months there is but rain and dirt. At this time of the year the people till the ground, sow wheat, tuturegan(?), peas, and all sorts of vegetables. Wine is kept in large skins (?) of Indian goat. (Unintelligible). . . .

Horses are fed on peas; also on *kichiris*, boiled with sugar and oil; early in the morning they get *shishenivo*, Horses are not born in that country, but oxen and buffaloes; and these are used for riding, conveying goods, and every other purpose.

Jooneer stands on a stony island; no human hand built it —God made the town. A narrow road, which it takes a day to ascend, admitting of only one man at a time, leads up the hill to it.

In the land of India it is the custom for foreign traders to stop at inns; there the food is cooked for the guests by the landlady, who also makes the bed and sleeps with the stranger. Women that know you willingly concede their favours, for they like white men. In the winter, the people put on the fata and wear it round the waist, on the shoulders, and on the head; but the princes and nobles put trousers on, a shirt and a kaftan (a long coat), wearing a fata on the shoulders, another as a belt round the waist, and a third round the head.

O God, true God, merciful God, gracious God.

At Jooneer the khan took away my horse, and having heard that I was no Mahommedan, but a Russian, he said: "I will give thee the horse and a 1000 pieces of gold, if

[1] Viz., in June.

thou wilt embrace our faith, the Mahommedan faith; and if thou wilt not embrace our Mahommedan faith, I shall keep the horse and take a 1000 pieces of gold upon thy head." He gave me four days to consider, and all this occurred during the fast of the Assumption of our Lady, on the eve of our Saviour's day (18th of August).

And the Lord took pity upon me because of his holy festival, and did not withdraw his mercy from me, his sinful servant, and allowed me not to perish at Fooneer among the infidels. On the eve of our Saviour's day there came a man from Khorassan, Khozaiocha Mahmet, and I implored him to pity me. He repaired to the khan into the town, and praying him delivered me from being converted, and took from him my horse. Such was the Lord's wonderful mercy on the Saviour's day.

Now, Christian brethren of Russia, whoever of you wishes to go to the Indian country may leave his faith in Russia, confess Mahomet, and then proceed to the land of Hindostan. Those Mussulman dogs have lied to me, saying I should find here plenty of our goods; but there is nothing for our country. All goods for the land of Mussulmans, as pepper and colours, and these are cheap.

Merchandise conveyed by sea is free from duty, and people that would bring it to us will give no duty;[1] but the duties are many. The sea is infested with pirates, all of whom are Kofars, neither Christians nor Mussulmans; they pray to stone idols and know not Christ.

We left Jooneer on the eve of the Assumption of the very holy (Virgin)[2] for *Beuruk* (Beder), a large city, and we were a month on the road. From there we went in five days to

[1] This sentence is not clear, and as it stands thus in the original, I did not venture to put on it any construction to explain the author's mind, the more so as the latter part of the sentence is left out in Mr. Stroef's impression. (Count Wielhorsky.)

[2] $\frac{15}{27}$th of August.

Kulongher, and in five days from the latter to Kelberg (Kulburga). Between these large towns there are many small ones: three for each day, and occasionally four; so many *kors*, so many towns. From Chivil to Jooneer it is 20 kors; from Jooneer to Beder, 40; from Beder to Kulongher, 9 kors; and from Beder to Koluberg, 9.

In Beder there is a trade in horses, goods, stuffs, silks, and all sorts of other merchandise, and also in black people; but no other article is sold but Indian goods, and every kind of eatables; no goods, however, that will do for Russia. And all are black and wicked, and the women all harlots, or witches, or thieves and cheats; and they destroy their masters with poison.

The rulers and the nobles in the land of India are all Khorassanians. The Hindoos walk all on foot and walk fast. They are all naked and bare-footed, and carry a shield in one hand and a sword in the other. Some of the servants are armed with straight bows and arrows.

Elephants are greatly used in battle. The men on foot are sent first, the Khorassanians being mounted in full armour, man as well as horse. Large scythes[1] are attached to the trunks and tusks of the elephants, and the animals are clad in ornamental plates of steel. They carry a citadel, and in the citadel twelve men in armour with guns and arrows.

There is a place *Shikhbaludin Peratyr*, a bazaar Aladinand,[2] and a fair once a year, where people from all parts of India assemble and trade for ten days. As many as 20,000 horses are brought there for sale from Beder, which is 20

[1] Weighing three pouds or 106 lb.

[2] Stroef gives it thus: "Shikhb-aludin piriatyr bazaar Aliadinand." Shikhuladin, as will be seen presently, appears to have been a man held in great veneration at that time. Ibn Batuta, the celebrated Arabian traveller, who visited India about the middle of the fourteenth century, relates that in coming to Bengal his chief object was to see a great saint who dwelt in the mountains of Karuru, which adjoins the mountains of

kors distant, and besides every description of goods; and that fair is the best throughout the land of Hindostan. Every thing is sold or bought in memory of Shikbaladin, whose fête falls on the Russian festival of the Protection of the Holy Virgin (1st October).

In that Aland (Aladinand ?) there is a bird, *gookook*, that flies at night and cries "gookook," and any roof it lights upon, there the man will die; and whoever attempts to kill it, will see fire flashing from its beak. Wild cats rove at night and catch fowls; they live in the hills and among stones. As to monkeys they live in the woods and have their monkey *kniaz*, who is attended by a host of armed followers. When any of them is caught they complain to their kniaz, and an army is sent after the missing; and when they come to a town they pull down the houses and beat the people; and their armies, it is said, are many. They speak their own tongues and bring forth a great many children; and, when a child is unlike its father or its mother, it is thrown out on the high road. Thus they are often caught by the Hindoos, who teach them every sort of handicraft, or sell them at night, that they may not find their way home, or teach them dancing.[1]

Spring begins from the Protection of the Holy Virgin (10th October). A fortnight after this festival they celebrate Shikbaladin and the spring during eight days. They make the spring three months, the summer three months,

Thibet, the *Shiekh Falal Oddin*. This saint treated him with attention, and placed on him at parting the fine goat's hair garment which he wore himself. (Cooley, i, 203.) Might he not be the same in whose memory everything was bought and sold at the Aladinand bazaar.

[1] The belief that these animals are but a variety of the human species, already existed among the Greeks of antiquity. Ibn Batuta informs us that he found the same belief established among pious and credible persons in India. He was assured that the monkeys have a chief, whom they treat as if he were a king, four monkeys with rods in their hands being constantly in waiting upon him, and supplying his table with all sorts of eatables. (Cooley, i, 202.)

the winter three months, and the autumn three months. Beder is the chief town of the whole of Mahomedan Hindostan; the city is large, and contains a great many people.

Description of Beder. The sultan. The sultan[1] (of Beder) is a little man, twenty years old, in the power of the nobles. Khorassanians rule the country and serve in war. There is a Khorassanian Boyar, Melik-Tuchar, who keeps an army of 200,000 men; Melik Khan keeps 100,000; Kharat Khan, 20,000, and many are the khans that keep 10,000 armed men.

The sultan goes out with 300,000 men of his own troops. *The nobles.* The land is overstocked with people; but those in the country are very miserable, whilst the nobles are extremely opulent and delight in luxury. They are wont to be carried on their silver beds, preceded by some twenty chargers caparisoned in gold, and followed by 300 men on horseback and 500 on foot, and by horn-men, ten torchbearers and ten musicians.

The sultan's hunts. The sultan goes out hunting with his mother and his lady, and a train of 10,000 men on horseback, 50,000 on foot; 200 elephants adorned in gilded armour, and in front one hundred horn-men, 100 dancers, and 300 common horses in golden clothing, 100 monkeys, and 100 concubines, all foreign (haurikies).

The sultan's palace. The sultan's palace has seven gates, and in each gate are seated 100 guards and 100 Mahommedan scribes, who enter the names of all persons going in and out. Foreigners are not admitted into the town. This palace is very wonderful; everything in it is carved or gilded, and, even to the smallest

[1] After the Mahommedan conquest the province of Beder was the seat of the Bhamener dynasty of Deccan sovereigns, the first of whom was sultan Allah ud Deen Houssun Kangoh Bhamenee, A.D. 1347, whose capital was Kalbergah. Beder was formerly noted for works of tutenague inlaid with silver. Before the Mahommedan invasion it was the capital of a Hindoo sovereignty. Near the ruins of the old Beder, Ahmed Shah Bhamenee founded the city Ahmedabad, which he made his capital in place of Kalbergah, and this is the modern Beder. (Hamilton, p. 105.)

stone, is cut and ornamented with gold most wonderfully. Several courts of justice are within the building.

Throughout the night the town of Beder is guarded by 1000 men *kutovalovies*,[1] mounted on horses in full armour, carrying each a light. *Beder and its people.*

I sold my stallion at Beder, and got by him 60 and 8 *footoons*, having kept him a whole year.

Snakes crawl about in the streets of Beder, in length two sajen (fourteen feet).

I came to Beder from Kulongher on the day of St. Philip (14th of November); sold my horse about Christmas and staid at Beder till Lent; and made acquaintance with many Hindoos, told them what was my faith; that I was neither Mahommedan nor . . . (caædronic, saiadenie?), but a Christian; that my name was *Ofonasey*, and my Mahommedan name *Khoza Issuf Khorossani*. After that they no more endeavoured to conceal anything from me, neither their meals, nor their commerce, nor their prayers, nor other

[1] The kouteval, like the police of our days, had to keep good order in the streets, especially during the night. Olearius, in describing the authorities of the city of Gomron, or Bunder Abbas (*Voyages du Sr. Jean A. Mandelslo, publiés par A. Olearius et traduits par De Wicquefort*, 2 vols., folio. Vol. i, p. 32), says, that the kouteval performed the duties of a *chevalier du guet*, or night guard. In the kingdom of Guzerat, according to the same authority (pp. 152, 153), his duty was also to decide petty suits, "But justice," remarks Olearius, "is administered there in a curious manner; for the person that begins the suit usually wins it, and the consequence is that in most cases it is the sufferer has to pay the fine. The capital crimes are judged by the governors of the cities, the executions devolving on the kouteval. There is almost no crime from which you may not be redeemed by money; so that it may be said of those countries, with more truth than of any other, that gibbets are erected there for the poor only. The crimes most severely punished are murder and adultery, especially when committed with a lady of high station. This is the only reason why houses of pleasure are tolerated, all of which pay a tribute to the kouteval, who in return extend to them such an efficient protection that they not only afford security, but also confer a certain amount of honour on their customers.

Religious creeds.

things; nor did they try to hide their women. And I asked them all about their religion, and they said: "We believe in Adam;" and they hold the *Budhs* to be Adam and his race. There are in all eighty-four creeds, and all believe in *Boot* (Buddha), and no man of one creed will drink, eat, or marry with those of another. Some of them feed on mutton, fowls, fish, and eggs, but none on beef.

Description of Pervottum.

Having spent four months at Beder, I agreed with some Hindoos to go to *Pervota*,[1] which is their Jerusalem; its Mahommedan name is *Gkhat Deikh Bootkhana*. We were a month on the route. A fair is held there during five days.

Budhkhana.

Bootkhana is a very extensive building, about the half of Twer, built in stone, and exhibiting in carvings on the walls the deeds of Boot. All around it are cut out twelve wreaths, in which are shown how Boot achieved miracles; how he appeared in different forms; first in the shape of a man, then as a man with an elephant's nose, then as a man with a monkey's face, and again as a man with the appearance of a savage beast and a tail rising a sajen (seven feet) above him.

People from all parts of the land of India congregate at Bootkhana, to witness the wonders of Boot. Old women and girls shave their hair at Bootkhana, and everyone coming there shaves his beard and head and whatever hair is on his body; and a tribute of two *mekshenies* is levied on each head for the sake of Boot, and also of four *fonties* on each horse. Twenty millions of people assemble at Bootkhana, but sometimes a hundred millions.

At Bootkhana, Boot is sculptured in stone of an immense size, his tail rising over him. His right hand is lifted up high and extended like that of Justian (Justinian?), emperor of Constantinople; his left holding a sword; he is quite uncovered, with only a small cloth round the loins, and has the appearance of a monkey. Some other budhs (idols) are

[1] See an account of Perwuttum and its pagoda, by Colonel Colin Mackenzie, in Asiatic Researches, vol. v, 304.

naked, without anything on their hinder parts, and the wives of Boot and their children are also sculptured naked.

A huge bull, carved in black stone and gilded, stands before Boot; people kiss his hoof and adorn him with flowers as well as Boot.

Hindoo meals.

The Hindoos eat no meat, no cow flesh, no mutton, no chicken. The banquets were all on pork; and pigs are in great abundance. They take their meals twice a day, but not at night, and drink no wine nor mead; but with Mahommedans they neither eat nor drink. Their fare is poor. They eat not with one another nor with their wives, and live on Indian corn, carrots with oil, and different herbs. Always eating with the right hand, they will never set the left hand to anything nor use a knife; the spoon is unknown. In travelling every one has a stone pot to cook his broth in. They take care that Mahommedans do not look into their pot, nor see their food, and should this happen they will not eat it; some, therefore, hide themselves under a linen cloth lest they should be seen when eating.

Hindoo mode of praying.

They offer their prayers towards the east, in the Russian way, lifting both hands high and putting them on the top of the head; then they lie down with the face to the ground, stretching their body to its full length, and such is their law.

They sit down to eat, and wash their hands and feet, and rinse their mouths before they do so.

Religious customs.

Their Bootookhanies (places of worship) have no doors, and are situated towards the east; and the budhs (idols) also stand eastward.

The bodies of the dead are burnt, and the ashes scattered on the waters.

When a woman is confined, her husband acts the midwife. He gives the name to a son, but the mother gives it to a daughter. Still there is no good about them, and they know not what is shame.

On meeting together, they bow to each other like the monks, touching the ground with both hands, but say nothing.

During Lent they go to Pervota, their Jerusalem. In Mahommedan it is named Koka, in Russian Jerusalem, in the Hindoo tongue *Tparvat*.

They come hither all naked, with only a small linen round their loins; and the women also naked, with a fota round the middle; but some are dressed in fotas, wearing necklaces of sapphire, bracelets round the arms, and golden rings, *ollooak*.

They drive into the Bootkhana on bulls, the horns of which are cased in brass. These animals, called "ach-chee," have their feet shod, and carry round the neck 300 bells. The Hindoos call the bull *father*, and the cow *mother*; with their excrements they bake bread and boil food, and with their ashes sign the images of these animals on their own faces, foreheads, and whole bodies.

On Sundays and Mondays they only eat once in the day. In India "pachektur a uchu zeder sikish ilarsen ikishitel akechany ilia atyrsen a tle jetelber bularadastor akul karavash uchuz charfuna khubbem funa khubesia kap karaam chuk-kichi khosh."[1]

From Pervota we returned to Beder, a fortnight before the great Mahommedan festival (Ulu Bairam). But I know not the great day of Christ's Resurrection; however, I guess by different signs, that the great Christian day is by nine or ten days sooner than the Mahommedan *Cagrim* (Cairiam). I have nothing with me; no books whatever; those that I had taken from Russia were lost when I was robbed. And I forgot the Christian faith and the Christian festivals, and know not Easter nor Christmas, nor can I tell Wednesday from Friday, and I am between the two faiths. *But I pray to the only God that he may preserve me from destruction. God is* one, king of glory and creator of heaven and earth.

[1] This, like the other untranslated passages in this narrative, are in Turkish, as they stand in the original, but are so corrupt as to be scarcely intelligible. Even when the meaning can be guessed at, it has sometimes, as in the present instance, been thought undesirable to supply it in English.

On my return to Russia I again adopted the Russian law. The month of March passed, and I had not eaten any meat for one month, having begun to fast with the Mahommedans on a Sunday. Abstaining from all animal or Mahommedan food, I fed myself twice a day with bread and water, abstained from female society, and prayed to God Almighty, who made heaven and earth; and no other god of any other name did I invoke. Bog ollo, Bog kerim, Bog garym, Bog khudo, Bog Akber, God, king of glory, Ollo-vareno ollo garymello, sensen olloty.

It takes ten days to go by sea from Ormuz to Golat (Kalat); from Kalat to Degh six days; from Degh to Moshkat (Muscat) six days; from Moshkat to Gujzrat ten days;[1] from Gujzrat to Combat (Cambay) four days; from Combat to Chivil (Chaoul) twelve days; and from Chivil to Dabyl (Dabul) six days.

Calicut. Ceylon. Shibat. Pegu. China.

Dabul is the last seaport in Hindostan belonging to the Mussulmans. From there to Colecot (Calicut) you have to travel twenty-five days, and from Colecot to Ceylan fifteen; from Ceylan to Shibait one month; from Shibait to Pewgu twenty days; and from Pewgu to China and Macheen one month: all this by sea. From China to *Kyt* you go by land six months, but by sea in four days....

Hormuz.

Hormuz is a vast emporium of all the world; you find there people and goods of every description, and whatever thing is produced on earth you find it in Hormuz. But the duties are high, one tenth of everything.

Cambay. Indigo.

Cambayat (Cambai) is a port of the whole Indian sea, and a manufacturing place for every sort of goods; as talach,[2] damask, khan,[3] kiota,[4] and there they prepare the blue stone colour. There also grows *lek daakhyk dalon.*

[1] The distances in days between Degh, Muscat, and Guzerat are given in Stroef's edition, but not in this manuscript.

[2] Long gowns, still worn by Tartars, of a striped material, half cotton half silk.

[3] A sort of satin from China.

[4] Blankets.

Dabul. Dabyl (Dabul) is also a very extensive seaport, where many horses are brought from Mysore, Rabast (Arabia), Khorassan, Turkestan, Neghostan. It takes a month to walk by land from this place to Beder and to Kulburgha.

Calicut. Articles produced. Calecot (Calicut) is a port for the whole Indian sea, which God forbid any craft to cross, and whoever saw it will not go over it healthy. The country produces pepper, ginger, colour plants, muscat, cloves, cinnamon, aromatic roots, *adrach* (?) and every description of spices, and everything is cheap, and servants and maids are very good.

Ceylon. Ceylon is another not inconsiderable port of the Indian Sea. There, on a hill, is the tomb of Adam, and in the vicinity are found precious stones, antimony, *fastisses*, agate, *cinchai*, crystal, *sumbada*.[1] Elephants and ostriches live there and are sold, the former by the size, the latter by the weight.

Shabat. Shabait, on the Indian Sea, is a very large place; a tribute of one *tenka*[2] a day is paid there to each Korossanee, big or small. And when he marries, then the sovereign of Shabat pays him 1000 tenkas for the sacrifice and as a tribute, and he eats for ten tenkas a month. At Shabat the country produces silk, sandal, gems, and everything is cheap.

Pegu. Pegu is no inconsiderable port, principally inhabited by

[1] A sort of mastich, used for shaving (?).

[2] The tankha appears to be the coin represented by the modern rupee, and, perhaps, when at its proper standard, was of about the same value. The rupee of Akbar (sixteenth century) contained 174·5 grains of pure silver, and was divided into forty dams or pusas (of 191½ grains of copper each). Queen Elizabeth's shilling contained 88.8 grains of pure silver; Akbar's rupee, therefore, was worth 1s. 11½d. of English money of his time. Akbar's standard remained almost unaltered all over the Mogul dominions until the breaking up of the empire, in the middle of the last century. (The Hon. M. Elphinstone's History of India, book viii, chap. II, note 19.) Hence the value of one tenka at the latter part of the fifteenth century may be fixed at about two shillings.

Indian dervishes. The products derived from thence are *manik, iakhut, kyrpuk,* which are sold by the dervishes.

The seaports of *Cheen* and *Machin* are also large. Porcelain is made there, and sold by the weight and at a low price. Women sleep with their husbands in the day, but at night they go to the foreign men and sleep with them and pay for it, besides waiting on them with sweetmeats and supplying them with food and drink, that the foreigners may love them, because they like strangers and white people, their own men being so very black. And when a woman conceives a child by a stranger, the husband pays him a salary. If the child is born white, the stranger receives a duty of eighteen tenkas; if it is born black he gets nothing, but is welcome to what he ate and drank.

Shabat is distant three months from Beder; but by sea it takes two months to go from Dabul to Shabat. Machin and Chim, where porcelain is made and everything is cheap, are four months distance by sea from Beder, and Ceylon two months by sea.

At Shabat nature produces silk, beads, gems, sandal, elephants, which are sold by the *lokot.* At Ceylon you find *ammone,* antimony, *fatisses*; at Lecot (Calicut?), pepper, muscat, cloves, Indian peas and colour plants; at Guzrat the Indigo colour; at Cambat the agate; at Rachoor[1] the diamond. *Cirkona danov konaj?* The parcel is sold at five roubles, but the best at ten; a parcel of rough diamond—*penech chekeni siaje charasheshkeni asipit ek tenka.* The diamond is found on a rocky hill, and the rough diamond from that hill is sold for two thousand pounds weight of gold per *lokot;* the *kona* diamond is sold at 10,000 pounds of gold per *lokot.* That district belongs to Melik-khan, a vassal to the sultan, and is thirty *kors* from Beder.—*a syto.*

The Jews call the people of Shabat Jews like themselves; but this is not true, for the people of Shabat are neither Jews,

[1] Orachoor, according to Stroef.

nor Mahommedans, nor Christians, but belong to a different Indian religion. They eat not with *Khuds* (Jews?) nor Mahommedans, and use no meat. Silk and sugar are cultivated at a low expense, and everything generally is cheap at Shabat.

Monkeys and wild cats infest the woods and attack the traveller on the highroads; nobody, therefore, attempts to travel at night, on account of the monkeys and wild cats.

From Shabat it is ten months by land and four by sea, *aukiikov.*

Musk deer. There is a kind of deer, which, when fattened, have their vesicles cut, and a liquid is generated therein. When wild they drop these vesicles, which give a very strong smell on the fields and in the woods, and any one attempting to taste the liquid would immediately die.

I kept the great day in May at Beder, the Mahommedan residence in Hindostan, having begun to fast on the first day of April; but the Mahommedans kept the Bairam in the middle of May.

O true believing Christians! He that travels through many countries will fall into many sins, and deprive himself of the Christian faith... (Two lines unintelligible.)

Four great Lent fastings and four great days (Easter days) have already passed by, but I, sinful man, do not know which is the great day, or when is Lent, or Christmas, or any other holiday, or Wednesday or Friday. I have no books; they were taken by those that plundered us. Driven by this great misfortune I went to India, for I had nothing to return with to Russia, being robbed of all my goods.

Places where Nikitin kept Easter days. The first great day I kept at *Kain* (Nain); the second at *Chebokhara,* in the country of Mazanderan: the third at Hormuz; the fourth in India, together with the Mussulmans; and there I wept bitterly because of the Christian faith.

A Mussulman called Melikh, forcibly exhorted me to go

over to the Mahommedan faith. But I said to him: "Master, thou *markylaresen menda namaz kilarmen ty bez namaz kilarsiz menda 3 kalaremen mengarib easen enchai.*"—But he replied: "Truly thou seemest not to be a Mahometan; but thou knowest not the Christian faith."

And I was then engrossed by many a thought, and said to myself: "Woe to me, obdurate sinner, who wandered from the path of truth, and who no more know where to go. Oh Lord Almighty, Creator of heaven and earth, turn not away Thy face from Thy servant, for I am near to despair in my trouble. Lord, bestow Thy glance upon me and have mercy upon me, for I am Thy creature; do not lead me, O Lord, from the path of truth, but direct my steps to wander in righteousness; for in my trouble I did no good for Thy sake, O Lord, and have spent the whole of my days in evil. *Ollo pervodiger, Ollo garym, Ollo tykarim, Ollo karim, Ollo ragymello, Akhalim dulimo.*"

I have already passed the fourth great day in the Mussulman country, and have not renounced Christianity. But what may come hereafter, that God alone knows: "O gracious Lord, on Thee I rely, and unto Thee I pray to save me from destruction."

(Three lines unintelligible.)

On the Mahometan Bairam, the sultan went out to *teferich*, and with him twenty high-viziers, three hundred elephants, clad in Damask steel armour, carrying citadels equally fitted in steel, and each holding six warriors with guns and long muskets. The big elephants are mounted by twelve men. Each animal has two large *probortsy* and a heavy sword, weighing a *kentar* (three pouds, about 100 lb.), attached to its tusks, and large iron weights hanging from the trunk. A man in full armour sits between the ears, holding in his hand a large iron hook wherewith he guides the animal.

But besides this there may be seen in the train of the sultan about a thousand ordinary horses in gold trappings, one hundred camels with torchbearers, three hundred trumpeters, three hundred dancers, and three hundred *kovre*.

The sultan, riding on a golden saddle, wears a habit embroidered with sapphires, and on his pointed headdress a large diamond; he also carries a suit of gold armour inlaid with sapphires, and three swords mounted in gold. Before him runs a Mussulman playing on the *teremetz*, and behind a great many attendants follow on foot; also a mighty elephant, decked with silk and holding in his mouth a large iron chain. It is his business to clear the way of people and horses, in order that none should come too near the sultan.

The brother of the sultan rides on a golden bed, the canopy of which is covered with velvet and ornamented with precious stones. It is carried by twenty men.

Mahmud sits on a golden bed, with a silken canopy to it and a golden top, drawn by four horses in gilt harness. Around him are crowds of people, and before him many singers and dancers, and all of them armed with bare swords or sabres, shields, spears, lances, or large straight bows; and riders and horses are in full armour. Some are naked, but wear a small garment round the waist.

At Beder the moon remains full three days. I found there no fresh vegetables.

The heat in Hindostan is not great; it is great at Hormuz; at *Katobagraim*, where gems are found; at Tid;[1] at *Bakh;* at Mysore; at *Ostan;* at Lar. In the land of Khorassan the climate is warm, but not to excess; it is, however, exceedingly hot in *Chegotan*, and in the cities of Shiraz, Yezd, and Kashan; but winds blow there sometimes. At

[1] Djid, near Mecca? The three following names, Bakh, Mysore, Ostan, are omitted in Stroef's impression, but replaced by the words "at Mahrab, and in Oroobstan", which appears the better reading, as the names referred to would indicate the first, Tid, a town on the Red Sea; Mahrah, a province in Arabia; and Oroobstan Arabia, that being the name given to that country by our traveller.

Ghilan the air is sultry and extremely warm; the same at Shamakha and at Babylon, at *Khumit*, at *Shamah* (or *Sham*). It is less warm at Lap.

But in Sevastihub (Sivas) and in the land of *Gurzyn*[1] there is abundance of everything, as well as in the lands *Tursk* and *Walosk*, where eatables are plentiful and cheap. The land of Podolia also abounds in every produce.

May God preserve the Russian land, God preserve this world, and more especially from hell; may He bestow his blessing on the dominions of Russia and the Russian nobility, and may the Russian dominion increase. O Lord, I rely upon Thee; spare my life. I have lost my road and know not where to go!

I can well get from Hindostan to Hormuz, but there is no road from there to Khorassan; nor to *Chegotay*, nor to *Kitabagraim*,[2] nor to Tezd;[3] for all these places have been conquered by the *Bulgack*,[4] and their kings expelled. Uzu-Assanbekh killed Taousho Murzah; Sultan Massait was poisoned; Uzu-Assanbekh took Shiraz; but the country refused to submit, and Ediger Mahmet did not appear (to make his allegiance), but continued in a state of defence. So there is no practicable way whatever.

If you proceed to Mecka you must take the Mahometan faith, and on account of this Christians do not like to go to Mecka. On the other hand, living in India is very expensive. I have spent the whole of my money, and being alone I spend daily for my food one-sixth of an altyn;[5] nor do I drink wine or *synda*.

[1] This may be Gruzia, the present name of that part of the Caucasus known to Europe as Georgia, a country which by its fertility would answer to the qualification given to it by our traveller. Stroef's reading is Qurmyz, namely Hormuz, which does not seem so good, as the author would not have called it a land, having described it as a town *standing on an island*.

[2] Here follows in Stroef's edition "*nor to Bodat*".

[3] Here follows in Stroef, "*nor to Arabostan*".

[4] In Stroef, "*Bulck*".

[5] About two-thirds of a farthing.

Melikh Tuchar took two Indian towns,[1] whose ships pirated on the Indian Sea, captured seven princes with their treasures, a load of precious stones, a load of diamonds and *kirpuks*, and a hundred loads of valuable goods; while the army took an immense quantity of various merchandize. The town had been besieged for two years by an army of two hundred thousand men, one hundred elephants, and three hundred camels.

Melikh Tuchar. Melikh Tuchar came with his army to Beder on the day of Kurbant-Bairam, in the Russian Calendar Peter's day; and the sultan sent ten viziers to encounter him at a distance of ten kors (a kor is equal to ten versts), each at the head of ten thousand warriors, and of ten elephants in full equipment.

His court. At the court of Melikh Tuchar five hundred people sit down to dinner every day; but three viziers only are admitted to his table, and with each vizier fifty people, and besides one hundred of his household boyars.

Two thousand horses stand in the stables of Melikh Tuchar, of which one thousand are always saddled and kept in readiness day and night; and also one hundred elephants. His residence is guarded every night by a hundred armed men, twenty trumpeters, and ten torchmen; while ten large kettledrums, each attended by two men, are alternately struck throughout the watch.

Myza Mylk, Mek-Khan, and Farat-Khan took three large cities, with an army of one hundred thousand men and fifty elephants of their own, and captured an immense quantity of precious stones, sapphires and diamonds, the whole of which was bought by Melikh Tuchar, who gave order that none of them should be sold to foreign traders. They came to Beder on the day of the Ascension.

[1] Probably situated on the coast of Malabar, whose inhabitants were noted as intrepid and ferocious pirates, and belonged to one of the most warlike tribes of India. (Mandelslo. ii, 263.)

The sultan goes out hunting on Tuesdays and Thursdays, and is accompanied by three viziers.

His brother, when in a campaign, is followed by his mother and sister, and two thousand women on horseback or on golden beds; at the head of the train are three hundred ordinary horses in gold equipment, and a great many troops on foot, two viziers, ten *vizierins*, fifty elephants in cloth coverings, carrying each four naked natives with a small garment round the waist. The women that follow on foot are equally uncovered; they carry supplies of water for drinking and washing. No man will drink with another from the same vessel.

Melikh Tuchar moved from Beder with his army, fifty thousand strong, against the Indians, on the anniversary of Sheikh Aladin, after the Russian calendar, on the Protection of the Holy Virgin. The sultan (of Beder) sent with him fifty thousand of his own army and three viziers with thirty thousand men, one hundred elephants fully equipped, and carrying each a citadel and four men, the latter armed with long muskets. With this force Melikh Tuchar went to fight against the great Indian dominion of *Chenudar*. But the king of Binedar possessed three hundred elephants, one hundred thousand men of his own troops, and fifty thousand horse.

The sultan left Beder on the eighth month after the great day (Easter), and with him twenty-six viziers, of whom twenty were Mussulmans and six Hindoos.

Army of the sultan of Beder.

There went out of the household troops of the sultan, one hundred thousand horse, two hundred thousand foot, three hundred elephants with citadels and clad in armour, and one hundred savage beasts led in double chains. The brother of the sultan took the field with one hundred thousand horse and one hundred thousand foot of his own troops, and one hundred equipped elephants.

Mal Khan led	20,000 horse,
	60,000 foot,
	20 elephants.
Beder Khan	30,000 horse.
His brother	100,000 foot,
	25 elephants.
The Sultan	10,000 horse,
	20,000 foot,
	10 elephants.
Vozyr-Khan	15,000 horse,
	30,000 foot,
	10 elephants.
Kutar-Khan	15,000 horse,
	40,000 foot,
	10 elephants.

Each vizier 10,000 or 15,000 horse and 20,000 foot.

The Indian *Ordonom* went out with forty thousand horse, one hundred thousand foot, forty elephants in full armour, each carrying four men with long muskets. The sultan mustered twenty-six viziers, each at the head of ten or fifteen thousand horse and thirty thousand foot.

There are in India four great Hindoo viziers, having each an army of forty thousand mounted men and one hundred thousand foot. The sultan, being indignant that the Indians had turned out so few, added to them twenty thousand foot, two hundred thousand horse, and twenty elephants. And this is the force of the Mahommedan sultan of India.

Mamet deni iaria arast deni khudodonot, and God knows the true faith, and the true faith bids us to know only one God and to invoke his name in every place.

On the fifth great day I thought of returning to Russia, and I set out from Beder a month before the Mahommedan Bairam. *Mamet deni rossolial.* Knowing no more the great Christian day, the day of Christ's resurrection, I kept Lent time with the Mussulmans and broke fasting with them on

Easter day, which I did at Kulburga, a city twenty kors from Beder.[1]

The sultan (of Beder) moved out with his army on the fifteenth day after the Ulu Bairam to join Melich-Tuchar at Kulburga. But their campaign was not successful, for they only took one Indian town, and that at the loss of many people and treasures.

The Hindoo sultan Kadam is a very powerful prince. He possesses a numerous army, and resides on a mountain at Bichenegher (Bijanagar). This vast city is surrounded by three *forts*,[2] and intersected by a river, bordering on one side on a dreadful *jungel*, on the other on a dale; a wonderful place, and to any purpose convenient. On one side it is quite inaccessible; a road goes right through the town, and as the mountain rises high with a ravine below, the town is impregnable. *Bichenagar.*

The enemy besieged it for a month and lost many people, owing to the want of water and food. Plenty of water was in sight, but could not be got at. *Besieged and captured.*

This Indian stronghold was ultimately taken by Melikh Khan Khoda, who stormed it, having fought day and night to reduce it. The army that made the siege with heavy guns, had neither eaten nor drunk for twenty days. He lost five thousand of his best soldiers. On the capture of the town twenty thousand inhabitants, men and women, had their heads cut off; twenty thousand, young and old, were made prisoners, and sold afterwards at ten tenkas and also at five tenkas a head; the children at two tenkas each. The treasury, however, having been found empty, the town was abandoned.

[1] In Stroef, "ten kors", which agrees better with the distance of nine kors, as given above between Beder and Kalburga.

[2] *Forts* may be the meaning of the Russian word "rogy", as given in this manuscript. In Stroef it is *rovy*, which alteration of a single letter makes a great difference, the latter meaning "ravines".

From Kulburga I went to *Kooroola*,[1] where the *akhik* is produced and worked, and from whence it is exported to all parts of the world. Three hundred dealers in diamonds reside in this place, but no *sulakhmyk*.

I stopped there five months and then proceeded to Calica (Calicut), which is a large bazaar; thence I went to Konakelburga, and from Konakelburga to Sheikh Aladin, and from Sheikh Aladin to Kamindria, and from Kamindria to Kynarias, and from Kynarias to Surah, and from Surah to Dabul, a port of the vast Indian Sea. It is a very large town, the great meeting-place for all nations living along the coast of India and of Ethiopia.

And there it was that I, Athanasius, the sinful servant of God the creator of heaven and earth, bethought myself of the Christian religion, of the baptism of Christ, of the Lent fastings ordained by the holy fathers, and of the precepts of the Apostles, and I made up my mind to go to Russia. So I embarked in a tava, and settled to pay for my passage to Hormuz two pieces of gold.

We sailed from Dabul three months before the great day of the Mahommedan Lent, and were at sea a whole month, during which I saw nothing. On the following month we descried the mountains of Ethiopia, and then those on board exclaimed:—"*Ollo bervogydir, Ollo kon kar bizim bishimudna nasip bolmyshti*," which in Russian tongue means:—"God our Lord, O God, O God, king of heavens, righteously hast Thou devoted us to destruction."

I remained five days in that country, and, by the mercy of God, met with no evil, but distributed among the natives a quantity of brynetz, pepper, and bread, in order that they might not plunder our ship.

From thence I reached Muscat in twelve days; and there I held the sixth great holiday. Nine days journey brought me to Hormuz, where I stayed twenty days.

[1] Stroef, Kulura.

From Hormuz I proceeded thus:—First to Lar, where I stopped three days; then in twelve days from Lar to Shiraz, stopped there seven days; in fifteen days from Shiraz to *Vergh*, stopped there ten days; in nine days from *Velergh* to Yezd, stopped there eight days; in five days from Yezd to Ispahan, stopped there six days; from Ispahan to Kashan, where I stopped five days; from Kashan I went by Koom, Sava, Sultania, Tabreez, and came to the orda of Assanbek. There I spent ten days, as there was no road further on.

The khan sent against the Turks an army of forty thousand men, who conquered the cities of Sevast (Sivas), burnt down Tokhat, took Amasiah, and plundered many smaller places, carrying the war to the land of Karaman.

Leaving the orda I went to *Arzizin*,[1] and thence to Trebizond, where I arrived on the festival of the Protection of our Lady the holy Virgin Mary. After staying there five days I went on board a ship and agreed to be conveyed to Caffa[2] for one coin of gold, the food to be paid at the end of the voyage.

I was very much annoyed at Trebizond by the pasha Shubasha. He ordered the whole of my lumber to be brought up to his residence on the hill; it was searched, especially for writings, as I was coming from the orda of Assanbek.

However, by the mercy of heaven, I here came to the third sea, the Black Sea, called in the Persian tongue Doria Stimbolskia. The wind was fair during the first five days, but having reached Vonada[3] we encountered a heavy northern gale, which drove us back to Trebizond. We lay for fifteen days at Platana, the weather continuing very bad, and then we twice attempted to sail and again met with a

[1] Perhaps Erzeroum.

[2] The old name of Theodosia, on the south coast of Crimea.

[3] Probably Cape Vona, about one hundred English miles west from Trebizond.

foul wind, that did not permit us to keep the sea: "Ollo ak, Ollo khudo' pervodiger," except that we know no other God. Having crossed the sea, we were carried first to Sukbalykae, and thence to Kzov (Azov), where we lay five days. At last, with God's blessing, I reached Caffa, nine days before the fast of St. Philip.[1]

Ollo pervodiger, through the mercy of God I have crossed three seas, *dighyt khúdo dono Ollo pervodiger donoamin milnarakhmam ragym Ollo-ak ber akshikhúdoilello, akshi khodo karúkholloalik Solom Olloakber akham dúlillo spúkúrkhúdo afatad bismilna girakmam rragym khúvomogulezi lailai sa illiagúia alimúl gaibi vashagaditikhúia rakhmanu ragymú khúbomogú liazi liai laga illiakhúia Almeliku Alakúdosú asalomú almúminú almúgaminú alazirú alchebarúalmúta kanbirú alkhalikú albariúú almúsavirú alkafarú alkakharú albakhadú alriazakú alfataghú alialimú alkabizú albasútú alkafizú alrrafiú almabifu almuzilú alsemiú albasirú aliakamú aliadaúliú alliatúfú.*

[1] The fast or eve of St. Philip is also the eve of Advent, i.e., the 13th of November.

ACCOUNT OF THE JOURNEY OF HIERONIMO DI SANTO STEFANO,

A GENOVESE,

ADDRESSED TO MESSER GIOVAN JACOBO MAINER.

ACCOUNT OF THE JOURNEY OF HIERONIMO DI SANTO STEFANO,

A GENOVESE,

ADDRESSED TO MESSER GIOVAN JACOBO MAINER.

ALTHOUGH it recalls many painful recollections, I will nevertheless, in compliance with your request, give you an account of our disastrous journey. You must know, then, that Messer Hieronimo Adorno and I went together to Cairo, where, having purchased a certain quantity of coral beads and other merchandize, we started for India, and at the end of a fortnight arrived at Cariz, and found a good port called Cane (Keneh). On our road we met with the ruins of many ancient cities, and many admirable buildings constructed in the time of the gentiles, in which several temples are still standing. Afterwards we departed from the abovenamed port of Cane, and travelled by land for several days through those mountains and deserts, wherein Moses and the people of Israel wandered when they were driven out by Pharaoh. At the end of these seven days we arrived at Cosir (Cosseir),[1] a port of the Red Sea, and here embarked on board a ship, the timbers of which were sewn together with cords and the sails made of rush mats. In this ship we sailed for twenty-five days, putting in

[1] The route from Cairo to India thus early described is the same which has been followed up to very recent times.

every evening at very fine but uninhabited ports, and ultimately arrived at an island called Mazua (Massawa), off the right shore of the said sea, distant about a mile from the land, where is the port of the country of Prester John: the lord of this island is a Moor. Here we remained two months and then departed. Sailing through the said sea in the manner described above for twenty-five days more, we saw many boats fishing for pearls, and having examined them we found that they were not of so good quality as the oriental pearls. At the end of the said twenty-five days we arrived at the city of Adem, situate on the left shore of the sea and on the mainland. This city is inhabited by Moors, and a very extensive traffic is carried on there. The lord of this country is so just and good, that I do not think any other infidel potentate can be compared with him. We abode in this city four months, whence we embarked for India in another ship, fastened together with cords, but the sails were made of cotton. We sailed for twenty-five days with a prosperous wind without seeing land, and then we saw several islands, but did not touch at them; and continuing our voyage for ten days more, with a favourable wind, we finally arrived at a great city called Calicut.

We found that pepper and ginger grew here. The pepper trees are similar to the ivy, because they grow round other trees wherever they can attach themselves; their leaves resemble those of the ivy. Their bunches are of the length of half a palm or more, and as slender as a finger: the grain grows very thickly around. The reason why pepper does not grow in our region is, that we have none of the trees to plant. It is not true, as reported amongst us, that the pepper is scorched in order that it may not grow. When it is ripe and gathered in it is green, like ivy; it is left to dry in the sun, and in five or six days it becomes black and wrinkled as we see it. For the propagation of ginger they plant a piece of a small fresh root, about the size of a small nut, which at the end of a month grows large: the leaf resembles that of the wild lily. The lord of the city is an idolater, and so likewise are all the people. They worship an ox, or the sun, and also various idols, which they themselves make. When these people die they are burnt: their customs and usages are various; inasmuch as some kill all kinds of animals excepting oxen and cows: if any one were to kill or wound these, he would be himself immediately slain, because, as I have before said, they are objects of worship. Others, again, never eat flesh or fish, or anything that has had life. Every lady may take to herself seven or eight husbands, according to her inclination. The men never marry any woman who is a virgin; but if one, being a virgin, is betrothed, she is delivered over before the nuptials to some other person for fifteen or twenty days in order that she may be deflowered. In this city there are as many as a thousand houses inhabited by Christians, and the district is called Upper India. We departed hence in another ship, made like the one above described, and after a navigation of twenty-six days we arrived at a large island called Ceylon, in which grow the cinnamon trees, which resemble the laurel even in the leaf. Here grow many precious stones, such as garnets, jacinths, cat's eyes, and other gems, but not of very good quality, for the fine ones grow in the mountains. We remained here only one day. The lord of the said island is an idolater, like one of the before-mentioned, and so likewise are his people. There are many trees here of the sort which bears the nut of India (cocoa-nuts), which also are found in Calicut, and are properly speaking like palm trees.

Departing thence after twelve days, we reached another place called Coromandel, where the red sandal wood tree grows in such abundance, that they build houses of it. The lord of this place is an idolater, like the preceding. There is another custom in practice here, that when a man dies and they prepare to burn him, one of his wives burns herself alive with him; and this is their constant habit. We remained in that place seven months. We departed thence in another ship, made after the fashion of the former, and after twenty days reached a great city called Pegu. This part is called Lower India. Here is a great lord, who possesses more than ten thousand elephants, and every year he breeds five hundred of them. This country is distant fifteen days' journey by land from another, called Ava, in which grow rubies and many other precious stones. Our wish was to go to this place, but at that time the two princes were at war, so that no one was allowed to go from the one place to the other. Thus we were compelled to sell the merchandise which we had in the said city of Pegu, which were of such a sort that only the lord of the city could purchase them. He is an idolator, like the before-mentioned. To him, therefore, we sold them. The price amounted to two thousand ducats, and as we wished to be paid we were compelled, by reason of the troubles and intrigues occasioned by the aforesaid war, to remain there a year and a half, all which time we had daily to solicit at the house of the said lord. While we were thus suffering from cold and from heat, with many fatigues and hardships, Messer Hieronimo Adorno, who was a man of feeble constitution, and greatly reduced by these afflictions combined with an ancient malady which tried him sorely, after fifty-five days' suffering, during which he had neither physician nor medicine, yielded up his spirit to our Lord God. This was at night, on the twenty-seventh day of December, St. John's day, in the year fourteen hundred and ninety-six. Although the sacraments of the church could not be administered to him, as there was no priest among us, nevertheless, such was his patience and contrition, that I am sure, judging from the excellent life which he had always led, that our Lord God will have received his soul into paradise, and to that effect have I prayed and continually do pray. His body was buried in a certain ruined church, frequented by none;

and I declare to you, that for many months I was so grieved and afflicted by his death, that it was a great chance I had not followed him; but afterwards, considering that the grief which had taken such hold of me could bring no remedy, and being consoled by some men of worth, I exerted myself to recover our property. In this I succeeded, but with great trouble and expense, and I set sail in a ship to go to Malacca, and after being on the sea twenty-five days, one morning, in not very favourable weather, we reached a very large island called Sumatra, where grows pepper in considerable quantities, silk, long pepper, benzoin, white sandal wood, and many other articles. As the weather was bad and unsettled, the captain took counsel with the other mariners and with the merchants, and it was resolved to unload our goods in that place. The chief is a Moor, but speaking a different language. In all the other countries where we had been they spoke different languages. As soon as our merchandize was landed this chief raised a quibble, asserting that, as my companion was dead, all the said merchandize came to him, and that he would have it, it being the custom of that country, and of every other place where the chief was a Moor, that when any one dies without sons or brethren the chief takes his property, and this he thought it right to do in my case. He thereupon ordered all my property to be seized, and caused all my person to be searched. There were found upon me rubies of the value of three hundred ducats, which I had bought. These they took, and the chief appropriated them to himself. The remainder of our merchandize they placed in a room and sealed it up until the truth was ascertained, and if there had not been an inventory which I had brought from Cairo, in which were specified all the goods which I had brought with me, and which inventory I brought forward in my defence, everything I had would have been taken away from me. As, however, there was a cadi in that place who was very friendly to me, and who had some knowledge of the Italian language, by the help of God and his assistance I cleared myself, but not without much expense and trouble. The rubies, as I have said, were never recovered, nor many other articles of ornament which I possessed. Whereupon, finding that that was not a desirable place to stay in, I determined to take my departure; and selling all my merchandize, I converted the value into silk and benzoin, and set sail in a ship to return to Cambay; and after being twenty-five days at sea in unfavourable weather, we reached certain islands called the Maldives, which are from seven to eight thousand in number, all desert,[1] small and low, through which the sea for the most part enters, the space from one to another being about a mile and a half; and there were seen in them an infinite number of people, all black and naked, but in good condition and courteous. They hold the faith of the Moors, and have a chief who rules over the whole of them. There are trees growing there which produce the cocoa nuts of large size. The people live on fish, and a little rice, which they import. We were obliged to stay here six months to wait for favourable weather for our departure. When it came, and the ship had got well out at sea on our voyage, my ill fate, not content with the aforesaid disasters which she had inflicted on me, but being resolved in every way to crush me, ordained that after eight days there should come a storm with rain, which lasted continuously for five days, so that the vessel, having no deck, became filled with water to such a degree, that there was no means of bailing it out, and it sunk, and those who could swim were saved and the rest were drowned. It pleased the Lord God that I was able to lay hold of a large plank of wood, on which I

[1] The original word "dishabitate" is thus rendered, as its more literal translation would involve a direct contradiction to the concluding clause of the sentence.

floated at the mercy of the waters from morning till evening, when, as it pleased the divine mercy, three ships which had parted from our company and had been five miles in advance of us, learning our disaster, immediately sent out their boats, which came and took in those men who remained alive, of whom I was one, and we were divided amongst them according to their pleasure, and thus I arrived in one of the said ships at Cambay, the chief of which is a Mahometan, and a great lord.

From this place are procured lac and indigo. Here I found some Moorish merchants of Alexandria and Damascus, by whom I was assisted with money for my expenses. I afterwards made an arrangement with a merchant, a sheriff of Damascus, and remained in his service one month, and then proceeded to Ormuz with some of his goods, in sailing to which place I was at sea sixty days. Having there paid all the dues on his merchandize which I had brought with me, and left them with his agent, I prepared to depart. In this place of Ormuz are found many good pearls and good merchandize. I started from thence in company with some Armenian and Azami merchants by land, and after many days reached the country of the said Azami, where I remained for the space of one month, waiting for the chance of accompanying the caravan. With this I afterwards came to Shiraz, where, on account of the war which was then waging, I stayed three months. Thence I went to Ispahan, and thence to Kazan. Thence to the city of Sultanieh, and finally to Tauris, where I stayed many days, because the roads were not safe on account of the wars. From Tauris I went to Aleppo, and in the middle of our journey, while with the caravan, we were attacked and plundered. Again I was assisted by some merchants of Azami, who were with the same caravan, and was enabled to proceed to Aleppo. Here many merchants came to me, beseeching me to return to Tauris to buy jewels, silks, and crimson stuffs, and made me very large offers to induce me to go; but as the roads were not safe I declined going.

Such are the events which in my disastrous journey befel me for my sins. If they had not happened to me, I might well have contented myself with what I had gained; for in such case I should have had no favour to ask from my equals. But who can contend with fortune? Nevertheless I render infinite thanks to our Lord God, for that He has preserved me, and shown me so great mercy. To His care and keeping I commend you.

Written at Tripoli, in Syria, on the first of September, 1499.

INDEX.

The large Roman figures in this Index refer to the individual documents as they stand in the work: thus, I refers to Abd-er-Razzák; II, to Nicolò de' Conti; III, to Nikitin; IV, to Hieronimo di Santo Stefano.

Abd-er-Razzák, ambassador from Shah Rokh, analysis of his travels, lxvii-lxxiv; sets out on his journey to India, I, 4; arrives at Ormuz, 5; proceeds by sea to Muscat, 7; stays at Kariat, 8; his illness there, 10; sails to Calicut, 13; his description of the city, 14-17; his interview with the sovereign, 18; he sails to Mangalor, 20; journey to Bijanagur, 19-22; his account of that city, 22-30; interview with the king, 31, 39-42; description of the Mahanadi, 35-38; he returns home, 43; meets with a storm at sea, 45; reaches Ormuz, 49

Abscharon, peninsula of, famous for naphtha springs, III, 7

Abu Abdallah Mohammed Ben Edris, surnamed Schafei, account of, I, 14

Adam, tomb of, III, 20

Adam's Peak, a mountain, lvii

Aden, II, 21; IV, 4

Adorno, Hieronimo, accompanies Hieronimo de Santo Stephano, his death, IV, 6

Aladinand, bazaar at, III, 12

Ala-eddin-Ahmed-Schah, king of Kalberga, I, 40

Albenigaras, a mountain producing diamonds, II, 29

Alexander the Great, results of his Indian expedition, iii

Alil-bek, a Kaitak chief, III, 6

Alkhedr, the prophet, anecdote of Moses and, I, 12

Ammianus Marcellinus, Indians noticed by, ix

Andaman Isles, II, 8

Animals of India, III, 13; of Ethiopia, II, 37-39

Annius Plocamus, stated by Pliny to have visited the island of Taprobana, II, 4

Antonio de Lisboa, his journey to Jerusalem, lxxxii

Ants, a Siamese delicacy, II, 13

Arabia, description of demons in, II, 4

Arabs: their advance into India, xiii; their trade with India, xiv-xvi

Aracan, II, 10

Army of the Sultan of Beder, III, 14, 26

Arotani, a river in Ceylon, strange fish in, II, 33

Assanbek, a Tartar ambassador, II, 4, 6

Astrakhan, III, 5

Atash Kudda, a Gheber temple, III, 7

Ava, account of, II, 11; IV, 6

Bachali, Indian priests, II, 24, 25

Bagdad, description of, II, 5

Bairam, ceremonies of the, III, 23

Baku, naphtha springs at, III, 7

Bamboos, magnitude of, II, 10

Bananas, II, 10

Baths, II, 29

Batman, a measure of weight, IV, 8

Beder, III, 11; trade of, 12; army of the Sultan, 14, 26; magnitude of the Court, 23; want of fresh vegetables at, 24

Belour, magnificent temple at, I, 20

Bells, unknown in part of India, II, 27

Bengal, kingdom of, invaded by the Sultan of Djounah-pour, I, 15

Benjamin of Tudela: his journey, xlv; his account of India, xlvi-l

Betel leaf, properties of the, I, 32

Bijanagur, city of: description of, I, 6, 23; its bazaars, 24; rose merchants, *ib.*; coins, 26; elephants, 27; women, 29; interview with the king of, 31; attempted murder of

the king by his brother, 33; description of the Mahanadi festival at, 35; splendour of the royal palace, 38; war between the kings of Bijanagur, and of Kalberga, 40; capture of the city, III, 29
Birds: description of gigantic birds by Sindbad and others, xxxvi-xl
Birds of Paradise, lxv; II, 17
Bizenegalia, city of: description of, II, 6; idols at, 28
Boa constrictor, description of the, II, 39
Book of Fates, consulted by Abd-er-Razzák, I, 45
Boris, a Russian saint, III, 4
Brahmins, account of the, II, 8, 25; incantations used by the, 26
Buddha, account of the religion of, III, 16, 18
Budhkhana, description of the temples and religious rites at, III, 16
Bulls of Buddha, III, 18
Bussorah, II, 5
Buzan, the river, III, 5

Cairo, route to India from, described by H. de Santo Stefano, IV, 3
Calicut, description of, I, 13; III, 30; religion and trade at, 14; the inhabitants of, 17; II, 20
Cambaleschia, *see* Pekin
Cambay, II, 20; III, 19; IV, 9
Camphor, Sindbad's account of, xxxii
Cannibalism, II, 8, 9
Cape of Good Hope, discovery of the, lxxxix
Caste, III, 17
Cathay, account of the province of, II, 14; the cities of Cambaleschia and Nemptai, 15
Ceylon, discovery of, iv; account of, II, 7, 8; IV, 5; tomb of Adam at, III, 20, 21
Chaoul, a seaport, III, 8
Chedad-ben-Ad, terrestrial paradise formed by, I, 21
Cheen, habits of people of, III, 29
China, route to India from, xx
Chinese houses like those of Italy, II, 15
Christians in India: the Vizier of Bijanagur a Christian, I, 41; the Nestorians, II, 7, 23, 33; they send to Rome, 34: Christians in Socotra, 20; in Ethiopia, 34
Cinnamon tree, description of, II, 7; IV, 5
Cities of India, magnitude of, II, 34
Civet, II, 38
Climate of India, III, 24
Cock fighting, fondness of the Javanese for, II, 16
Conspiracy at Bidjanagur, I, 33
Conti, Nicolò de': analysis of his travels, lx-lxvii; account of, by Poggio Bracciolini, II, 3; his departure from Damascas with a caravan, 4; reaches the Euphrates and sails down the river to the Persian Gulf, 5; resides at Calacabia and sails to Cambay, *ib.*; and to Helly, 6; journeys to Bizenegalia, *ib.*; his description of Ceylon, 7; Sumatra, 8; remains there a year and then sails to Tenassarim, 9; voyage up the Ganges, 10; returns and visits Aracan and Ava, 11; description of Cathay, 14; of Pegu and Java, 15; of Malabar, 17; Calicut and Cambay, 20; Aden, 21; sails to Ethiopia and returns to Venice by Egypt, 21; his account of India, 21-33
Coromandel, account of, IV, 5
Cosseir, account of the vessels of, IV, 3
Covilham, Pedro, account of, by F. Alvarez, lxxxii; his journey to the East, lxxxiv-lxxxvii; his claim to the discovery of the Cape of Good Hope, lxxxix
Cows, respect paid to, I, 19

Dabul, III, 20, 30
Daiang, Vizier of Bijanagur, I, 35; his expedition to Kalberga, 40
Dancing girls, I, 37
Dâralaman, a name given to Ormuz, I, 7
Dead, burial of, II, 23; mourning for, 25
Debtors sold as slaves, II, 31
Demons seen in the Arabian Desert, II, 4
Derbend, III, 6, 7
Diamonds, Sindbad's account of the valley of, xl; a singular method of procuring them, II, 30; their value in India, III, 21
Diaz, Bartholomew, rounds the Cape of Good Hope, lxxxii

Diou-rai, king of Bijanagur, I, 19; interview of Abd-er-Razzák with, 31; attempt to assassinate, 33; war with Kalberga, 40; his treatment of Abd-er-Razzák, 41, 42
Djafa-Sadek, the Book of Fates composed by, I, 45
Djoghis, Hindú ascetics, I, 17
Djounah-pour, Ibrahim, king of, invades Bengal, I, 15
Dreams, reflections of Abd-er-Razzák on, I, 18
Dress of Indians, III, 9, 10, 18
Duties levied in India, III, 11, 19

Egypt, a description of, by certain Ethiopians, II, 35
Elephants, an anecdote about, I, 28; mode of capturing, 27; II, 12; feats performed by, I, 37; used in Siam, II, 11; in Ethiopia, 37; used in battle, III, 12, 23
Embalming of corpses, xlviii
Epiphanius, archbishop of Salamis, his account of the mode of finding jacinths in Scythia, xlii
Ethiopia, account of, II, 35-39
Euphrates, Conti's voyage down the, II, 5
Expense of living in India, III, 25

Fan palm, size of the leaves, II, 7, 13
Festivals, account of, in India, I, 35; II, 28; III, 13
Fever, cured by the smoke of Ibex horns, II, 38
Fish, fever produced by the touch of, II, 33
Flying cats and serpents, II, 18
Foreigners, feeling of Indians towards, III, 21
Funeral rite, II, 23; III, 17

Ganges, Conti's voyage up the, II, 10
Genoese, their Indian commerce, xvii
Geomantia, an art practised by the Brahmins, II, 26
Georgia, III, 25
Ghebers, a resort of, at Baku, III, 7
Ginger plant, account of, II, 6; IV, 4
Giraffe, description of the, II, 38
Gleb, a Russian saint, III, 4
Gookook, a wonderful bird, III, 13
Guzrat, indigo trade at, III, 21

Hair, modes of wearing, II, 23
Heat of the weather, I, 9, 40; III, 24
Herat compared with Bijanagur, i, 23
Herodotus, mention of India by, i, ii
Hindoo viziers of India, III, 28
Hiouen-thsang, a Chinese traveller, his journey to India, xix, xxiii
Hippalus, route to India discovered by, vi
Hippopotamus, not found in Sumatra, xxxii
Hole, R., his remarks on Sindbad's voyages, xxxvi
Hormuz, *see* Ormuz
Horses, food of, III, 10
Hossein, death of, III, 7

Ibex horns, fevers cured by the smoke of, II, 38
Ibn Batuta, his travels in India, liv-lix; III, 12
Ibrahim, Sultan of Djounah-pour, invades Bengal, I, 15
Icepe, monsters called, II, 19
Idols, III, 16; immolation to, II, 27
Incantations of the Brahmins, II, 26
India: earliest information regarding India, ii; the expedition of Alexander, iii; the narrative of Megasthenes, iii, iv; communication with Egypt under the Ptolemies, v; Pliny's account of the route to India, vi; Ptolemy's description of, viii; Persian commerce with, x; the description of, by Cosmas, xii; advance of the Mussulmans into, xiii-xvi; the Genoese and Venetian traders, xvii. Voyages to India: the route of Hiouen-thsang from China, xix-xxiii; voyage of Soliman, a Muhammedan merchant, to India, xxiii-xxx; the narrative of *Sindbad the Sailor*, xxx-xlv; of Benjamin of Tudela, xlvi-l; of Marco Polo, l-liii; of Ibn Batuta, liv-lix; of Nicolò de' Conti, lx-lxvii; of Abd-er-Razzák, lxvii-lxxiv; of A. Nikitin, lxxvii-lxxx; of H. de Santo Stefano, lxxx; of Pedro Covilham, lxxxiv-lxxxvii. Journey of Abd-er-Razzák, ambassador from Shah Rokh to India, i, 4-13; description of Calicut, 13; appearance of the people, 17; trade, 14, 19; account of temples near

Mangalor, 20; and at Belour, 21; description of the city of Bijanagur, 22-26; the Mahanadi festival, 35. Early travellers to India, II, 4; voyage of Nicolò de' Conti to India from Bagdad, 5; description of various cities in, 6; of Ceylon, 7; Sumatra, 8; account of his voyage up the Ganges, 10; description of Ava, 11; fruits and animals, 13; description of Java, 15; of Calicut and Cambay, 20; general account of India, 21; manners and customs of the people, 22-32; Nestorian Christians in India, 7, 33; Nikitin's journey from Russia to India, III, 3-8; he reaches Chaoul, 8; and winters at Jooneer, 9; account of the people and their religion, 9-10; account of Beder, 11-15; of strange animals in India, 12; description of the temples at Perwuttum and the Hindoo religion, 16-17; distances between the Indian cities, 19; Ormuz, *ib.*; Dabul, Calicut, and Ceylon, 20; Shabat and its diamond mines, 21; of the climate in India, 24; account of the Sultan of Beder, 24, 26, 28; description of Bijanagur, 29; Kooroola, 30; journey of H. di Santo de Stefano from Cairo to India, IV, 3; his account of Massawa, Aden, and Calicut, 4; of Ceylon and Coromandel, 5; of Pegu and Ava, 6; of Sumatra, 7; the Maldive Isles, 8; his route home by Persia, 9-10

India, inhabitants of: Abd-er-Razzák's account of the natives of Calicut, I, 17; of Bijanagur, 24; their writings, 25; the Mahanadi festival, I, 35; dancing girls, 36; Conti's account of Suttee, II, 6; of the Brahmins of Ceylon, 8; of the natives of Sumatra, 8, 9; Cannibalism, 9; customs of Ava, 11; of Siam, 13; serpents and ants esteemed a delicacy, *ib.*; cruelty of the Javanese, 16; their fondness for cock fighting, *ib.*; manners and customs at Calicut, 20: Indian merchants, 21; wine unknown to the Indians, 22; manners and dress of the natives of Central India, *ib.*; funeral rites, 23; Suttee, 24; mourning for the dead, 25; priests, Bachali and Brahmins, *ib.*; navigation and ship building among the Indians, 26; religious worship 27; human sacrifices to idols, 28; weddings, 29; modes of obtaining precious stones, 30; divisions of time, *ib.*; money, *ib.*; weapons, 31; legal proceedings, *ib.*; magnitude of Indian armies, 32; Nestorian Christians in North India, 33; Nikitin's account of the dress of the people about Bombay, III, 9; a prince carried by men, *ib.*; inns, 10; costumes, *ib.*; religion of the inhabitants of India, 11; trade at Beder, 12; the nobles and the people, 14; night watchmen, 15; Buddhists religion, 16; temples of Perwuttum, 16; religious ordinances, 17-18; coins, 20; customs of the people of Pegu, 21, price of diamonds, *ib.*; inhabitants of Shabat, *ib.*; splendour of the Sultan's court at Beder, 24; camp-followers, 27; the Indian army, 28; treatment of prisoners, 29; Hieronimo de Santo Stefano's account of the inhabitants of Calicut, IV, 5; of Coromandel, *ib.*; of the Maldive Isles, 8

Indigo, III, 8, 19

Inns in India, III, 10

Irawaddy, Conti's voyage up the, II, 11

Irem, an earthly paradise, I, 21

Ivan, Grand Duke of Russia, III, 3, 5

Jacinths, strange mode of finding in Scythia, xlii

Jack tree, II, 18

Java, account of, II, 15; cruelty of the inhabitants, 16; a wonderful tree in, 32

Jews, natives of Shabat said to be, III, 21

John II, king of Portugal, his missions to the East, lxxxii

Jugglers, I, 37

Julien, Stanislas, his Pelerins Bouddhistes, xix

Jurufgan, great heat at, I, 49

Kaitaks, a Tartar tribe, III, 6

Kalahat, city of, I, 10

Kalberga, account of the city of, I, 6; war with Bijanagur, 40

Kalila and Dimna, a Persian work, I, 23
Kariat, great heat at, I, 8-9
Kazan, III, 5
Kêlâ, probably Keydah, Sindbad's account of, xxxiii
Kerman, a ruined city in the desert of, I, 4, 5
Khotbah, a Mahometan sermon, I, 15
Koliasin, convent of the Holy Trinity at, III, 4

Langlès, M., remarks on his translation of Abd-er-Razzák's travels, lxix
Legal proceedings in India, II, 31
Longevity of Brahmins, II, 25; of Ethiopians, 36

Madagascar, gigantic birds of, xxxix
Mahanadi, a Hindoo festival, description of, I, 35
Maha-raja, origin of the title, xxvii
Mahommedan Sultan of India, III, 28
Mahommedan religion in India, III, 11
Maldive Islands, account of the, IV, 8
Mangalor, magnificent temple near, I, 20
Mango tree, II, 19
Megasthenes, account of India by, iii
Melikh-Tuchar, his army, III, 26, 27
Money at Bijanagur, I, 26; coins of India, II, 30
Monkeys, a kingdom of, III, 13; travellers attacked by, 22
Moses, anecdote of Alkheda and, I, 12
Mountains of the Moon, II, 39
Mud volcanoes, III, 7
Muscat, I, 49
Musk deer, III, 22

Nacous, probably Nicobar, Sindbad's voyage to, xxxiii
Naphtha springs at Baku, III, 7
Navigation, Indian knowledge of, II, 26
Nauruz, Mahometan New Year's day, I, 14
Nestorians, account of the, II, 23; in Malabar, II, 7; in Socotra, 20; in North India, 33
Nikitin, Athanasius, account of the manuscript of his travels, lxxiv; analysis of them, lxxvii-lxxx; he starts from Twer, III, 3; stays at Nijni-Novgorod, 4; descends the Volga, 5; to Derbend, 6; thence to Bokhara, 7; and to Ormuz, 8; thence to Muscat, Gujrat and Cambay, *ib.*; his description of Chaoul, 9; he winters at Jooneer, 10; attempt to make him a Mahommedan, 11; he proceeds to Beder, 12; spends the winter there, 15; his description of Perwuttum, 16; religious remarks by, 18, 23; places where he kept Easter Days, 22; he commences his homeward journey from Beder, 28; voyage from Dabul to Ormuz, 30; journey to Trebizond, 31; arrives at Caffa, 32
Nile, Ethiopian account of, II, 35
Nimek-pezir, a Christian, Vizier of Bijanagur: his treatment of Abd-er-Razzák, I, 41

Oaths, mode of administering, II, 31
Old Man of the Sea, Sindbad's account of the, xxxiv
Omar Saad, curse brought upon Rhey by, III, 7
Onesicritus, Ceylon first described by, iv
Onore, length of the voyage to Ormuz from, I, 49
Orda, the name given to the seats of the Tartar rulers of Russia, III, 5
Ordeal, trial by, II, 31
Ormuz, city of, account of, I, 5; trade of, 6; character of the inhabitants of, 7; length of the voyage from Onore to, I, 49; duties levied at, III, 19; heat at, III, 8
Ostrich, described, II, 39

Paintings on the temple of Belour, I, 21
Palace at Beder, description of, III, 14
Panconia, description of the city of, II, 15
Parrots, II, 17; xl
Payva, A. de, his journey to the East with Covilham, lxxxii
Pearl fishery in the Red Sea, IV, 4
Peas, horses fed on, III, 10
Pegu, III, 20; IV, 6
Pekin, account of the city of, II, 14
Pepper trees, description of, xxxiii; IV, 4
Persian Gulf, storm in the, I, 46
Persians: their aversion to the sea,

iv; success of their commerce with India, x
Perwuttum, account of, III, 16
Pestilence unknown among the Indians, II, 31
Phœnix, account of the, II, 32
Pictures, I, 36
Pirates in the India Seas, III, 11
Pliny's account of the route to India, vi; of Taprobana, II, 4
Polo, Marco, sketch of his travels in India, l-liii; his account of the Rukh, xxxviii
Population of India, II, 32
Porcelain, III, 21
Posting regulations in Russia, III, 4
Prayers, Russian custom of prefacing a journey by, III, 3; Hindoo, 17
Precious stones, mode of procuring, II, 30
Prester John, IV, 4
Ptolemies, communication between India and Egypt under the, iv
Ptolemy, the geographer, his account of India, viii

Rachoor, a diamond hill at, III, 21
Red Sea, pearl fishery in, IV, 4
Reinaud, M., his edition of Soliman's voyage to India, xxiii-xxx
Religion of the Indians, I, 19; II, 27; III, 11, 15, 16; IV, 5; temples, I, 20; religious service, 22; festivals, II, 28
Rhey, account of the ruins of, III, 7
Rhinoceros, description of the, II, 13
Riha, peninsula of, mentioned by Sindbad, xxxii
Roc, *see* Rukh
Roman trade with India, viii
Roses, partiality of the people at Bidjanagur for, I, 24
Route to India described by Pliny, vi; from Cairo, described by H. di Santo Stefano, IV, 3
Rukh, a gigantic bird, remarks on Sindbad's description of the, xxxvi; Marco Polo's account of it, xxxviii; mentioned by Ibn Batuta, lviii
Rupee, value of the, III, 20
Russia, religious practices of travellers in, III, 3; posting regulations, 4

Santo Stefano (H. di), analysis of his travels, lxxx; his route from Cairo to India, IV, 3; his account of Calicut, 4; goes to Ceylon and Coromandel, 5; Pegu and Ava, 6; death of his companion, *ib.*; sails to Sumatra, 7; is detained at the Maldive Islands, 8; shipwrecked, *ib.*; reaches Cambay and returns home by Ormuz, Ispahan, and Aleppo, 9, 10
Sameri, title of the sovereign of Calicut, I, 17; interview of Abd-er-Razzák with the, 18
Santy, a sort of aloe-wood, xxxiv
Sarai, a ruined city on the Volga, III, 5
Schafei, Mussulman sect of, I, 14
Scythed elephants, III, 12
Selaheth, probably Sumatra, described by Sindbad, xxxii
Semerida, the Indian Phœnix, II, 32
Sensitive plant, description of the, II, 29
Sepulchres, II, 23
Serendib, or Ceylon, Sindbad's voyage to, xxxv
Serpents, Sindbad's descriptions of, xl; the Siamese eat them, II, 3; their fondness for children, II, 18; flying serpents, *ib.*; serpents fifty cubits long, II, 39
Shabat, produce of, III, 20
Shikhuladin, a saint, III, 12
Ships, Indian, II, 27; IV, 3
Shirvanshah, present of falcons made by the Grand Duke of Russia to, III, 4
Siam, province of, II, 11
Silkworms introduced into Europe, xii
Sindbad the Sailor: Walckenaer's opinion as to the authenticity of Sindbad's voyages, xxx; Sindbad's first voyage, xxxi; second and third voyages, xxxii; fourth voyage, xxxiii; fifth voyage, and his account of the Old Man of the Sea, xxxiv; his sixth and seventh voyages, xxxv; observations on his stories by R. Hole, xxxvi; his account of the roc, xxxvii-xl; of the valley of diamonds, xl-xliii; of a huge tortoise, xliii-xlv
Slavery, II, 31
Smoke of Ibex horns a cure for fever, II, 38
Snakes at Beder, III, 15
Socotra, island of, II, 20

Soliman, a Muhammedan merchant, his voyage to India, xxiii-xxx
Solomon, treasure obtained from India by, ii
Sour, a place near Kalahat, I, 10
Storm in the Persian Gulf, I, 46
St. Philip, fast of, III, 32
St. Thomas, burial place of, II, 7
Suicide by fire, xlix
Sumatra, probably described in Sindbad's voyages, xxxii; account of, II, 4, 8; produce of, IV, 7
Suttee, II, 6, 24; IV, 5, 6

Taprobana, *see* Sumatra
Teak trees, xxvi
Temples, II, 27; magnificence of at Mangalor and Belour, I, 20; at Perwuttum, III, 16
Tenka, a coin, III, 20
Throne of gold at Bijanagur, I, 38
Tides in the Persian Gulf, II, 5
Time, divisions of in India, II, 30
Tortoises, account of gigantic, xliii
Tortoise-shell, churches made of, II, 33
Trade, account of at Ormuz, I, 6: at Calicut, I, 14; at Beder, III, 12
Trebizond, III, 31

Venetian trade with India, xvii
Vines, want of, in India, II, 15
Volga, cities on the, III, 5

Walckenaer, Baron, his opinion as to voyages of Sindbad, xxx
Watchmen in India, III, 15
Weapons used by Indians, II, 31
Weddings, celebration of, II, 29
Wild cats, attacks on travellers by, III, 22
Winter, account of, at Jooneer, III, 10
Women of India, II, 20; III, 10, 12, 21; IV, 5; courtezans at Bijanagur, I, 29; the king's harem, 32; dancing girls, 37; polygamy, I, 17; an island inhabited by, II, 20; modes of wearing their hair, 23; Suttee, II, 6, 24; IV, 6
Writing, Indian modes of, I, 25; II, 31

THE

HAKLUYT SOCIETY.

President.

SIR RODERICK IMPEY MURCHISON, G.C.St.S. F.R.S., D.C.L.
Mem. Imp. Acad. Sc. St. Petersburg, Corr. Mem. Inst. Fr., &c. &c.

Vice-Presidents.

THE MARQUIS OF LANSDOWNE.
REAR-ADMIRAL C. R. DRINKWATER BETHUNE, C.B.

Council.

REAR-ADML. SIR F. BEAUFORT, K.C.B., F.R.S.
RT. HON. LORD BROUGHTON.
JOHN BRUCE, ESQ., F.S.A.
THE LORD ALFRED SPENCER CHURCHILL.
THE RIGHT REV. THE LORD BISHOP OF ST. DAVID'S.
CHAS. WENTWORTH DILKE, ESQ.
RT. HON. SIR DAVID DUNDAS.
SIR HENRY ELLIS, K.H., F.R.S.
LIEUT.-GEN. CHARLES RICHARD FOX.
R. W. GREY, ESQ., M.P.
JOHN WINTER JONES, ESQ., F.S.A.
HIS EXCELLENCY THE COUNT DE LAVRADIO.
P. LEVESQUE, ESQ., F.S.A.
RT. HON. ROBERT LOWE, M.P.
SIR ERSKINE PERRY, M.P.
SIR HENRY RAWLINSON, K.C.B.
THE REV. W. WHEWELL, D.D.

Honorary Secretary.—R. H. MAJOR, ESQ., F.S.A.

Bankers.—MESSRS. RANSOM, BOUVERIE, AND CO., 1, PALL MALL EAST.

THE HAKLUYT SOCIETY, which is established for the purpose of printing rare or unpublished Voyages and Travels, aims at opening by this means an easier access to the sources of a branch of knowledge, which yields to none in importance, and is superior to most in agreeable variety. The narratives of travellers and navigators make us acquainted with the earth, its inhabitants and productions; they exhibit the growth of intercourse among mankind, with its effects on civilization, and, while instructing, they at the same time awaken attention, by recounting the toils and adventures of those who first explored unknown and distant regions.

The advantage of an Association of this kind, consists not merely in its system of literary co-operation, but also in its economy. The acquirements, taste, and discrimination of a number of individuals, who feel an interest in the same pursuit, are thus brought to act in voluntary combination, and the ordinary charges of publication are also avoided, so that the volumes produced are distributed among the Members (who can alone obtain them) at little more than the cost of printing and paper. The Society expends the whole of its funds in the preparation of works for the Members; and since the cost of each copy varies inversely as the whole number of copies printed, it is obvious that the Members are gainers individually by the prosperity of the Society, and the consequent vigour of its operations.

New Members have, at present, *the privilege of purchasing the complete set of the publications of the Society for previous years for six guineas, but have not the power of selecting any particular volume.*

The Members are requested to bear in mind that the power of the Council to make advantageous arrangements, will depend, in a great

1,11,57.

measure, on the prompt payment of the subscriptions, which are payable in advance on the 1st of January, and are received by the Secretary, RICHARD HENRY MAJOR, Esq., British Museum; and by MR. RICHARDS, 37, Great Queen Street, Lincoln's Inn Fields, who is the Society's agent for the delivery of its volumes. Post Office Orders should be drawn on the *Charing Cross Post Office*.

It is especially requested, that all subscribers who shall not have received their volumes within a reasonable period after the payment of their subscription, will notify the same to the Secretary.

ALREADY PUBLISHED.

The Observations of Sir Richard Hawkins, Knt.

In his Voyage into the South Sea in 1593. Reprinted from the edition of 1622, and edited by Capt. C. R. DRINKWATER BETHUNE, R.N., C.B.

Select Letters of Columbus.

With Original Documents relating to the DISCOVERY of the NEW WORLD. Translated and Edited by R. H. MAJOR, Esq., of the British Museum.

The Discoverie of the Empire of Guiana,

By SIR WALTER RALEGH, KNT. Edited, with Copious Explanatory Notes, and a Biographical Memoir, by SIR ROBERT H. SCHOMBURGK, Phil. D., etc.

Sir Francis Drake his Voyage, 1595,

By THOMAS MAYNARDE, together with the Spanish Account of Drake's Attack on Puerto Rico, edited from the Original MSS., by W. D. COOLEY, Esq.

Narratives of Early Voyages

Undertaken for the Discovery of a Passage to CATHAIA and INDIA, by the Northwest, with Selections from the Records of the worshipful Fellowship of the Merchants of London, trading into the East Indies; and from MSS. in the Library of the British Museum, now first published, by THOMAS RUNDALL, Esq.

The Historie of Travaile into Virginia Britannia,

Expressing the Cosmographie and Commodities of the Country, together with the Manners and Customs of the people, gathered and observed as well by those who went first thither as collected by William Strachey, Gent., the first Secretary of the Colony; now first Edited from the original manuscript in the British Museum, by R. H. MAJOR, Esq., of the British Museum.

Divers Voyages touching the Discovery of America,

And the Islands adjacent, collected and published by RICHARD HAKLUYT, Prebendary of Bristol, in the year 1582. Edited, with Notes and an Introduction, by JOHN WINTER JONES, Esq., of the British Museum.

A Collection of Documents on Japan,

With a Commentary, by THOMAS RUNDALL, Esq.

The Discovery and Conquest of Florida,

By DON FERDINANDO DE SOTO. Translated out of Portuguese, by Richard Hakluyt; and Edited with Notes and an Introduction, by W. B. RYE, Esq., of the British Museum.

Notes upon Russia,

Being a Translation from the Earliest Account of that Country, entitled RERUM MOSCOVITICARUM COMMENTARII, by the Baron Sigismund von Herberstein, Ambassador from the Court of Germany to the Grand Prince Vasiley Ivanovich, in the years 1517 and 1526. Two Volumes. Translated, and Edited with Notes and an Introduction, by R. H. MAJOR, Esq., of the British Museum.

The Geography of Hudson's Bay.

Being the Remarks of CAPTAIN W. COATS, in many Voyages to that locality, between the years 1727 and 1751. With an Appendix, containing Extracts from the Log of CAPT. MIDDLETON on his Voyage for the discovery of the North-west Passage, in H.M.S. "Furnace", in 1741-2. Edited by JOHN BARROW, Esq., F.R.S., F.S.A.

Three Voyages by the North-east,

Towards Cathay and China, undertaken by the Dutch in the years 1594, 1595, and 1596, with their Discovery of Spitzbergen, their residence of ten months in Novaya Zemlya, and their safe return in two open boats. By GERRIT DE VEER. Edited by C. T. BEKE, Esq., Ph.D., F.S.A.

The History of the Great and Mighty Kingdom of China and the Situation Thereof.

Compiled by the Padre JUAN GONZALEZ DE MENDOZA. And now Reprinted from the Early Translation of R. PARKE. Edited by SIR GEORGE T. STAUNTON, BART. With an Introduction by R. H. MAJOR, Esq. 2 vols.

The History of the Tartar Conquerors who Subdued China.

From the French of the Père D'Orleans, 1688. Translated and Edited by the EARL OF ELLESMERE. With an Introduction by R. H. MAJOR, Esq.

The World Encompassed by Sir Francis Drake,

Being his next Voyage to that to Nombre de Dios. Collated with an unpublished Manuscript of FRANCIS FLETCHER, Chaplain to the Expedition. With Appendices illustrative of the same Voyage, and Introduction, by W. S. W. VAUX, Esq., M.A.

A Collection of Early Documents on Spitzbergen and Greenland,

Consisting of: a translation from the German of F. Marten's important work on Spitzbergen, now very rare; a translation from Isaac de la Peyrère's Relation de Groenland, and a rare piece entitled "God's Power and Providence showed in the miraculous preservation and deliverance of eight Englishmen, left by mischance in Greenland, anno 1630, nine mouethe and twelve days, faithfully reported by Edward Pelham." Edited, with Notes, by ADAM WHITE, Esq., of the British Museum.

The Voyage of Sir Henry Middleton to Bantam and the Maluco Islands.

From the rare Edition of 1606. Edited by BOLTON CORNEY, Esq.

Russia at the close of the Sixteenth Century.

Comprising "The Russe Commonwealth" by Dr. GILES FLETCHER, and SIR JEROME HORSEY'S Travels, now first printed entire from his manuscript in the British Museum. Edited by E. A. BOND, Esq., of the British Museum.

The Travels of Girolamo Benzoni, in America, in 1542-56.

Translated and edited by ADMIRAL W. H. SMYTH, F.R.S., F.S.A.

Other Works in Progress.

INDIA IN THE FIFTEENTH CENTURY. A collection of documents, comprising, "The Travels in India of the Venetians NICOLO DE' CONTI and HIERONIMO DI SAN STEFANO." Translated from the Latin and Italian by J. WINTER JONES, Esq., of the British Museum. "The Travels of ABD-ER-RAZAK, ambassador from Shah-Rokh in the years 1441-2-3. And, "The Travels of the Russian traveller ANASTASIUS NIKITIN." Translated by Count WIELHORSKY, late Secretary to the Russian Legation at the Court of St. James's, from a Russian MS. procured from a monastery near Moscow. The work to be edited by R. H. MAJOR, Esq., of the British Museum, F.S.A.

AUSTRALIA PRÆDICTA; a Collection of Documents shewing the Early Discoveries of Australia to the time of CAPTAIN COOK. Edited by R. H. MAJOR, Esq., of the British Museum, F.S.A.

The FIFTH Letter of HERNANDO CORTES, being that describing his Voyage to Honduras in 1525-6. Now first Translated and to be Edited by W. R. STEET, Esq.

The Voyage of VASCO DE GAMA round the Cape of Good Hope in 1497, now first Translated from a cotemporaneous manuscript, accompanied by other documents forming a monograph on the life of DE GAMA. To be translated and edited by RICHARD GARNETT, Esq., of the British Museum.

The first Voyage of the Dutch to the East Indies. To be translated from various documents, and edited by GEORGE ASHER, Esq., LL.D.

A Collection of Documents forming a monograph of the Voyages of HENRY HUDSON. To be edited by N. E. S. A. HAMILTON, Esq., of the British Museum, with an Introduction by GEORGE ASHER, Esq., LL.D.

Works suggested to the Council for Publication.

FRESCOBALDI.—The Travels of Frescobaldi in Egypt and Syria, in 138 . Translated from the Italian text as edited by Manzi.

BETHENCOURT.—A History of the Discovery and Conquest of the Canary Islands, made by Jean de Béthencourt, in 1402-25. From the French Narrative of his Chaplains, Pierre Boutier and Jean le Verrier.

CA DA MOSTO.—The Voyages of Ca da Mosto along the Western Coast of Africa in 1454. Translated from the Italian text of 1507.

VIRGINIA.—Virginia in the years 1484-1600; comprising the Narratives of Arthur Barlowe, Ralf Lane, Thomas Harriott, etc.

CADIZ.—A Brief and True Report of the Honourable Voyage to Cadiz, 1596. From the suppressed edition of 1598, with additions.

COLONIZATION.—Pamphlets on Colonization. By Sir William Alexander (afterwards Earl of Sterline), and James Hagthorpe.

GALVANO.—Tratado dos descobrimentos antigos e modernos feitos até a era de 1550, composto pelo famoso Antonio Galvaõ. Lisboa, 1731.

Laws of the Hakluyt Society.

I. The object of this Society shall be to print, for distribution among its members, rare and valuable Voyages, Travels, Naval Expeditions, and other geographical records, from an early period to the beginning of the eighteenth century.

II. The Annual Subscription shall be One Guinea, payable in advance on the 1st January.

III. Each member of the Society, having paid his subscription, shall be entitled to a copy of every work produced by the Society, and to vote at the general meetings within the period subscribed for; and if he do not signify, before the close of the year, his wish to resign, he shall be considered as a member for the succeeding year.

IV. The management of the Society's affairs shall be vested in a Council consisting of twenty-one members, namely, a President, two Vice-Presidents, a Secretary, and seventeen ordinary members, to be elected annually; but vacancies occurring between the general meetings shall be filled up by the Council.

V. A General Meeting of the Subscribers shall be held annually, on the first Thursday in March. The Secretary's Report on the condition and proceedings of the Society shall be then read, and, along with the Auditor's Report, be submitted for approval, and finally, the Meeting shall proceed to elect the Council for the ensuing year.

VI. At each Annual Election, six of the old Council shall retire; and a list of the proposed new Council shall be printed for the subscribers previous to the general meeting

VII. The Council shall meet ordinarily on the 3rd Tuesday in every month, excepting August, September, and October, for the despatch of business, three forming a quorum, and the Chairman having a casting vote.

VIII. Gentlemen preparing and editing works for the Society, shall receive twenty-five copies of such works respectively.

IX. The number of copies printed of the Society's productions shall not exceed the estimated number of Subscribers; so that after the second year, when the Society may be supposed to have reached its full growth, there shall be no extra copies.

X. The Society shall appoint Local Secretaries throughout the kingdom, empowered to enrol members, transmit subscriptions, and otherwise forward the Society's interests; and it shall make such arrangements with its correspondents in the chief provincial towns, as will insure to subscribers residing in the country the regular delivery of their volumes at moderate charges.

Rules for the Delivery of the Society's Volumes.

I. The Society's productions will be delivered without any charge, within three miles of the General Post Office.

II. They will be forwarded to any place beyond that limit, the Society paying the cost of booking, but not of carriage; nor will it be answerable in this case for any loss or damage.

III. They will be delivered by the Society's agent, Mr. Thomas Richards, 37, Great Queen Street, Lincoln's Inn Fields, to persons having written authority of subscribers to receive them.

IV. They will be sent to the Society's correspondents or agents in the principal towns throughout the kingdom; and care shall be taken that the charge for carriage be as moderate as possible.

LIST OF MEMBERS

OF

THE HAKLUYT SOCIETY.

Admiralty (The), 2 *copies*
Ainslie, Philip Barrington, Esq., St. Colme
Allen, Mr. E., 12, Tavistock-row, Covent-garden
Allport, Franklin, Esq., 156, Leadenhall-st.
Amsterdam, de Bibliothek van het Collegie Zeemanshoop.
Antiquaries, the Society of
Arlt, Mr., Moscow
Army and Navy Club, 13, St. James's-square.
Arrowsmith, John, Esq., 10, Soho-square
Ashton, J. Y., Esq., Liverpool
Asher, A., Berlin
Athenæum Club, The, Pall Mall
Athenæum Library, Boston, U.S.
Atkinson, F. R., Esq., Oak House, Pendleton, Manchester

Baillie, David, Esq., 14, Belgrave-square
Bank of England Library and Literary Association
Baring, Hon. Francis, M.P., 16, St. James's-square
Barrow, J., Esq., F.R.S. F.S.A., 7, New-st., Spring-gardens
Batho, J. A., Esq., 49, Upper Charlotte-street, Fitzroy-square
Beaufort, Rear-Admiral Sir Francis, K.C.B., F.R.S., 11, Gloucester-place, Portman-square
Becher, Captain, R.N.
Beck, Dr., New York State Library, Albany
Beke, Charles T., Esq., Phil. D., Mauritius
Belcher, Captain Sir Edward, C.B., R.N.
Bell, Reverend Thomas, Berbice
Bell, Robert, Esq., Norris Castle, East Cowes, I.W.
Belfast Library
Berlin, The Royal Library of
Betencourt, Alonzo, Esq., Philadelphia
Bethune, Rear-Admiral C. R. Drinkwater, C.B., 56, Westbourne-terrace
Bibliothèque Impériale, Paris
Biden, Captain
Blackie, Dr. Walter G., Villafield, Glasgow
Blyth, James, Esq., 24, Hyde-park-gardens
Bois, H., Esq., 110, Fenchurch-street
Bombay Geographical Society
Bone, J. H. A., Esq., Cleveland, Ohio, U.S.
Booth, B. W., Esq., Manchester
Boston Athenæum, The
Botfield, Beriah, Esq., Norton Hall, Northamptonshire
Bowring, Sir John, LL.D., Hong Kong
Bradshaw, Lieut. Lawrence, Woolwich
Brevorst, J. C., Esq., New York
Brodhead, J. R., Esq., New York
Broome, Major A.
Broughton, Lord, 42, Berkeley-square
Brown, George, Esq., 41, Rochester-row
Brown, J., Esq., Newcastle-pl., Clerkenwell
Brown, W. H., Esq., Chester
Brown, John Carter, Esq., Providence, Rhode Island
Bruce, John, Esq., F.S.A., 5, Upper Gloucester-street, Dorset-square
Brussels, Royal Library of
Burnett, W. F., Commander, R.N., Royal Naval College, Portsmouth

Cambridge University Library
Campbell, R. H. S., Esq., 5, Argyle-place, Regent-street
Cannon, Charles, Esq., British Museum
Carlton Club, Pall Mall
Chapman, Mr. John, Strand
Chapman, William, Esq., Richmond
Chauncey, Henry C., Esq., New York
Chichester, J. H. R., Esq., 40, Wimpole-st.
Christie, Jonathan Henry, Esq., 9, Stanhope-street, Hyde-park-gardens
Churchill, Lord Alfred S., F.R.G.S., 27, Chapel-street West
Colledge, Dr., Lauriston House, Cheltenham
Collier, John Payne, Esq., F.S.A.
Colonial Office (The)
Congress, Library of the, United States
Cooley, W. D., Esq., 33, King-street, Bloomsbury
Corney, B., Esq., M.R.S.L., Barnes-ter.
Costello, Dudley, Esq., 54, Acacia-road, St. John's Wood
Cotton, R. W., Esq., Barnstaple
Cracroft, Capt., R.N.
Cranstoun, G., Esq., Corehouse, Lanark
Crawford, R. Wygram, Esq., 71, Old Broad-street
Crowninschield, E. A., Esq., Boston, U.S.
Cunard Edward, Esq., New York

Dalrymple, Arthur, Esq.

Dalton, J. Stuart, Esq., for the Liverpool Free Public Library
Deane, Charles, Esq., Boston, U.S.
Dilke, C. Wentworth, Esq., 76, Sloane-st.
Dilke, C. W., Esq., Jun., 76, Sloane-street
Drake, Samuel G., Esq., Boston, U. S.
Dry, Thos., Esq., 25, Lincoln's Inn Fields
Dundas, Rt. Hon. Sir David, 13, King's Bench Walk, Temple
Dundas, George, Esq., 9, Charlotte-square, Edinburgh
Dundas, John, Esq., 25, St. Andrew's-square, Edinburgh
Dupart, M. B., Paris

East India Company, The Hon. the Court of Directors of the, 20 *copies*
Ecky, John H., Esq., Philadelphia
Ellice, Rt. Hon. Edward, M.P., 18, Arlington-street
Elliot, J. B., Esq., Patna
Ellis, Sir Henry, K.H., F.R.S., &c., 24, Bedford square
Elphinstone, Lord
Elphinstone, Lieut., 3, Chesham-place, Belgrave-square

Flagg, Geo. W., Esq., Charleston, South Carolina
Fletcher, Wm. Younger, Esq., British Museum
Foley, Lord, 26, Grosvenor-square
Folsom, Hon. George, New York
Foote, John, Esq.
Force, Colonel Peter, Washington, U.S.
Foreign Office (The)
Forster, John, Esq., 46, Montague-square
Fox, General, Addison-road, Kensington
Freer, W. E., Esq.

Galignani, M., Paris
Garnett, Richard, Esq., British Museum
Gawler, Colonel, United Service Club
Giraud, R. Hervé, Esq., Furnival's-inn
Gladdish, William, Esq., Gravesend
Glendening, Robert, Esq., 5, Britain-st., Portsea
Graham, Robert, Esq., 18, Heriot-row, Edinburgh
Grant & Griffith, Messrs. 21, Ludgate-st.
Graves, Robert Edmund, Esq., British Museum
Grey, R. W., Esq., M.P., 47, Belgrave-sq.
Grylls, —, Esq.
Guild, G. F., Esq., Boston, U.S.
Guillaume, Mr., Chester-square
Guise, W. V., Esq., Elmore-ct., Gloucester

Hale, J. H., Esq., Park-road, Stockwell-common
Harcourt, Egerton, Esq., Carlton Gardens
Harker, Turner James, Esq., 10, Northampton Park, Islington
Hawes, Sir Benjamin, 9, Queen's-square, Westminster
Hawkins, Edward, Esq., British Museum
Henderson, Dr., 6, Curzon-st., Mayfair
Hodgkin, Thomas, Esq., M.D., 35, Bedford-square
Hollond, R., Esq., M.P., 63, Portland-pl.
Holmes, James, Esq. 4, New Ormond-street, Foundling
Home Office (The)
Horner, Rev. J. S. H., Wells Park, Somersetshire
Hull Subscription Library
Hunter, David, Esq., Blackness, Dundee

Jacob, Major John, Bombay
Johnston, Alex. Keith, Esq., Edinburgh
Jones, J. Winter, Esq., F.S.A., British Museum
Jukes, J. B., Esq., 51, Stephen's-green, Dublin
Junior United Service Club, Pall Mall

Kennedy, Robt. Lenox, New York
Kerslake, Mr. T., Bristol

Labouchere, the Rt. Hon. Henry, M.P., 27, Belgrave-square
Laird, John, Esq., Birkenhead
Lansdowne, the Marquis of, 54, Berkeley-square
Lavradio, His Excellency the Count de, 12, Gloucester-place, Portman-square
Law, William, Esq., 103, Piccadilly
Leicester Permanent Library
Lemon, Sir C., Bart., M.P., 46, Charles-street, Berkeley-square
Lenox, James, Esq., New York
Levesque, Peter, Esq., 29, Guildford-st.
Little and Brown, Messrs., Boston, U.S.
Liverpool Free Public Library
Logan, A. J., Esq., Singapore
London Institution, Finsbury Circus
Lott, Capt. E. P., 159, Parliament-street, Liverpool
London Library, 12, St. James's-square
Lowe, Rt. Hn. Robt., M.P., Vice-President of the Board of Trade, 34, Lowndes Square
Lyceum Library, Hull

Mackenzie, John W., Esq., Edinburgh

Macready, W. C., Esq., Sherborne House, Dorset
Madan, Capt. Frederick, H.C.S., 5, Northwick-terrace, St. John's Wood
Madras Literary Society
Major, R. H., Esq., F.S.A., British Museum
Malcolm, W. Elphinstone, Esq., Burnfoot
Marett, Charles, Esq., 50, Chancery-lane
Markham, Clements R., Esq., 24, St. George's-road, Eccleston-square
Marlborough, His Grace the Duke of, Blenheim
Marsh, Hon. George P., Constantinople
Massie, Captain T. L., R.N., Chester
Maxse, Lieut. Frederick, A., R.N., 40, Upper Grosvenor-street
Melbourne, Public Library of, per Mr. Guillaume
Montriou, W., Esq., Bombay
Muller, F., Esq., Amsterdam
Munich Royal Library
Murchison, Sir Roderick Impey, F.R.S. &c., 16, Belgrave-square
Murphy, Hon. C. H., Brooklyn, New York
Murray, Lord, Great Stuart-st., Edinburgh
Murray, John, Esq., Albemarle-street

Newcastle-upon-Tyne Literary and Scientific Institute
New York Mercantile Library
Nicholls, Sir G., K.C.B., 17, Hyde Park-st.
Nimmo, Thomas, Esq., Demerara
Norris, Edwin, Esq., Sec. Asiatic Society, 5, New Burlington-street

Oriental Club, Hanover-square
Ouvry, F., Esq., F.S.A., 66, Lincoln's Inn Fields

Paine, W. Dunkley, Esq., Cockshutt-Hill, Reigate
Parker, J. W., Esq., West Strand
Pasley, Major-General Sir C. W., K.C.B., 12, Norfolk Crescent, Hyde Park
Patmore, C. K., Esq., Highwood-cottage, Fortis-green, Finchley
Pemberton, Mrs.
Pennington, John, Esq., Philadelphia
Pennsylvania, Historical Society of
Perry, Sir Erskine, M.P., Eaton-place
Petit, Rev. J. Louis, the Uplands, Shiffnal
Petit, Miss
Platt, T. Clayton, Esq., Philadelphia
Plowden, W. H. Chicheley, Esq., F.R.S.
Porter, G. W., Esq., British Museum
Portland, His Grace the Duke of
Portsmouth, the Royal Naval College
Pourtales, Count Albert, Berlin
Powis, Earl of, 45, Berkeley-square
Prescott, Rear Admiral H., C.B., Portsmouth Dockyard
Putnam, G. R., Esq., New York

Rawlinson, Colonel, C.B., 21, Langham-place
Reed, F. J. Esq., Friday-st., Cheapside
Richard, John E., Esq., Wandsworth, Surrey
Richards, Mr., 4, St. Alban's-road, Kensington
Richardson, Sir John, M.D., F.R.S., Haslar, Gosport
Richardson, Ralph, Esq., Greenfield Hall, Holywell, Flintshire
Riggs, G. W., Esq., Washington, U.S.
Ritter, Professor Karl, Berlin
Robinson, Lieut. Walter F., R.N., F.R.G.S., Junior United Service Club
Royal Academy of Delft
Royal Geographical Society, 3, Waterloo-place
Royal Society, Somerset House
Roys, Thos. Wm., Esq., Southampton, Long Island, New York
Rowsell, E. P., Esq., 29, Finsbury-circus
Rumbold, C. E., Esq., 1, Eccleston-square
Rundall, Thomas, Esq., East India House
Rushout, Miss, Tetbury
Rye, W. B., Esq., British Museum

Scarth, J., Esq., Canton
Schomburgk, Sir Robert, St. Domingo
Sedgwick, the Rev. Adam, Woodwardian Professor, Cambridge
Sheffield, Earl of, 20, Portland-place
Shillinglaw, —, Esq., Admiralty
Simpson, Lieutenant
Singapore Library
Smith, Andrew, Esq., M.D., St. James's-place
Smith, Edmund, Esq., Hull
Smith, George, Esq., 21, Russell-square
Smith, G., Esq., Hague-ter., Kingstown, Dublin
Smith, J., Esq., Bombay
Smith, J. P. G., Esq., Everton, Liverpool
Somers, Earl, 45, Grosvenor-place
Sotheby, S. Leigh, Esq., the Woodlands, Norwood
Stanley of Alderley, Lord
Stanley, Hon. Henry E. J., Athens
Staunton, Sir G. T., Bart., D.C.L., F.R.S., 17, Devonshire-street, Portland-place
Stuart, R. L., Esq., New York
Stuart, Alexander, Esq., New York
St. Andrew's University

St. David's, the Right Rev. the Lord Bishop of, Abergwili, Carmarthenshire
Stevens, H., Esq., Boston, United States
Stirling, Wm., Esq., of Keir, 128, Park-st.

Talbot, Earl
Ternaux-Compans, Mons. H., Paris
Thomas, Rev. Vaughan, High-st., Oxford
Thompson, Thos., Esq., Solicitor, Hull
Thomas, W. A., Esq., 50, Threadneedle-street
Todd, R. B., Esq., M.D., F.R.S., 26, Brook-street, Grosvenor-square
Trade, the Board of, Whitehall
Travellers' Club, 106, Pall Mall
Trinity House, Tower Hill

Union Society, Oxford
United Service Institution
Upham & Beet, Messrs. 46, New Bond-st.

Victoria Library and Reading Rooms, Hong Kong
Vienna Imperial Library
Van Ryckevorsel, H., Consul de Venezuela, Conseiller à la Régence de Rotterdam
Von Siebold, Col. Ph. Fr., Leyden

Waite, Henry, Esq., 68, Old Broad street
Walker, J., Esq., 31, Keppel-street
Walker, Joshua, Esq., Jun., 50, Upper Brunswick-place, Brighton
Waters, J. S., Esq., Baltimore, U.S.
Watts, Thomas, Esq., British Museum
Weir, William, Esq., 30, Great Coram-st.
Wensleydale, the Rt. Hon. Lord, 56, Park-street, Grosvenor-square
Whateley, W., Esq., Q.C., 6, Park-street, Westminster
Whewell, the Rev. W., D.D., Master of Trinity College, Cambridge
White, R., Esq., Cowes, Isle of Wight
Whiteman, J. C., Esq., Theydon Grove, Epping
Wilkinson, John, Esq., 8, Wellington-st., Strand
Williams, T., Esq., Northumberland-house, Strand
Wilson, Edward S., Esq., Hull
Wolff, H. Drummond, Esq., 44, Half-moon-st., Piccadilly
Woodd, Basil T., Esq., 14, Gt. Cumberland-street
Wood, Lieutenant John, H.E.I.C.S., 137, Leadenhall-street
Wright, H., Esq., Cheltenham
Wyld, James, Esq., Strand

Young, G. F., Esq., 80, Cornhill

RICHARDS, PRINTER, 37, GREAT QUEEN STREET.